Contents

Acknowledgements 7

Foreword 9

CHAPTER 1   'Full of Bogs and Marshes': The Making of Whitburn Parish 11

CHAPTER 2   The Cunynghames and the Baillies 16

CHAPTER 3   The New Village of Whitburn 21

CHAPTER 4   The Church – Patrons and Grave-robbers 28

CHAPTER 5   Working in the New Village: Cotton Weaving and a Distillery 31

CHAPTER 6   Everyday Life 36

CHAPTER 7   Radicals, Riot and Revolution 43

CHAPTER 8   Coaching Days 54

CHAPTER 9   The Weavers – From Riches to Rags 59

CHAPTER 10   The Baillies Acquire Whitburn 63

CHAPTER 11   Mining, 1750–1850 67

CHAPTER 12   The New Polkemmet Pit 73

CHAPTER 13   'Shake off the Galling Chain' – More Whitburn Radicals 83

CHAPTER 14   Whitburn: Occupations, Incomers and Emigrants 88

CHAPTER 15   Whitburn becomes a Burgh 95

CHAPTER 16   The Later Baillies, the Baillie Institute and Polkemmet Estate 102

CHAPTER 17   Railways and Roads 111

CHAPTER 18   The Churches After 1820 115

CHAPTER 19   Housing 122

CHAPTER 20   Industry After 1945 131

CHAPTER 21   Schools   139

CHAPTER 22   A Frozen Postman, a Bank Scandal and
Some Shops and Pubs   146

CHAPTER 23   Poverty, Poor Relief and Self-help   152

CHAPTER 24   Keeping Whitburn in Order and in Health   157

CHAPTER 25   Whitburn at War   160

CHAPTER 26   Sports and Leisure   165

CHAPTER 27   Some Famous Natives and Local Notables   170

Index   179

Whitburn

A Scottish Town's Fight to Survive Change

SYBIL CAVANAGH

Luath Press Limited
EDINBURGH
www.luath.co.uk

First published 2019

ISBN: 978-1-913025-40-3

The paper used in this book is recyclable. It is made from low
chlorine pulps produced in a low energy, low emission manner from
renewable forests.

Printed and bound by Ashford Colour Press, Gosport

Typeset in 11 point Sabon by Lapiz

The author's right to be identified as author of this work under the
Copyright, Designs and Patents Act 1988 has been asserted.

SYBIL CAVANAGH grew up in Fife and is a graduate of the University of St Andrews. She worked in the public library service in Wigan, Glasgow and West Lothian, and along the way gained a Diploma in Scottish Historical Studies at the University of Glasgow and a fascination with Scottish and local history. She was the Local History Librarian with W. othian Council for 26 years.

.h now retired, she is still obsessed with local history and tries .re that enthusiasm through talks, books and other publications. .as joint organiser and contributor to *The Bathgate Book: a new .ory* (2001), editor and joint author of *Pumpherston: the story of a shale oil village* (Luath Press, 2002) and wrote *Blackburn: West Lothian's Cotton and Coal Town* (Luath Press, 2006) and *Old Bathgate* (Stenlake Publications, 2007), as well as booklets on subjects as diverse as Linlithgow Poorhouse, cholera in West Lothian and West Lothian's many links with slavery and the slave trade.

She is syllabus secretary for the West Lothian History and Amenity Society, enjoys walking, is trying to re-capture her lost French, has been a church organist for 30 years (without any noticeable improvement), volunteers with the Riding for the Disabled charity and has taken up carriage driving.

Acknowledgements

GRATEFUL THANKS ARE due to the many people who gave up their time to speak to the author about Whitburn past and present, or provided useful sources of information: Allison Gilchrist, Dave Gillan, Tracy Johnston, the Rev Dr Angus Kerr, Scott McKillop, Blair Martin, Nancy Mickel, Emma Peattie, the Rev Dr Sandy Roger, Stephen Roy, Alex Smith, Craig Statham, Meg Stenhouse, Ian Tennant, Father Sebastian Thuruthipillil, Jennifer Tortolano; and to Elizabeth Henderson, Roy Calderwood and Charlie Edwards for their practical help, support and encouragement.

The resources of the West Lothian Local History Library in Linlithgow Partnership Centre, and of the National Records of Scotland in Edinburgh were invaluable in researching this book. The author is grateful to the former for permission to reproduce some of the photographs in this book. The West Lothian Archives and Records Centre and West Lothian Museums Service at Kirkton Service Centre, Livingston, also provided much useful information, as did the National Library of Scotland and the Almond Valley Heritage Centre; and the staff of Linlithgow Library were always helpful.

A much longer version of this book showing sources of information and full references will be available for consultation from July 2020 in Whitburn Library and in the West Lothian Local History Library at Linlithgow Partnership Centre.

Foreword

DESPITE A MULTITUDE of changes during the last 300 years, numerous threads connect those who live in Whitburn today with those who have gone before. Its people have repeatedly had to cope with upheavals over which they had no control – the agricultural changes of the 18th century, the industrial changes of the 19th century, the decline of handloom weaving, the hardships of the inter-war period, the huge growth of Whitburn after 1920, the end of the mining industry and the ravages of Thatcherism. All these caused great turbulence and hardship to those who lived through them. The book records these changes and their effects on the local people but also uncovers the things that remain the same in every century – the struggle to find work, to find a home and raise a family; the urge to retain independence, to worship, to learn, to help others – and not least, to relax and enjoy life.

The south-west has always been the poorest part of the county of West Lothian, isolated from the centre of power whether that was in Linlithgow, Bathgate or Livingston. The area remains less prosperous than the more northerly parts of the county and some pockets of deprivation are to be found in Whitburn. In some ways, the town is typical of former mining communities anywhere in Scotland – a close-knit community suffering some hardship, unemployment and loss of identity, with large council housing schemes, decaying high street and tracts of degraded post-industrial land. In other ways, Whitburn's history has proved to be distinctive – in its strong radical leanings and its lack of deference to all forms of authority. This radical streak, which has not been found to such a marked degree in other West Lothian communities, runs right through Whitburn's past, helping it to confront and overcome its many difficulties.

Population of Whitburn		
	Parish	Village/Burgh
1755	1,121	
1801	1,537	500
1821	1,693	
1831	1,900	
1841		798
1851		808
1861		1,362
1871		1,432
1881		1,200
1891		1,185
1901		1,442
1911		1,876
1921		1,971
1931		2,440
1941 (estimate)		4,000
1951		5,232
1961		5,904
1971		10,175
1981		11,965
1991		10,860
2001		10,391
2011		10,527
2013 (estimate)		10,873

CHAPTER 1

'Full of Bogs and Marshes':
The Making of Whitburn Parish

A NOT UNCOMMON complaint heard in Whitburn these days is that Livingston has ruined Whitburn – the New Town is said to have sucked the life out of surrounding communities. As we'll see, however, Whitburn people resented Livingston much earlier in their history! For over five centuries, Whitburn was part of the parish of Livingston. A parish was a small area where a church and a priest were based; to pay for the building of the church and the maintenance of the priest, a tax was levied on the local landowners – in effect, they paid for their own church.

The boundaries of these early parishes followed natural features such as rivers and burns and did not change greatly over the centuries. The parish was the basic unit of church life and became, too, the basic unit of local government. Scottish parishes survived intact until they ceased to have any significance after the local government reorganisation of 1975.

Livingston parish was one of the largest parishes in West Lothian – some 11 miles long and four miles broad at its widest. It extended from Knightsridge and Dechmont Law in the east, to Fauldhouse and the county boundary with Lanarkshire in the west, and it included the area where Whitburn is situated. The church for the whole parish was at Livingston Village – almost as far east as it could be, and some ten miles away from the west end of the parish. In those days of poor roads and few horses and carts, it was a considerable journey for the people in the west of the parish to reach the church even on a mild day in mid-summer; in the worst of winter weather, it was impossible. There was certainly a chapel in the Whitburn area by the 1620s and probably before that, but the people there felt isolated from their parish kirk at Livingston Village. In 1630, Linlithgow Presbytery received a 'supplication' from 'the people of the west end of the said parish, regrating [regretting] the incommodious situation of the said kirk', and asking for the church to be moved towards the west end of the parish.

Nothing was done, so in 1647 they again petitioned the Presbytery. This time, the Presbytery arranged a perambulation of the whole parish, as a result of which, they conceded that the parish was populous enough to be divided in two. The boundaries for a new parish of Whitburn were drawn up and a site for a new church was chosen at Tounhead of Whitburn. But despite this preparatory work, the scheme fell through: national events intruded.

In 1650, Scotland was invaded by Cromwell's forces. The kirk session records of Livingston parish stop abruptly in September 1650, when English soldiers of occupation were stationed in Livingston and other parishes. The soldiers destroyed Livingston Peel and badly damaged the church. They also plundered for food, and the kirk session recorded the eyewitness account of a young woman: 'about fourtein days before Yule, she did see an Inglish foot soldier with two hens under his oxters.' After the withdrawal of the English troops, the kirk session records resume in May 1651:

> No Session before this day keipt by reason of the trouble, howbeit always preaching (except about a month) either at Whitburne or Ffoulshiells.

What sort of building was in use for the preaching at Whitburn is not clear. The Whitburn chapel mentioned earlier may have been still in use, or the preaching may have taken place in private houses. However, in 1658, a new 'Meeting House' was built at Whitburn, known simply as the New House. Its location was the site of the present South church and parts of that original building may well have been incorporated into the present church. The landowners of the whole of Livingston parish would have shared the cost of building this new meeting house.

The population at the west end of Livingston parish was growing slowly and by 1718, the meeting house needed to be repaired and enlarged. At this point, the local heritors [landowners] petitioned Presbytery yet again for Whitburn to be created a separate parish: the common people, they wrote, were

> not only separated from their own Church by the Water of Almond and from all other Neighbouring churches by the Waters of Almond and Breigh, but the Interjacent Ground is so Mairish [marshy] and full of Bogues [bogs] and Marishes [marshes], that in the Winter time and Rainy seasons the ways are unpassable... and it is Impracticable for the Minister of Livingstone sufficiently to oversee and Instruct the people...

Why should the heritors have voluntarily sought the expense of building a new church? Setting up Whitburn as a separate parish would have two benefits for them: they would have a church nearby and they would be able to choose their own minister. In Livingston parish, as in the majority of Scottish parishes, the chief heritor was the 'patron' of the parish – in other words, he chose the minister and 'presented' him to the parish. If Whitburn could be set up as a new parish and the heritors jointly paid for the new church, manse and stipend of the minister, then, they assumed, they would have the legal right to choose their own minister.

Religious radicalism

In the days before political radicalism arose, radicalism was often to be found in the form of opposition to the powerful Church. Certainly, two incidences of local religious radicalism can be found even before Whitburn came into being as a village. In the reign of James IV (1488–1513), the owner of Polkemmet estate, Adam Shaw, was an adherent of the religious group known as the Lollards. In 1494, 30 prominent supporters of Lollardism (a forerunner of Protestantism) were summoned before James IV to answer charges of heresy. Shaw of Polkemmet and the others were admonished but were fortunate in that no further action was taken against them.

And during the Covenanting period of the 1680s, when the more rigid Presbyterians resisted great pressure to conform to the Episcopal form of worship and church government, the Baillie family (who had bought Polkemmet estate from the Shaws) seems to have had sympathy for the persecuted Covenanters. The minister of Livingston parish (of which Whitburn was still a part during the Covenanting period) was an Episcopalian and royalist, hated by Covenanters and strict Presbyterians. Whitburn had a number of active Covenanters, who met in the large tracts of lonely moorland which were ideal for secret open-air conventicles, hidden from government dragoons.

Covenanters saw their obedience to the civil authorities (ie the king) as a form of contract or covenant. As long as the king kept *his* part of the bargain (which they took to be support of true religion, ie Presbyterianism), they would keep *their* side (ie submission to the king's earthly authority). So they already understood authority to be not absolute but conditional on its proper exercise. If power was not correctly exercised, then there was no obligation to obey it. This way of thinking took firm hold in Whitburn and can be traced in its subsequent story.

The desire of Whitburn people to choose their own minister fits this pattern and by making Whitburn a separate parish, the landowners assumed they would avoid patronage. The main mover was William Wardrope, probably the son of the owner of the small estate of Cult (sometimes spelled Quilt), who worked in the Grassmarket in Edinburgh as an apothecary – a pharmacist with some medical knowledge. In April 1719, he went to the trouble and expense of consulting with a judge,

Lord Grange, as to who would have the patronage of the proposed new parish. The judge's opinion was that the new parish of Whitburn would have no patron and that not just the heritors but the whole congregation (males only, of course) would be entitled to choose its own minister.

'Excluding thereby all patrons...'

Led by Wardrope the apothecary, the Whitburn heritors formed themselves into a trust to raise funds. Money was also raised 'by a voluntary subscription all over Scotland' (which would have taken the form of a special offering uplifted in churches throughout the country).

> Several of the heritors were liberal in subscribing, active in procuring subscriptions, and zealous in carrying out the process of creation before the Court of Teinds, from entertaining the idea that the minister was to be chosen by the parish at large.

By the start of 1722, the trustees had raised enough money to buy the meeting house and the land adjoining it and they rebuilt and extended it into a new church and churchyard. In addition, the trustees bought land for a manse and for the glebe – that is, farmland for the minister's own use:

> ...these six acres of arable land going in a straight line north from the meeting house and Kirkyard to the headrig,... all lying on the West side of the said Driftloan [ie Drove Loan, ie Longridge Road] – for the 'Gleib.'

The minister would also have the right to take turf (for building walls or roofs), and dig peat from Whitrigg Moor for the use and service of his family.

The land was purchased from the owner of Wester Whitburn, Sir John Houstoun of Houstoun in Renfrewshire, on the clear understanding that he gave up all rights of patronage over the new parish. The ministers were to be chosen by the kirk session, heritors and heads of families of Whitburn,

> providing they be such as are of the presbyterian persuasion and are not grossly ignorant or profane... excluding thereby all patrons or other persons whatsomever expressly from the power of presenting, or nominating any person whatsomever to be Minister of the said Parish...

One final matter was attended to: two farms in Shotts parish were purchased, the rent from which would be used to make up the minister's stipend if necessary, and to buy wine and bread for communion services. So the trustees were confident that they had covered every possible contingency, secured the financial future of the new parish and definitively excluded any power of patronage over it.

Convinced by the energy and commitment shown by the heritors, Linlithgow Presbytery recommended the Whitburn people to apply to the Court of Session for the new parish to be set up. This was done in 1726, and the long process was finally completed on 23 June 1731 when the Lords Commissioners of Teinds erected Whitburn into a new parish. It was some six miles long and four miles broad, with a population of about 1,000.

The first minister

Meanwhile the parishioners had not been idle. Work began on building the new church in 1729 and was finished the following year. William Wardrope, by now a surgeon-apothecary, donated to the new church two brass collecting plates and a handbell for the church officer to make public announcements through the town (like a town crier) or to ring as a mortbell to give notice of a death. In 1731, the men of the congregation set about choosing its first minister and they decided on the Rev Alexander Wardrope, minister at Muckhart, probably a cousin of the surgeon-apothecary. The 'call' of the congregation was sent to Wardrope at Muckhart and accepted by him. Then to the undoubted dismay of all those who had struggled so hard to set up the new parish, Sir James Cunynghame of Milncraig claimed the right of patronage of Whitburn parish, based on his being patron of Livingston parish; Whitburn being carved out of Livingston parish, he must also be patron of Whitburn. The Presbytery of Linlithgow heard submissions from both sides and came down on the side of the Whitburn folk: 'there can be no patron of that [Whitburn] paroch'.

There the matter was shelved for the time being since Sir James Cunynghame agreed that Wardope of Muckhart was the right man for the job. But it was a dispute that would raise its head again and cause division in the parish and village of Whitburn.

CHAPTER 2

The Cunynghames and the Baillies

THE CUNYNGHAME FAMILY had acquired the barony of Livingston in the late 17th century. Until the mid-1720s, their land extended from Dechmont, across most of the area covered by the present new town of Livingston and as far west as Seafield. In 1725, Sir James Cunynghame bought the barony of Whitburn from the Houstoun family who had owned it from at least the 1540s. The purchase extended the Cunynghames' estates to the west end of Whitburn – a huge tract of land. Being the major landowner in Livingston parish, Sir James had the right to choose its minister; a valuable right, as he could offer the post in exchange for loyalty or service of some sort and he would be sure to present a man who agreed with his own religious and political views. It was for this reason that the Cunynghames were keen to acquire the patronage of the new Whitburn parish as well.

The Barony of Whitburn

Until the mid-18th century, the owner of a barony had the legal right to hold courts and to sentence wrong-doers. By the 1720s and 1730s, these courts had declined into agricultural courts at which rents were paid and local disputes over boundaries, terms of lease, debts, etc settled. Various old documents mention the Head Court of the barony of Whitburn, and the ordinary Baron Court. These 'hereditary jurisdictions' were abolished in 1747; thereafter, a barony was merely an estate.

The Cunynghames and the Baillies

When they acquired Polkemmet estate c.1620, the Baillies of Polkemmet did not become the lairds of Whitburn. In fact, compared to the Cunynghames, the Baillies were minor landowners until the early 19th century. Around 1770, the Cunynghames' Livingston and Whitburn estates had a valuation of nearly £3,000; Polkemmet's was a mere £735. The relative status of the Baillies and the Cunynghames is revealed by the fact that Thomas Baillie was for a time the factor of the Livingston estate – a paid employee of the Cunynghames. And in that same year, 1735, William Baillie, son of the Polkemmet laird, became an apprentice wright [carpenter] in Edinburgh. None of the Cunynghame sons would have been sent to learn a trade but it was acceptable in the mid-18th century for the younger son of minor gentry like the Baillies to become a craftsman. For the wealthy Cunynghames, only the law, the army or Parliament were fit occupations for their sons.

Making improvements

The farms of the early 18th century were based on fermtouns – clusters of poor thatched cottages, whose inhabitants farmed the land together. The ground was open and unenclosed by hedges or dykes; stony, marshy and unsheltered by trees. The 'infield' land nearest the fermtoun was fertilised with dung and divided by deep drainage ditches into long narrow riggs – strips of cultivated land some 20 or 30 feet broad. The remains of these ploughed riggs and ditches can still be seen today, most easily in aerial photographs.

A stone dyke divided the infield from the outfield, which was poor quality land only fit for rough grazing. Again, there were no enclosures. Young children had the task of herding the beasts and keeping them from wandering too far away. With little winter fodder available, most animals were killed and salted in the autumn as food for the coming months.

> **Amang the Riggs o' Barley**
>
> Another use for the ditches between riggs is noted in Whitburn Kirk Session minutes of 29 December 1734: Margaret Bogle 'has relapsed in uncleanness', this time with 'young Patrick in Easter Whitburn; that he had carnal dealing with her... in the month of July last betwixt two of his father's bear [barley] Ridges about Mid Day, as she was going to Bickertoun to fetch a scythe...'

Just a few animals were kept over the winter to breed from in the spring. Houses were low, dark, smoke-filled, with thatched or turf roofs, often consisting of just a single room housing both humans and animals – the latter provided much-needed warmth. Farming in the early 18th century was a hard, punishing life, constantly on the brink of destitution and hunger should a harvest fail or a winter be exceptionally severe.

Poor land had low rental value. For example, the lease of Damhead on Polkemmet estate to William Bishop in 1738 brought Thomas Baillie an annual rental of only £9 sterling and also 'six good and sufficient hens' and several days unpaid work for the laird. Rent was paid partly in money, partly in kind and partly in labour and this remained common until nearly the end of the 18th century. Subsistence farming meant that little surplus produce was left that could be sold to create some profit.

From about the middle of the 18th century, landowners and farmers began to study farming in a scientific way with a view to increasing the fertility of their land and improving their livestock. Startling growth in the income yielded by estates could be achieved, provided the landowner had the money to make the initial improvements and the patience to wait several years before a profit was made. Agriculture became focused on producing a surplus for the market: profit, not mere self-sufficiency, became the aim. Open land that had been farmed in common by a group of small tenants was enclosed into large farms of regular fields, farmed by a single tenant employing a few workers. Such an agricultural revolution was not achieved without major disruption: it was the poor and power-less who suffered – the small tenants, cottars and labourers – as they were pushed off the land.

As part of the process of enclosure, the right of access to common land was lost to the ordinary people. A commonty or common muir was rough ground owned jointly by several different proprietors. It was not owned by all the people in common but many of them had the right to graze their beasts there or to dig peat and turf. As early as 1709, there had been a proposal to divide up Whitburn's common muir at Whitrigg among the various proprietors but it came to nothing. However, the right of locals to take free peat and turf from the common muir seems to have been lost in the later 18th century; presumably because the common was divided up and fenced off by its owners.

Sir James Cunynghame's father David was one of the early 'improv-ers' of land: in the records of the old Scots Parliament of 1705, there is a petition submitted by him to Parliament, in which he:

> humbly sheweth, that he, having inclosed a considerable quantity of ground to the south of his house of Livingston, which will require the changeing of the high way, which at present goes straight by his door and is both uneasie to him and bad of itself...

He gained Parliament's petition to close up the road that came too close to his mansion house of Livingston and to build a new road, 'twenty foot broad, except where it goes betwixt houses...' Like most landowners, Sir David had begun by enclosing the land around his own house and then worked outwards to the land held by his various tenant farmers. This was an expensive process, so his son James and his successors increased their income by selling off small plots of lands but retained the right to levy annual feu duty on the land.

'A solitary house in a desolate country'

One of the first recorded feus was sold (in 1735) to William Wardrope, the Edinburgh surgeon apothecary, despite his being Sir James Cunynghame's main opponent in the Whitburn patronage dispute. Evidently, an armed truce had been reached and relations between the two sides had not broken down completely. The land sold to William Wardrope was:

> Tounhead of Whitburn with houses, biggings, yards... parts, pendicles thereon... the lands of Dykehead... the lands of Brounhill... lying within the barrony of Whitburn.

Then Cunynghame feued two plots of land to James Storrie, a Bathgate merchant: 'that room and lands of Whytburn commonly called Yatehouses with houses, biggings, yards..., parts, pendicles'. The purchase agreement gave Storrie the right to dig peat on the common moor of Whitrigg and take turf for repairing the houses already on the land. The following year, 1736, the same James Storrie feued:

> all haill the little house and yaird... bounded betwixt... his lands of Yatehouses upon the west and north, the high causey or loan leading from the miln [ie Whitburn Mill] to the Church on the East, and the highway leading from Edinburgh to Glasgow upon the [south?]

– ie the northwest corner of the Cross. (The site of Whitburn mill has vanished under the motorway – it was close to what's now the junction of Ellen Street and Armadale Road.)

But Whitburn was not yet a village, just a scattering of houses along the high road. Accounts of Whitburn in the early years are few and far between. The earliest is perhaps that of Alexander Carlyle, one of the leading Church of Scotland ministers of his day. As a young student in November 1744, Carlyle walked from Edinburgh to the university in Glasgow. On the second day of his journey, he set out from Kirkliston some 16 miles away:

> I walked to Whitburn at an early hour, but could venture no further, as there was no tolerable lodging-house within my reach. There was then not even a cottage nearer than the Kirk of Shotts, and Whitburn itself was a solitary house in a desolate country.

By a solitary 'house', Carlyle probably meant a 'change-house' or inn but
the impression left on his mind was certainly that of isolation and desolation. The desolation was compounded by the lack of trees to provide
shelter from the winds, the poor condition of the roads and its height
above sea level (620 feet). When Carlyle started his wintry journey, he
could walk easily on the frozen roads but, on the following morning:

> the frost was gone, and such a deluge of rain and tempest
> of wind took possession of the atmosphere, as put an end
> to all travelling. The wet thaw and bad weather continuing,
> I was obliged to remain there for several days, for there was
> in those days neither coach nor chaise on the road, and not
> even a saddle-horse to be had. At last, on Sunday morning,
> being the fourth day, an open chaise returning from Edin-
> burgh to Glasgow took me in, and conveyed me safe.

For the traveller then there was no public coach service and no horses for
hire; only the kindness of the owner of a private carriage (chaise) allowed
Carlyle to finish his journey. Given such conditions, only the very determined would travel any distance; and poor roads also impeded trade, for
it was extremely difficult and costly to bring in or send out goods any
distance on such bad roads.

Another difficulty for travellers was the scarcity and badness of inns.
At the inn where Carlyle stayed:

> I passed my time more tolerably than I expected; for though
> the landlord was ignorant and stupid, his wife was a sensi-
> ble woman and in her youth had been celebrated in a song
> under the name of the 'Bonny Lass of Livingstone' [later
> collected and re-worked by Robert Burns]. They had five
> children, but no books but the Bible and Sir Richard Black-
> more's epic poem of 'Prince Arthur'... When I came to pay
> my reckoning, to my astonishment she only charged me 3s
> 6d for lodging and board for four days. I had presented the
> little girls with ribbons I bought from a wandering ped-
> lar who had taken shelter from the storm. But my whole
> expense, maid-servant and all, was only 5s; such was the
> rate of travelling in those days.

CHAPTER 3

The New Village of Whitburn

Two more Cunynghames: Sir David and Sir William

IN 1747, Sir James Cunynghame died unmarried and the estates of Livingston and Whitburn passed to his brother Sir David Cunynghame, the 3rd baronet. David was an army officer and had also managed to raise the family's social status by marrying the daughter of the Earl of Eglinton. Sir David continued his military career, so he was often an absentee landlord, though not an uninterested one. He administered his estates through his factors and through his wife, Lady Mary Cunynghame.

A few letters survive from Sir David to the factor of his estate, Thomas Baillie of the Polkemmet family, which show an active interest in the improvement of his estate.

> I shall be glad to know if Mr Robertson has begun any repairs at the House of Whitburn. I am sure he has one of the best bargains ever man had. I beg of you to write me more frequently.

The John Robertson mentioned at the House (ie 'change house' – a small inn) of Whitburn is probably the inn-keeper whom Carlyle had described as 'ignorant and stupid' some ten years before. Since he had managed to get his lease as a best bargain from his landlord, perhaps he wasn't so stupid! During the 20 years of Sir David Cunynghame's ownership (1747–67), the feuing of a few small plots of land continued but not to any great extent. By the time that William Roy surveyed the Whitburn area as part of his Great Military Survey in 1752–5, Whitburn was a cluster of perhaps a dozen houses along the high road, east of the Armadale road. The Military Survey provides the first evidence that a new village was being built in Whitburn parish but, oddly enough, it's East Whitburn which is captioned 'New Whitburn' and (Wester) Whitburn does not appear at all on the map. No evidence exists of a new village at East Whitburn, so clearly this was a mistake by the military surveyors: it was Whitburn which should have been captioned New Whitburn.

Sir David died of 'gout in the stomach' in October 1767 and was succeeded by his son, Sir William Augustus Cunynghame, the true founder of Whitburn.

Sir William Augustus Cunynghame

Born in 1747 and educated at Oxford, Sir William, like every young man of fortune, went on the Grand Tour of Europe to study classical and European art and civilisation. After his father's death in 1767, he became the fourth baronet at the age of 20. He was a wealthy young man who moved in fashionable circles and was something of a ladies' man. At the age of 21, he married Frances, daughter and heiress of Sir Robert Myreton of Gogar, said to be the 'the most inveterate swearer in Scotland. He could not speak a sentence without an oath.' She produced three children but died young. After another few years abroad, Sir William came back to Scotland and was elected MP for Linlithgowshire in 1774.

In 1767, Sir William Cunynghame's sister Margaret married James Stuart, second son of the third Earl of Bute who was prime minister 1762–3. With such influential in-laws, Sir William moved in high social and political circles. He took another wealthy heiress as his second wife, much of whose fortune derived from her father's estate and slaves in Grenada in the West Indies. They produced another five children.

> ## Highwaymen
>
> A 19th century book called *Social Gleanings* records an anecdote of Sir William Cunynghame and his wife while in London with a friend, Col. Graham. 'They were driving down Park Lane to a ball or concert at the Palace, when the carriage was stopped by two footpads' [highwaymen]. 'Col. Graham, who was in uniform, instantly sprang from the carriage on the opposite side to the footpad, and, hurrying round, made a thrust with his sword... The... robbers made a precipitate retreat; and Lady Cunynghame's magnificent diamonds... escaped, and the party proceeded... to enjoy the attractions and hospitality of the Palace.'

Unlike his Bute relations, Sir William was on the Whig side in politics but also something of a maverick, who 'stood forth as the indefatigable champion of Scottish interests'. That he was hot-tempered is revealed by an incident at a political dinner during an election contest in Linlithgowshire. Lord Hopetoun (a Tory) proposed a toast, 'Up with the Hopes, and down with the Cunynghames'. Sir William Cunynghame rose up and was pushing his way towards Lord Hopetoun to protest when William Baillie of Polkemmet stepped between them to make peace. The irate Cunynghame punched Baillie on the head, causing Baillie to cry out, 'My lord, he's gi'en me a gowf on the lug!' Baillie (another Tory) challenged Cunynghame to a duel, which was fought without bloodshed on either side. In 1877, more than 50 years after Sir William's death, his legendary hospitality was still remembered – some 15 or 20 carriages on a Sunday afternoon lining the drive up to his mansion house. This then was the man who created Whitburn – vain, wealthy, quick-tempered, patriotic and independent-minded.

New villages

The founding of new villages was taking place all over Scotland at this time: between 1720 and 1850 perhaps as many as 490 were formed. In West Lothian, Blackburn was one such and Whitburn another. Small farm tenants and labourers thrown off their land by the improvements were sold or leased land and perhaps given some materials to build a house in the new village. What was the benefit to the landowner of founding a new village? The new villagers would still be available for farm work at busy times such as harvest but had to make their own living the rest of the year. It was also a profitable exercise for the landowner: if land was feued off, money was got from its sale and the new owners had to pay him feu duty (an annual payment in perpetuity to the feudal superior). A boggy tract of worthless ground could be used for a new village, creating a market for the increased produce of the land and leading to growth of population and trade which would eventually benefit both the local community and the local landowner.

Feuing out the new village

Frequently the founding of a new village amounted to little more than the public announcement in a newspaper that a town now existed on a particular site and that ground was available for feuing. Once they had feued a piece of ground, the new residents built their houses generally with free stone and turf from the landowner's quarries and moorland. The proprietor would allow – indeed, encourage – the local people to engage in trade within the new village, open shops or set up businesses. Some landowners built public buildings such as an inn or even set up a business to provide work for new settlers.

The first certain indication of the establishment of a village at Whitburn (rather than just a few new houses) is in the *Edinburgh Advertiser* of 6–9 October 1772:

> Sir William Augustus Cunynghame of Livingstone having finished a large and commodious building at WHITEBURN, on the great road half way between Edinburgh and Glasgow, for the purpose of a market-place and Granaries, proposes to establish a WEEKLY MARKET there, for the sale of meal, barley, all kinds of grain, beef, flax, etc, and every other article of merchandise any person shall think proper to expose, FREE

OF CUSTOM. To commence the first Tuesday of November
next and continue regularly every Tuesday thereafter.

Here we have evidence of Sir William taking steps to establish a firm
economic basis for his new village. By providing a market place and
granaries for storing grain, he is attempting to make Whitburn the
agricultural market centre for the surrounding district. To encourage
merchants to rent one of his granaries, he offers to forego his right to
duty on the sale of the grain 'for some time'. The present Market Inn
is a reminder of the site of the market place and granaries in the new
village of Whitburn.

The same newspaper article also states:

> several parcels of land, lying adjacent to the town and very
> convenient for feuars, will be let by roup [auction] upon the
> first market day.

Those interested were directed to apply to Allan Gilmour, shoemaker at
Whitburn, who would show them the available sites. The advertisement
for the new town of Whitburn probably appeared several times in the
Scottish newspapers of the time. It was the usual way in which a landowner alerted the public to the fact that land was for sale or lease and
that new residents, traders and merchants would be coming to the area,
creating business opportunities for entrepreneurs.

Further evidence that a village now existed at Whitburn is to be found
in a legal document of 1773 which specifically mentions the 'village and
lands of Wester Whitburn' and also the public house on the lands of
Wester Whitburn, 'possest by Bethia Wright, relict of John Robertson,
vintner at Whitburn'. And a newspaper advert for the sale of Croftmalloch farm in 1775 states that the land lies close to the 'new town of
Whitburn'. In 1778, Sir William was said to be about to set up a woollen manufactory in Whitburn – further proof of his efforts to provide
employment for the village and to increase his rental income by raising
the general prosperity of the area and attracting new residents.

Early villagers

Among the people who might be considered the earliest villagers of
Whitburn were William Kinloch, wright (joiner); William Frame,
shoemaker; Alexander Russell, tenant farmer of the Dales; John
Robertson, the inn-keeper, probably the son of the 'ignorant and
stupid' bargain-maker, and his wife, Bethia Wright; and Allan Gilmour,
shoemaker. All of these people feued land in the new village.

From 1780, there was an increase in the feuing of land at Whitburn. In 1781, it's recorded that houses or land in Whitburn were purchased by James Houlden, servant to Bethia Wright, the inn-keeper's wife; James Easton, victual merchant; Robert Brown, schoolmaster; and James Dick, weaver. In the following few years, land in the village was feued to John Hamilton, mason; William Brice, tenant farmer; Bethia Robertson (running the inn after her husband's death); sisters Agnes, Jean and Nelly Mains; James Barry, baker; James Taylor, another baker; John Robertson again, by this time a brewer in Whitburn; and James Brown, servant. The new residents of the village had come from within Whitburn parish or a fairly small radius around it – West Calder, Carstairs, Carnwath and Cambusnethan were the most common, plus a few from Bathgate and Torphichen, one from Queensferry and one or two from Glasgow.

Writing for the First *Statistical Account* in 1793, the minister of Whitburn remarks that:

> the cot-houses, which were formerly scattered through the parish, are now almost all demolished, and those who possessed them have removed to the village.

The minister also commented on the number of incomers:

> A person who has resided long in a public station in the parish, remarks, that not above a third part of the present heads of families are natives of the place.

However, the number of people *leaving* the parish is also quite high – presumably some of those who were being cleared off the land preferred to try their luck elsewhere. Compared with the forcible evictions of the Highland clearances, the Lowland clearances resulted in fewer cases of hardship and resistance. Proper provision was generally made for the families being moved off their land, and alternative work was available in the growing industrial towns and cities. Despite the difficulties caused to many, the rising standard of living throughout the 18th century meant that by 1800, ordinary people were markedly better off than they had been 50 or 100 years before.

Building control

Those who bought feus in the Cunynghames' new village were required to build to a certain standard. A surviving legal document relating to a plot on the south side of the turnpike road (later 33–39 West Main Street) provides some interesting detail. The plot was 78 feet wide and extended 100 feet back from the road. The feu was taken in 1769 by Alexander Russell, tenant farmer at Dales farm, and by the terms set by Sir William Cunynghame, Alexander was obliged to build a house on his plot within ten years. The house was to be of stone and lime and it must extend the whole width of the north front excepting for a passageway no more than ten feet wide through to the back area, if need be. He was not permitted to build his house nearer than ten feet from the side of the turnpike road; and the side walls must be at least eight feet high with hewn stone facings around the doors and windows. Slate is not mentioned, so it's likely that the early houses were thatched. Thus, as well as controlling the sale of building plots in his new village, Sir William Cunynghame also controlled the size and appearance of the housing to ensure that the houses were of a decent standard and not the clay or turf huts of earlier times.

The roads

In documents of the 18th century, the north-south road through Whitburn was usually referred to as the loan, and the east-west highway as the causey (ie causeway, a road at least partially paved with cobblestones) or later as the Great Road. Villagers apparently referred to 'up the loan or doun the loan' and 'east the causey or west the causey'. The north-south route was also sometimes known as the drove loan, as it formed part of one of the age-old routes by which cattle were driven in great droves from the major cattle markets at Crieff and Falkirk, south towards the Borders and England.

It's probable that the location for the new village was chosen because it was at a crossroads where the new Great Road crossed the north-south loan. This Great Road was the second of the three Glasgow-Edinburgh turnpike roads that were built across West Lothian in the 18th century. First was the road via Linlithgow and Falkirk, which was upgraded to a turnpike road from 1751; next was the Shotts turnpike road via Livingston, Blackburn, Whitburn, Kirk o' Shotts and Newhouse, begun in 1753; third came the Bathgate and Airdrie turnpike of the 1790s.

The north-south loan was a local road leading south to the church and Longridge or north to Whitburn mill. In 1779, ironworks were established at Cleugh near Wilsontown, from where the ironmasters sent their iron to the port at Bo'ness. The route they used was upgraded to a turnpike road in 1781 and named the Cleugh Road. From Wilsontown, it passed the Breich crossroads and through Longridge to Whitburn – thus the north part of the loan (now Manse Road) became part of this busy Cleugh turnpike road. At the Cross, the Cleugh Road turned east to East

Whitburn, where it turned north on the road now severed by the M8 motorway, crossed the River Almond at Stepends Bridge, and so to Bathgate, Linlithgow and Bo'ness. Thus, East Main Street and its continuation to East Whitburn formed part of two turnpike roads – the Shotts and the Cleugh turnpikes.

Essential for travellers on these early roads was an inn where refreshments could be got, or a bed for the night, or a change of horses for the carriage. As we have seen, there was certainly an inn in Whitburn parish by 1744 when Alexander Carlyle stayed there. By 1764, John Robertson and his

> **Highway code**
>
> The convention of driving on the left was not yet firmly established, so the Cleugh Road trustees had to specify in 1816 that every rider or coach driver must drive 'to his own left hand, or what is commonly called holding to the near side.'

wife, Bethia Wright were the inn-keepers and the Heritors' records of 7 June 1764 include a claim from John Robertson junior, on behalf of his mother, 'for the entertainment of the Ministers during the vacancy' and for the dinner when Mr Porteous was inducted as the new minister of the parish church.'

A new Whitburn inn (replacing the original one, possibly in the Blaeberryhill area) was built, probably by Sir William Augustus Cunynghame, to take advantage of the increased traffic on the Great Road. He wished to protect the business by giving it a monopoly of travellers' trade, so his early feus banned the use of any other houses as inns or taverns 'for the reception of travellers in machines [horsedrawn vehicles] or on horseback during the currency of the present tack of the farm and Inn of Whitburn'. There was another inn, but it was on the Baillie family's property at the gates to Polkemmet House, so was outwith the Cunynghames' control. It took its name Halfway House from its position on the Edinburgh and Glasgow road – 21 miles from each city – and it was in business by at least 1774, probably catering for the carters, carriers and hawkers who travelled the Great Road. Whitburn Inn, however, catered for the prestige travellers – mail coaches, commercial coaches and private travellers.

CHAPTER 4

The Church – Patrons and Grave-robbers

THE MINISTER WHOSE call by the congregation provoked the Cunynghames' claim to the patronage of Whitburn parish, the Rev Alexander Wardrope, turned out to be popular with all sides. In the earlier part of his ministry

> multitudes, for twenty miles round, attended his ordinary ministrations, as well as on sacramental occasions. His preaching was clear, evangelical and useful.

But there was evidently already dissatisfaction in Whitburn with the established Church of Scotland, for the great English dissenting preacher, George Whitefield, included Whitburn in his hectic tour of Scotland in 1741, probably by invitation of William Wardrope, the surgeon-apothecary.

After Alexander Wardrope's death in 1759, the Rev William Porteous was presented to the charge of Whitburn by Lady Mary Cunynghame; her husband Sir David was abroad on military service. In the 1760s, the patronage of Whitburn parish was confirmed by the courts as belonging to Sir David Cunynghame, to the fury of those who had worked so hard and paid for the making of the new parish and church of Whitburn. Their anger led to many parishioners leaving the Church of Scotland in Whitburn and setting up the two seceding churches.

The new minister, Mr Porteous, was:

> a man of much practical ability and energy – one of the early supporters of the British and Foreign Bible Society, and [after leaving Whitburn] a vigorous and successful organiser of Sabbath Schools.

In 1770, Porteous moved to a parish in Glasgow.

As patron of the parish, Sir William Cunynghame notified the kirk session that he was to present the minister of Wamphray to be the new minister. The session decided:

> Considering that Mr Barron is little known in this Country... that Thomas Marshel... should go to Wamphray and make

what Inquiry he should think necessary to discover
Mr Barron's ministerial Character...

Marshel went diligently to work, drawing up a questionnaire about
Barron which he put to five neighbouring ministers, and was paid 7s 3d
for his expenses on the journey.

Whether the session liked him or not, Mr Barron came to Whitburn
but proved to be more interested in scholarship than the day-to-day work
of the parish. Many years later, an old man remembered him as:

the driest of all dry preachers... who used to say in my
remembrance 'I preached 20 minutes, and by that time the
people were tired of me and I of them.'

As well as his scholarly research, he published *An essay on the mechanical
principles of the plough* (1774) but allowed the kirk session to lapse that
same year − probably after he had lost some of his elders and members
to the new Burgher Secession congregation at Longridge. This departure
was triggered by Mr Barron's pay rise: the heritors, having ensured that
the rent of two farms near Shotts would pay the minister's stipend, were
angry when told they were liable to pay for his 'augmentation of stipend'.
In 1778, Mr Barron departed unlamented to be professor of Rhetoric and
Logic at the University of St Andrews.

Grave-robbers in Whitburn

Sir William Augustus Cunynghame then presented the Rev Dr James Somerville, who came to Whitburn after a period as minister of the Scots Kirk in
Rotterdam. Somerville moved on after ten years and was followed by the
Rev James Rhind, minister from 1790 until 1808 (again a Cunynghame
presentee). It was Rhind who wrote the report on Whitburn parish for the
first *Statistical Account* in the 1790, which shows that he had some knowledge of the village and parish. He was followed by the Rev James Watson
from 1809 till 1823. During both these ministries, the church records were
badly kept, or have gone missing, so that little is known about them. James
Watson, however, was remembered in the reminiscences of an elderly
Whitburn man in 1901. It seems that his outgoings exceeded his income,
and he decided to claim for himself the money raised for church funds by
the hire of the mortcloths. Samuel Greenshiels, the session clerk, rightly
refused to release the money but when Mr Watson came to his house with
a gun under his arm, he prudently handed it over. Watson was neither
devout nor evangelical and certainly offended his more godly parishioners.

This was the time of the grave-robbers (c.1800–32), so Watson arranged for a rota of people to keep watch at night over newly buried bodies in the churchyard and told the watchers to ring the bell if any resurrectionists were spotted and he would come and shoot them. Certainly, a possible bullet hole can be seen in a headstone in the churchyard. According to an old man reminiscing in 1901, a rumour went about in 1845 (long after grave-robbing had generally ceased in 1832) that a body recently buried had been stolen by the Martins, a family of weavers. A warrant was obtained to open the grave, and more than 50 years later the old man could

> still see Martin seize a big quarry-pick, leap on the coffin lid, tear it open, and by putting the pick under the body, prize it up and almost make it stand on its legs. The police declared this satisfactory, and that the *fama* [allegation] was without foundation.

CHAPTER 5

Working in the New Village:
Cotton Weaving and a Distillery

Occupations

WHAT WORK WAS available to those who settled in the new village of Whitburn? The earliest information on Whitburn's industry was produced by David Loch who made a tour of the *Trading towns and villages of Scotland* on behalf of the government in 1778. Whitburn, he wrote, was:

> A pleasant rising village, the property of Sir William Cunningham [*sic*], Bart. There are 27 looms at present employed at this place, in the winter at woollen, and in summer at linen.

This confirms that weaving was already an important trade in Whitburn, as it was also in Bathgate.

David Loch goes on to say that Sir William

> and some of his friends are immediately to lay out a considerable sum to establish a woollen manufactory here, of coarse cloths, druggets, sarges, camblets, and such goods. There is a true public spirit among the gentlemen in this neighbourhood...

At this period, many textile ventures were set up in Scotland but most were small and underfunded. With the further handicaps of limited local markets, poor roads to larger markets and an inexperienced workforce, few survived for very long. There is no evidence that Sir William Cunynghame's woollen manufactory was ever established and nothing more is heard of it.

Cotton manufactory

Fifteen years later (1793), however, the minister of the parish mentions the existence of a 'cotton manufactory, employing about 30 or 40 hands, at about 1s a day...' Confirmation of this is found in a document of 1792, when John Dick of Whitburn insured with the Sun Fire Office his 'Cotton Jeanie House... no stove therein [ie no fire hazard]... for a sum not exceeding one hundred pounds'. It was under the same roof as his dwelling house, which also operated as a draper's shop, but its location in Whitburn is not certain. Dick's 'cotton jeanie' was a mechanised spinning jenny (jenny or gin being an abbreviation for engine), which allowed one spinner to do the work of eight hand spinners and turned large quantities of cotton yarn into thread ready for the handloom weavers. It seems likely that the enterprising John Dick spun the thread, put it out to local weavers, then sold the completed cotton cloth for clothing.

The mechanisation of cotton spinning created work for armies of handloom weavers and the cotton industry was expanding rapidly in late 18th century Scotland. There was a cotton spinning mill in Blackburn by 1794, powered by the water of the River Almond and employing some 120 workers. Whitburn's 'manufactory' was on a much smaller scale but would have given employment to some of the displaced farmworkers and may have brought more people into the village. A writer in 1807 mentions the 'considerable cotton manufactory' in Whitburn but there is no further record of it. It may have been too small to compete against larger mills like Blackburn and made obsolete by the invention of the spinning mule. It was significant, however: the cotton spinning jenny was the first mechanisation of manufacturing processes – mechanisation that drove the Industrial Revolution that changed the world and made Britain the richest and most powerful nation in the world in the 19th century. In the cotton 'manufactory' of Whitburn, the Industrial Revolution arrived in West Lothian.

Traders and soldiers

The minister listed the trades in the parish of Whitburn in 1793:

Shopkeepers	3	Public-houses	4
Cotton manufactory	30 or 40	Alehouses	6
Surgeon	1	Weavers	20
Physician	1		
Masons and wrights	15	Muslin flowerers	50
Shoemakers	6	Clergymen	3
Baker and butcher	2	Landowners	26

A number of local men worked as carriers, taking farm produce by horse and cart to Edinburgh for sale. Others took grain from Leith and Dalkeith to Glasgow, often bringing back a load of pig-iron from the ironworks of the west for selling in Edinburgh.

At least a dozen Whitburn men joined the regular army, many of them during the Peninsular Wars, and some of them fought at Waterloo in 1815. Archibald Mackenzie served in the Waterloo campaign, though not in the actual battle. So, too, did James Flemington, remembered as 'the finest-looking man in Whitburn... tall, well-knit and erect in his bearing'. He served in the Life Guards and guarded two monarchs, George IV and William IV, 'of neither of whom did he speak in high praise'. After discharge, the old soldiers were entitled to a pension, payment of which was usually admin-

> **Whitburn distillery**
>
> A submission to the House of Commons drawn up c.1798 for Scottish lowland distillers notes that 'A distiller at Whitburn, using a twenty Gallon Still, appears to have made weekly, with this small Still, 200 Gallons of good Spirits from Malt.' So small a venture would not have required a purpose-built distillery, and as no further mention has been found of it, it was presumably a minor and short-lived venture.

istered through the local kirk session. Davie Richardson of Whitburn served in the 21st Fusilier Guards, was captured during the Peninsular Wars and kept a prisoner of war in France for five years. After release in 1814, he survived a shot through the leather collar of his uniform at the Battle of New Orleans in January 1815 during a short war between Britain and the United States. His collar with the bullet hole was proudly on show in his daughter Mrs Leggatt's house in Whitburn until her death in 1913.

Starch works

An advert appeared in an Edinburgh newspaper in 1805, 'To be let: the premises in the village of Whitburn lately erected and sometime occupied as a STARCH WORK.' The equipment to be sold included two 'Yetling Cockells [cast iron stoves] and five large oak casks. This was yet another venture of John Dick, cotton jeanie owner and pioneer of the Industrial Revolution in West Lothian.

Starch was commonly produced from potatoes and was used mainly in paper-making and in textiles. It's likely that the starch works was set up to provide starch for the cotton mill at the west end of Blackburn (established 1794) and for the weavers of Whitburn and Bathgate, who used starch to reduce breakages of their yarn. The starch works is unlikely to have given work to more than three or four people, and no further mention of it has been found after 1805.

Weavers

The Old *Statistical Account* lists some 20 weavers and another 50 flowerers (probably the wives and daughters of the weavers), indicating that 70 of the economically active persons in the parish were already dependent on the weaving trade in the 1790s. The earliest Whitburn weavers probably combined weaving with other work, mainly agricultural, and wove locally produced linen or wool into cloth for local use. When cotton was introduced and the spinning process was mechanised, huge quantities of cotton thread was produced and there were not enough weavers to weave the amount of thread being produced. Weavers were in demand: their wages went up to unprecedented heights – far more than other workers could earn.

Such high wages attracted newcomers to weaving, many of them agricultural workers who had lost their land or their jobs as a result of the changes and improvements being made to farming. They were doubtless glad to find a trade like weaving that could be fairly quickly learned and would allow them to stay in their own areas. With high wages and working independently at home, they could stop and start as they pleased and still make enough money without having to work long hours. They had time to spend on reading books and newspapers and became noted for their interest in current affairs, politics, theology and the natural world. They could afford to educate their sons and daughters, thus reinforcing the weavers' reputation as the most literate of all working-class groups. The weavers valued their independence. Their literacy made them politically aware and radical and gave them the confidence to stand up to the establishment, gentry and clergy: a significant proportion of Scottish handloom weavers were seceders (ie members of churches other than the Church of Scotland).

The years from 1790 till 1810 are considered the golden age of handloom weavers in Scotland. The earning and spending power of the Whitburn weavers contributed to the growth of Whitburn in its first half century; the prosperity of the village was closely linked to the fortunes of the weaving industry.

The women and children of weaving families were also involved in the trade. Younger children were employed as pirn winders – winding the yarn onto the bobbins ready for their fathers to place the bobbin in the shuttle for weaving. Wives and daughters were likely to be tambourers, who embroidered woven cotton using a frame shaped like a tambourine; or flowerers, who did fine embroidery in flower patterns – skilled work but sore on the eyes. In his *Statistical Account* of Whitburn parish in 1793, the minister noted that 'about 50 young people, from nine to 30 years of age, are employed in the flowering of muslins for Glasgow, earning usually about 10d or 1s a day'. The tambouring webs for embroidering were delivered from a Glasgow firm to Peter Murray's father's house at 87 West Main Street and he recalled that 'many of the ball dresses of silks and satins for the London Ladies passed through the skilful hands of the Whitburn tambourers'.

By the end of the 18th century, Whitburn was firmly established: it had the weaving industry to employ its inhabitants, and tradesmen to service the village and surrounding farms. With increased population came the need for more professionals – medical men, clergy and teachers – more tradesmen such as bakers, masons and wrights and also a few shopkeepers; so here we can see the start of the rise of the middle class of Whitburn. And to assist the population to spend its limited disposable income, there were ten public houses in the parish.

CHAPTER 6

Everyday Life

Farming & food

BY THE 1790s, the land around Whitburn was mostly 'improved'. Most of it was pasture for cattle; on the arable land, the main crops were oats and potatoes, with almost no wheat grown at all. Small quantities of flax were raised (there was a lint [flax] mill at Swineabbey near East Whitburn) to make linen for local needs and some horses were bred for sale, as well as black cattle – the small, hardy breed that was prevalent in Scotland at the time. Sheep were seldom found in Whitburn parish. It was a fairly self-sufficient economy but already the farms were prosperous enough to yield a surplus – calves, poultry, milk, cheese and butter – which was taken by horse and cart to Edinburgh to be sold.

Farming became geared to the needs of the towns and cities and, being halfway between Edinburgh and Glasgow, Whitburn was well-placed to benefit from these. The agricultural improvements had been begun by the great landowners like the Cunynghames and the Baillies but their success encouraged the smaller farmers to follow suit. Enclosures and other improvements could double or treble the yield of crops and livestock and the outlay could be recouped by a skilful farmer within a few years. However, there was still the Scottish weather to contend with and, as the minister observed in 1793, Whitburn parish was notably wet, especially on its higher southern ground. Poor harvests in 1772–3 and again in 1782–3 brought many of the poor close to starvation – but even those years could not prevent the upward trend in living standards. Rents rose but profits rose by a still higher rate, so in general everyone was better off. By 1800, the poor were still poor but not quite as poor as their forefathers had been.

Although the population of the landward part of Whitburn parish had dropped by the end of the 18th century, the population of the parish as a whole was rising, thanks to the village. The gradual change from a rural to an urban population in Scotland can be seen in microcosm in Whitburn.

James Trotter provided a glimpse of life for West Lothian folk in 1808. The usual working hours for labourers and farm workers in summer was

6.00am till 6.00pm; and in winter, from dawn till dusk. Women domestic servants had the longest hours: from 5.00am or 6.00am till 8.00pm or 9.00pm. Oats and potatoes were the staple foods.

> The usual food of the common people is – oatmeal porridge for breakfast; for dinner, broth made of barley... and of vegetables, sometimes with butcher meat, and sometimes without it; and for supper, potatoes two-thirds of the year, and porridge the remaining third. Oat cakes is the common bread.

It was a healthy albeit a monotonous diet. 'The use of tea and of wheat bread,' wrote James Trotter of West Lothian in 1808, 'has of late crept in among the lower classes, and is rather gaining ground. It is an unlucky practice. The new food is more expensive than the old, and is not more nourishing.'

Keeping the peace

Life in the 18th century was not a crime-free, rural idyll. For example, a newspaper reported in 1730 that 'Moore, the Ringleader of a notorious Gang of Thieves, was apprehended at Whitburn, and carry'd to the Prison of Linlithgow.' Law and order was maintained by the baron court of the barony of Whitburn, to which people could be summoned (either as the accused, as witnesses or as jurors). The barony officer or bailie was the nearest thing to a law officer at that time – a cross between a magistrate and a policeman. The bailies tended to be respectable working men, like Henry Kinloch, a Whitburn mason who was held the post in 1736. Also at the baron court, rent was gathered in for the landlord, disputes between neighbours or between tenants and landlord were settled and wrongdoers fined.

The sinners of Whitburn

The Church had the power to supervise many aspects of everyday life and to judge the moral conduct of the people. To marry, have a child baptised or move into or out of the parish required a certificate testifying that the holder was in good standing with the church. Without this certificate, they could not receive poor relief, baptism or communion. The majority accepted the discipline; a few chafed against it but had to accept it eventually.

The responsibilities of the kirk session were wide-ranging. Some of its many activities in the 18th century were: listing the parish poor and paying allowances to them; building a school and school-house; taking up a collection to help build a new pier at Bo'ness, and a bridge over the River Stinchar in Ayrshire; buying communion cups and plates and a 'paper book' for recording baptisms; paying for the education of several poor children, including 'John Eastoun, a fatherless boy', and 'George Nicol, whose parents are not able to educate him'; ordering up coffins for the poor; making payments to John Wilson, 'his family being in distress' and to 'four objects [ie objects of pity] barbarously used by the Algerines' – probably sailors who had been captured and mutilated by Algerian pirates in the Mediterranean; and paying a sick man, William Edmiston in Easter Whitburn, 'a shilling per month... to continue until he either recover or be removed by Death'.

In addition to their charitable work, the kirk session often acted as a court to try minor misdemeanours such as drunkenness, blaspheming and sexual misconduct. Witnesses were cited to appear, as in a civil court, and evidence was taken. In a case heard by the session in 1734, a man accused of fornication called 16 witnesses to prove his alibi and was cleared of the charge. Sexual misdemeanours were the most common cases, probably because the outcome of them was often a very visible pregnancy. The very first case to come before the new Whitburn kirk session in 1731 was alleged adultery between Alexander Anderson, weaver in Mossburgh, and Agnes Wilson, servant to John Meek in Easter Whitburn. Anderson tried to deny it but witnesses were heard and Agnes' evidence was detailed. She:

> confessed she was one night with him in the said house and that after she had received a drink of warm ale, a woman in the house having sucked her breast [Agnes had recently given birth], she went to bed, but did not put off her clothes and left the said Alex Anderson drinking at the fireside, and that after she was fallen asleep, he came to the bed where she was lying and lay down without her knowledge.

The couple were found to be guilty, Agnes Wilson appeared eight times at the place of public repentance in the church and was 'absolved' from the scandal of adultery. The slate was wiped clean and she was again in good standing with the church. Anderson appeared on the place of public repentance but instead of submitting to a public rebuke from the minister, 'he behaved in a most rude and indecent Manner to the great offence of the Congregation.' However, he too eventually submitted to church discipline.

The prurient interest of the session was because of the need to establish who the father was in order to ensure that he took financial responsibility for the child's upkeep. If no father was known, then the Church became responsible for the child's upkeep. Thus we read of Isabella

Lockie, 'servitrix' to David Martin in Wester Whitburn who in 1735 had 'brought forth a child in uncleanness'. She named Robert Weir junior in Burnwynd as the father. He denied it but she:

> declared that he had carnal dealing with her in Polkemmet's Crops sometimes in July last about the Magdalene fair in Linlithgow, as she was cutting grass, also that he committed uncleanness two several times with her before, among the Whin be-west his father's house in Burnwynd.

She continued to accuse and he to deny, so the Lockie case was left 'till God in his providence give further light therein' – which happened very quickly, as the following week Robert Weir came to the minister and admitted paternity.

Sometimes the detail given is startlingly explicit: in June 1781, the kirk session considered the case of James Smart in Whitburn and Elizabeth Marshel, spouse to John Thornton. In her defence, Elizabeth Marshel declared that:

> James Smart came west that day with a cock to her mother's house, that he and her mother went down to the watter with her, and that her mother went home, and she saying to James Smart she durst not bath herself in the watter, he took hold of her and said he would duck her, upon which she pulling herself from him, fell backward and said James Smart fell upon her... she also worried she could not say but her clothes might be up, but could not say how they were.

The witnesses cited were Alex Wallace at Halfway House and John Calder, his apprentice. Alex Wallace said:

> that as he and John Calder were going to their work upon Friday last they saw a man and woman lying by the watter side at a saugh [willow] bush, the woman with her clothes up and the man above her betwixt her bare thighs, and that he saw the man's shirt out, and they immediately upon seeing the Declarant changed their posture, and the Declarant said to James Smart, Have you got your pipe blown? James Smart said, No, and he said to him, You were in a fair way for it.

The kirk session minutes remain fascinating today for they provide glimpses of ordinary lives, hardships and pleasures, innocent as well as guilty – a drink of warm ale, dozing at the fireside, smoking a pipe,

washing clothes by the water side, attending the Lammas Fair in Bathgate. Life was hard and pleasures were simple – being in company with
friends and plenty of drinking. And occasionally the authentic voice of
the 18th century poor is heard – as when Thomas Marshel is accused of
swearing at others with the oath, 'Deil stap out your E'en!' Or the farm
servant who was woken one morning before dawn to deal with an errant
servant girl: 'I mused a little and took a pipe, and before I had done, the
light was coming down the Lum.'

Sabbath Observance and the actress

The Sabbath was strictly observed. In 1782, 89 parishioners of Whitburn
met in the parish church and drew up a petition to be sent to the Sheriff
of Linlithgow, asking that the drivers of the 'New Castle Waggon' should
not be allowed to drive through the parish on Sundays. The Newcastle wagon was the long-distance freight lorry of its day, carrying goods
between Scotland and the north of England and following a set route and
timetable. In reply to the petition, the wagon's owners explained that it
generally arrived on the boundary of Whitburn parish between 6.ooam
and 7.ooam on Sundays but there was no public house where the drivers
and their horses might stop; therefore, they drove on a few miles into
the parish, 'passing the small village of Whitburn long before the time of
divine service'. They reached an inn at 8.ooam and did not stir from there
till Monday morning. The outcome of the petition is not known.

By the 1790s, some passenger coaches apparently did run on Sundays, to the great annoyance of the more devout residents. Archibald
Bruce, Whitburn's Antiburgher minister, strongly objected to the distur-
bances caused by Sabbath drivers and passengers:

> the loud vociferations, the damnable oaths and drunken mer-
> riment of an intemperate crew, which often are superadded to
> the rattling noise of coaches and post chaises…; one may now
> see no less than ten or twelve carriages at once convened about
> the door of… the inns…

Another example of strict Sabbath observance in Whitburn comes in the
Memoirs of Mrs Charlotte Deans, an actress with a travelling theatre
company. About 1805, during a two-year tour of Scotland, the company
had the misfortune 'to languish and starve at Bathgate and Whiteburn.'
Mrs Deans, aged about 37, was heavily pregnant with her 13th child.
After performing at Bathgate on a Saturday night, they set off on foot

for Whitburn on the Sunday morning, 'carrying each our little bundle of dresses'. On the way, they were:

> repeatedly stopped by the good kirk-going folks, to give an account why we were travelling on the Lord's day, whether it was the work of necessity... some threatened to take us before the Bailie...

The actors responded that they would gladly go before the Bailie and stay there the whole day, if their accusers would pay the expenses – 'which they universally declined'. The actress tartly remarks that the local people were 'Christians enough to pronounce damnation against us for breaking the sabbath' but not Christian enough to 'sacrifice their world's wealth to promote their religion.'

At Whitburn, Mrs Deans continues: 'we had a severe time of it, as my situation disabled me from performing; here I remained a month, expecting every day to be confined, and at last was compelled to go forward'. On the very next day, at Lanark, her child was born.

'the abominations of popery'

The population was not uninformed about what was going on in the wider world. The gentry, clergy and schoolmaster would have read the weekly national newspapers and disseminated the information via the pulpit, the school and by word of mouth. For example, at the kirk session meeting on 22 June 1746:

> the Min[iste]r read from the ... Act for a Thanksgiving day Thursday next for the Victory at Culloden when the Rebels were scattered. As also the Duke of Cumberland His proclamation warning People from harbouring of Rebels was read.

Whitburn was too Covenanting and Presbyterian to have any sympathy for the Jacobite rebels and no Whitburn men are known to have served with the Jacobite army – unlike Bathgate or Linlithgow.

In 1779, local people had heard that:

> a bill is intended to be brought into parliament, for repealing the penal statues against Roman Catholics in Scotland, and that in all probability, the same might pass into a law, without a spirited opposition took place.

So some Whitburn residents drew up a petition opposing greater toler-
ance for Catholics. Their opposition seems to have been based on a belief
that Catholicism was an authoritarian religion and that greater influence
for the Catholic Church would lead to the loss of civil and religious liberties. The Whitburn petition states that:

> We also feel the weight of the obligation of our national
> covenant, wherein we, in our fathers, did most solemnly
> renounce the abominations of Popery, and bound ourselves
> to oppose these.

It was an opposition based on a deep-rooted and tribal fear, rather than
on dislike of any members of the local population: there was probably
not a single Catholic in the whole parish of Whitburn at the time.

The resolution was published in a newspaper and submitted to an
Edinburgh Committee which was co-ordinating the campaign against
repeal. It is unsigned, but the mix of learned political and theological
objections have the stamp of one man – the Rev Archibald Bruce who
is still remembered in Whitburn today in the name Brucefield. This is
the more probable in that the following year (1780), Bruce published
a book called *Free Thoughts on the Toleration of Popery*, in which he
argued against toleration for Catholics. This book 'procured Mr Bruce
the friendship of Lord George Gordon... who, a year or two later, visited
Mr Bruce at Whitburn.' This unstable nobleman was the instigator of
the huge 'No Popery' petition of June 1780, which was followed by the
violent and destructive Gordon Riots in London.

CHAPTER 7

Radicals, Riot and Revolution

The Unlikely Radicals: Bruce and Brown

WILLIAM WARDROPE OF Cult, no doubt still angry that the Cunynghames had the right to choose Whitburn's minister, offered land to the Associate Synod (Antiburgher) denomination for the building of a church in Whitburn parish. (Antiburghers refused to sign the Burgess Oath, which required holders of public office to swear approval of the Established Church. They viewed the oath as a case of the state interfering in religious freedom of conscience.) Archibald Bruce, born near Denny, was chosen by the new congregation as their first minister in 1768 when he was just 22 and he remained there for the next 48 years. The Antiburghers were a small denomination whose divinity students were few in number, so their college and its library of books followed its professor of divinity. When Archibald Bruce was appointed professor in 1786, his church with its clay floor and high-backed pews, had a second floor built over it for the divinity students and became known as the barracks (ie communal accommodation). The building survived until the 1930s and stood in the gusset between the Longridge road and Dixon Terrace.

In 1806, Bruce and three other ministers found themselves at odds with the doctrine of their Church on its relations with the state and were deposed from its ministry. The four formed themselves into an even smaller denomination, which they called the Constitutional Associate Presbytery (known mockingly as the Auld Licht Antiburghers). Bruce continued as its professor of divinity, though the number of his students seldom exceeded half a dozen.

He was a scholar and writer whose collected works filled nine volumes, and he could read Latin, Greek, Dutch, German and French. One of his books satirised patronage in the Church of Scotland: 'What is the chief end of modern clergyman? To obtain a presentation and enjoy the benefice and the favour of the patron all the days of his life.' His interests were not confined to theology but included science, for his published work included *An historical account of the most remarkable earthquakes and volcanic eruptions from the beginning of the world to the present time.*

Such a man does not sound a typical radical but in fact he was dangerously radical in some of his political writings. It has to be remembered that in the 18th century, reforming left-wing politics were widely associated with what we would now think of as right-wing religious attitudes; whereas the more tolerant and broad-minded Church of Scotland was decidedly Tory in its politics.

The French Revolution broke out in 1789 and in 1793–4 descended into great savagery. The aristocracy and gentry were guillotined in their thousands, the Church was abolished and the established order was turned upside down. The British government and ruling classes were deeply afraid that the contagion would reach Britain. A series of measures were passed which restricted freedom of speech and banned political meetings, calls for reform or even criticism of existing institutions. Radical writers like Thomas Paine were arrested and tried; in Scotland, several prominent radicals were convicted of sedition and harshly punished. Even publishers, printers and booksellers were prosecuted for daring to issue publications calling for reform. In response to these measures, Archibald Bruce wrote a pamphlet entitled *A peacable declaration* opposing the outbreak of war between France and Britain and severely criticising the government for restricting freedom of speech, describing it as rotten and 'tottering on its last expedients of force and terror'. Lawyers advised him that he risked trial, imprisonment or transportation to Botany Bay. It has been said that Bruce brought a printer to Whitburn to publish his own works because he was so prolific a writer. In fact, it's almost certain that it was because Bruce was unable to find an established printer willing to print his dangerous writings that he brought a printing press and printer from Edinburgh to Whitburn. John Fin(d)lay was not a skilled printer: his output was poor and his paper cheap. However, his work allowed Bruce to self-publish his writings at a time of severe restrictions on freedom of speech. Bruce's most dangerous writings were printed without the author's or printer's names – though they would have been easy enough to trace – like his 1794 work, *Reflections on the freedom of writing*, complete with a tabloid-style strapline on its title page: 'What Britons dare to think, he dares to tell':

> He [Bruce] scarce thought it possible that in our days, the
> old frenzy of tyrannical imposition and persecution should
> in any degree recur, or that Britons should ever be in danger
> of losing acquaintance with their darling liberty or their
> high estimation for it, or that they should tamely suffer any
> portion of it either to be stolen or wrested from them.' 'Civil
> and religious liberty are but two great branches of the same

expanded tree.' The threat of prosecution for sedition 'is the great political scare-crow, hung out to terrify the slavish herd, and keep the unthinking populace at a due distance.

Bruce was evidently a bold man; however, as a seceder, he lacked credibility among the intellectuals and upper class of his day. His works never reached a wide audience and the title of one of them may suggest why: *A Historico-Politico-Ecclesiastical Dissertation on the Supremacy of Civil Powers in Matters of Religion; particularly the Ecclesiastical Supremacy annexed to the English Crown.* He survived the dangerous years of 1792–5 perhaps simply because, as both a writer and preacher, he was too dull to be dangerous.

As a divinity professor, he was effective and respected but in the pulpit, he was slow and tedious and attracted a very small congregation:

> With a spare, erect figure... and wearing the full-bottomed wig, long cane and large shoe buckles of olden time, he presented to the last the polite bearing of the gentleman with the sedateness of the scholar and the minister.

He lived on an annual stipend of just £50, less than many a farm servant. Since he was able to employ a printer for several years, he presumably had private means to pay him. 'The delicately modest recluse of Whitburn' died suddenly at the age of 70. It seems a pity that so independent and fearless a man, who placed such a high value on liberty, should have tied himself into ever narrower denominations and anti-Catholicism.

Rev John Brown

Almost a contemporary of Archibald Bruce was the Rev John Brown, minister of the Whitburn Burgher congregation. The Associate Synod Church, which split off from the Church of Scotland in 1733, split again in 1747 over the Burgess Oath. The Burghers (who felt able to swear the oath) set up a congregation at Longridge in the parish of Whitburn in 1774 and the congregation chose the Rev John Brown as their minister. Inducted in 1777 (like Bruce, at the age of just 22), Brown remained there till he died in 1832 – a ministry of 56 years. He was the son of the well-known Rev John Brown of Haddington and the grandfather of the writer Dr John Brown who enjoyed great popularity during the Victorian age with sentimental tales like *Pet Marjorie* and *Rab and his Friends*.

Brown was not so narrow in his religious views as Bruce, nor so political, and his denomination was more tolerant. Bruce was respected but Brown was loved and he attracted large congregations to his small church in Longridge. Many anecdotes about him survive: riding to Haddington on his Shetland pony to preach at a communion service, he overtook an elderly member of his own congregation walking the 40 miles to Haddington to hear him. She had nowhere to stay overnight, so that afternoon he enquired from the pulpit 'Whaur's the auld wifie that followed me frae Whitburn? I have fund ye a bed; ye're to sleep wi' Johnnie Fife's lass.' A line from the florid inscription on his gravestone in Whitburn churchyard sums him up: 'His cheerful piety and active benevolence endeared him to all who knew him.'

Whitburn had among the highest proportion of seceders in the whole of Scotland. The fact that the two seceder churches in Whitburn parish claimed two thirds of church attenders, and the established Church of Scotland only one third, suggests the independence of the local people. As self-employed tradesmen and weavers, they need not be deferential to the established church or the laird. Some had experienced the upheaval of lowland clearances, which had severed their ties to the landowners. And of course, the patronage dispute had infuriated them, with the result that 'not many, even of the most sensible in the parish, can talk, with any degree of patience, of patronage or augmentation of stipends.' With their intellect honed on abstruse points of Presbyterian doctrine, they were well able to grasp political, radical and social issues of the time.

Slavery

Whitburn people demonstrated their radicalism by confronting two issues which greatly agitated public and political opinion during the last few years of the 18th century – slavery and reform.

Slavery was a burning topic in the 1780s and 1790s, with many beginning to realise its cruelty and calling for its abolition. A Scot called William Dickson was among the leading figures in the abolition campaign. He had witnessed the appalling treatment of slaves while working in the West Indies and in 1792 he embarked on a ten-week tour of Scotland to enlist support for abolition. In each town he sought out the leading figures – clergy, lairds, councillors – gave them a copy of an anti-slavery report and encouraged the ministers to preach about the horrors of the trade.

Travelling to Glasgow on 17 January 1792, Dickson stopped to dine at the inn at Whitburn and got into conversation with some travellers. In his diary, he noted:

> One of the gentlemen I found had been in the West Indies. Asserted negroes better off than British poor, that descriptions of their condition greatly exaggerated, that our

evidence applied to state of things 20 and even 30 years ago... thought that the trade however was a horrid one and ought to be abolished, but for the sake of the planters, gradually abolished. I defeated him on every tack as the company... were pleased to say. Negroes universally labouring under the whip like cattle had great effect. The poor ladies, one of them pretty, absolutely looked pale. I begged pardon, but said necessary to speak out the truth... In short, my antagonist who behaved well and like a gentleman on the whole, when we rose up, took a glass and drank to gradual abolition. I drank to immediate [abolition]...

The travellers may not have been Whitburn residents but the extract indicates that the issue was widely known and discussed. It may have been as a result of his brief visit that Whitburn took a stance on the issue two months later.

In an era when only the wealthy and land-owning class had the vote, publishing petitions in a newspaper was the usual way for towns or organisations to make their views known; it was one of the few ways in which ordinary people could make their voices heard. If public opinion as expressed through petitions in newspapers became vociferous, the government might think it wise to listen. On the matter of slavery, 185 Scottish towns and parishes published pro-abolition petitions in 1792, (proportionately far more than from England,) thus making it fairly clear to the government that the balance of Scottish public opinion was on the side of abolition. In West Lothian, West Calder, Bathgate and Whitburn all declared in favour of abolition. Whitburn's declaration appeared in the *Caledonian Mercury* newspaper of 10 March 1792:

Whitburn, 2 March 1792

A number of the inhabitants of Whitburn, and places adjacent, in consequence of the public attention being called to the consideration of the African Slave Trade, having consulted together on the subject, unanimously agree in declaring–

That the Slave Trade has ever appeared to them... to be highly unjust, inhuman, and perfectly incompatible with that improved civilisation, and those principles of liberty in which Britons glory, as well as with the spirit and laws of that religion which we profess...

Referring to slaves as 'our fellow men', the writers express 'their abhorrence and indignation' at it and continue:

> They heartily approve of the vigorous efforts of those, whether societies or individuals, who have taken a decided part in opposition to this abominable system and who are still persisting in their endeavours to have it abolished, notwithstanding of the powerful opposition against which they have been obliged to contend.

And what's more, the people of Whitburn were willing to put their hands in their pockets for the cause, as they had already subscribed £360 to be sent to the Committee for Abolition in Edinburgh. A committee had been formed in Whitburn, comprising the two dissenting ministers, Bruce and Brown, together with Robert Brown, the local schoolmaster and it was they who drew up the declaration. Unfortunately, the names of the 360 local people who signed the declaration are not given and nothing further is recorded about the Whitburn committee for the abolition of slavery. However, following national campaigning led by William Wilberforce, the government abolished trading in slaves in 1807 and emancipated the slaves in all of Britain's colonies in 1833.

The 360 names on the Whitburn declaration are unlikely to have included the Baillies of Polkemmet, for the Baillies had links with slavery, albeit later ones. In 1817, William Baillie's sister Penuel, who was 25, was married off to Farquhar Campbell, a man of 57, who owned the estate of Ormsary in Argyll. In addition, he owned the estates of Melville Ormsary and Strath Campbell in Demerara, a British colony on the north coast of South America. After Campbell's death in 1829, Sir William Baillie his brother-in-law was one of the executors of his will and, as such, applied for and won compensation for the loss of the slaves on Campbell's estates at emancipation in 1834. The number of Campbell's slaves was 197 and the compensation paid the following year (not to the slaves but to the owners, Campbell's trustees) was nearly £10,800. By the terms of the will, the money was divided among Sir William and three others. Penuel's husband had three illegitimate sons, at least one of whom was of mixed race and was educated in Scotland. Presumably the boy's mother was one of his father's slaves. And William Baillie himself married into the family of Dennistoun, of Dennistoun, Buchanan & Co, one of the big six sugar companies in Scotland, making their money through the labour of slaves in Britain's West Indian plantations. Even the ordinary people of Whitburn were not untouched: Whitburn's weavers wove with cotton imported from the West Indian slave plantations and later from the plantations of the American South. And some of their cloth, once woven, would very probably have been exported to clothe the multitudes of African slaves in the West Indies.

Friends of the People

Another radical movement attracted supporters from Whitburn in the 1790s. Towards the end of 1792, the French king was deposed and imprisoned, and France declared itself a republic. The ruling classes were deeply afraid that the revolution might spread to Britain and, during this febrile period, opinion in Britain polarised between those who called for similar reforms here and those who feared any change at all.

In July 1792, the first convention of the Societies of the Friends of the People in Scotland met in Edinburgh to call for reform. Many branches of this political society had been established in the preceding months throughout Scotland, with membership mainly drawn from artisans, particularly weavers. Led by Thomas Muir of Huntershill, the convention made fairly moderate demands: the vote for all adult males and more frequent general elections. However, it borrowed the language of the French Revolution, calling its meetings a General Convention and its members Citizens. Among the dozens of branches in Scotland were at least three in West Lothian: Mid Calder, Linlithgow and Whitburn. The president of the Whitburn branch was John Stark, who owned the lands of Gateside and Doghillock; and the secretary was James Shaw – nothing is known of him. Shortly after the Convention, many of the societies published 'resolutions' in the Edinburgh newspapers. Whitburn's was published in the *Caledonian Mercury* and the *Edinburgh Gazetteer* of 5 February 1793:

> A number of the inhabitants in this town and parish having previously formed themselves into an association, under the name and designation of the Friends of Liberty and of the People,
>
> Resolves unanimously,
>
> 1. That this association correspond with other associated Friends of the People throughout Great Britain, who are engaged in the patriotic design of proposing and promoting a Reform by all peaceable and regular means.
>
> 2. That they particularly express their hearty concurrence with them in the design of obtaining a more equal representation of the people in parliament; more frequent

meetings of parliament, and of promoting free, full, and useful information on all subjects, connected with public Reform.

3. That the present representation, in which so few of the community have any sort of concern, can hardly be considered as any thing else than nominal, a mockery of language, and an insult on the people at large....

In addition, they called for freedom of the press and the right to meet freely to discuss political questions – hardly rebellion but dangerous stuff at that time. The resolution was made available for local people to sign, then presumably was sent in to the leaders of the movement who would present it to Parliament as a petition for reform.

Alarmed by this new involvement of the lower classes in calls for political reform, the government arrested Thomas Muir and other leaders and, after show trials designed to intimidate, condemned them to transportation to Australia for 14 years, proceedings which shocked even diehard members of the English establishment.

Despite the fate of Muir and his associates, the Scottish Friends of the People planned a second convention in late 1793. Each society was asked to send a delegate to the convention: 28 did so, including the Whitburn branch. George Waddell (a local merchant) attended to represent Whitburn. The reformers attending the convention were literate, skilled, respectable men who clearly had some knowledge of political affairs and the writings of Thomas Paine. The meetings of the convention consisted of a great deal of administrative business, lengthy speeches raising awareness of political inequality, and the preparation of a petition to the House of Commons for parliamentary reform. By the second week, attendance was in decline: many delegates could not afford to miss work for long. Despite a demand from the leadership that the delegates 'remain at their posts', George Waddell was one of many who had ceased to attend by the twelfth day.

As the government considered 'the word Reform as tantamount to Rebellion', this second convention was dispersed and the remaining moderate members withdrew in alarm. The House of Commons rejected their petition, the societies lost heart and most folded. Nothing more is heard of any of the three West Lothian branches.

The bravery of these West Lothian men should not be underestimated. Most communities in West Lothian published not calls for reform but loyal declarations setting out their adherence to the current political set-up that were critical of the reformers: Linlithgow did so, as did Kirkliston,

Bo'ness, Abercorn and Ecclesmachan. William Baillie of Polkemmet called a meeting of the landlords and gentry of Linlithgowshire

> to consider of the proper modes to counteract the effect of the seditious and inflammatory publications industriously circulated, and other means used among the lower classes of people, to stir up discontents against the Constitution and Government.

The meeting drew up a loyal resolution to be submitted to the government and published it in an Edinburgh newspaper:

> We will... exert our utmost endeavours to assist the civil Magistrate in quelling every appearance of riot and disorder, and in apprehending and bringing to justice all those who... shall attempt to disturb the public peace... if any grievances or abuses do exist at present, the increasing prosperity of the country, and the happiness of all ranks of people, demonstrate that they cannot be of so pressing a nature, as to justify us in calling for a Reform at this time, because we are convinced that a number of seditious and designing men are ready to avail themselves of such an opportunity to attempt the total destruction of our present Constitution.' They declared their readiness to 'stand by his Majesty with our lives and fortunes against all enemies foreign and domestic... to assist the Civil Magistrates in quelling any disorder...'

Robert Purdie and the Militia Riot

The prosecution that might have befallen Archibald Bruce or the Whitburn Friends of the People happened in reality to Robert Purdie, Whitburn's surgeon. In those days, a country surgeon was not a highly trained professional but Purdie was earning enough to keep a horse for getting about on and to buy a house in Whitburn. In August 1797, he was involved in a huge demonstration on Bathgate Muir against new legislation allowing the government to conscript men for service in the militia (an army for home defence). The crowd, said to number some 2,000, became disorderly and demanded that William Baillie, depute Lord Lieutenant of the county, promise not to enforce the act. A deputation (including Robert Purdie) forcibly brought Baillie to the meeting and obliged him to sign a pledge that he would not assist in carrying out the conscription. They even forced him to pay the 19 shillings of stamp tax on the paper used!

Two months later, Purdie and three others were arrested and tried for rioting. The prisoners admitted they had been present but

> had committed no violence and that they had been from inno-
> cent motives at the meeting, one of them to get the names of
> his sons struck out of the list, another to get payment of a bill
> from a person who was on the Moor at the time.

Considering the vagueness of the charges, it's heartening to read that the charges were deemed not proven and the men were released.

Four days after the Bathgate events, a similar demonstration against the Militia Act in Tranent, Midlothian, was violently dispersed by a troop of cavalry; 12 men, women and children were slaughtered.

The gentry and middle class of West Lothian were acutely aware of the discontent of the 'lower ranks'. West Lothian farmer James Trotter wrote in 1808 that:

> it is undeniable also, that since the era of the French revolu-
> tion, an extraordinary degree of irritation has existed in the
> minds of men among the lower classes...

The depute lieutenants of each county were even more wary of calls for reform, as part of their role was to 'inform themselves respecting the dispo-sitions of those living in their districts'. In other words, it was the duty of William Baillie of Polkemmet to report to the government any signs of dis-affection in West Lothian. The presence of so powerful a 'Government man' in the district must have discouraged all but the bravest from showing their disaffection, particularly in Whitburn where they would be known to him.

After the failure of the Friends of the People, a more radical group was formed, the United Scotsmen, whose membership had a high pro-portion of weavers and seceders. Since Whitburn was full of both, it may have had a number of United Scotsmen but no records exist. The organ-isation was banned in 1799. The government was perhaps right to fear that these demands for reform were the thin end of the wedge: these were the first stirrings of political awareness and demands for extension of the vote, leading eventually to today's democracy.

The Whitburn Volunteers

An ordinary man suspected of sympathising with reform or revolution might well find himself discriminated against or put out of his home or his job. It was wise for ordinary people who were dependent on the powerful, to demonstrate their loyalty. One way of doing so was by joining the Volunteers, an amateur military body set up by the government in April 1794, when a French invasion was feared. Robert Burns joined the Volunteers in Dumfries, perhaps because he was a known supporter of reform. John Findlay, the printer brought to Whitburn by Archibald Bruce, also joined the Volunteers, perhaps to prove that although printing controversial works, he remained loyal to the crown.

Robert Purdie the surgeon also thought it wise to show his loyalty by joining the Volunteers. In addition, he paid five shillings to insure himself against being called up into the militia. To 'buy' a substitute to serve in your place cost 12 guineas, far more than ordinary people could afford. Therefore, many of the men in Whitburn parish set up a joint fund which, in the event of their name being selected in the ballot, would pay for a substitute. George Waddell, the former Friend of the People, also subscribed 2s to the fund in May 1798. Only the relatively well-off could afford to pay the shillings required for this insurance; therefore, the burden of militia conscription and service fell, as ever, on the poorest in society.

Though formed to prevent French invasion, the underlying purpose of the Volunteers was probably to ensure internal peace and deal with radical uprisings. Their duties were not onerous: they were required to undertake about 28 days of exercises and drills in the course of a year, for which they received a small payment. The Volunteers were funded by a small local tax on local landowners: for example, in November 1804, James Waddell, laird of Crofthead, was told to pay £3 5s 6d

> as the amount of an assessment upon the lands of East side of Fallhouse belonging to you and others, for providing Clothing and Appointments to the Volunteers of the County of Linlithgow.

Whitburn's company, commanded by that same James Waddell of Crofthead, was part of the Royal Linlithgowshire Volunteers, and was trained in drill and target shooting by Drill Sergeant Whitford, probably a former regular soldier. In 1803, Whitburn's Volunteers numbered some 130, drawn from the whole parish, and included Hugh Munro, labourer, who was just three feet eight inches tall.

Once the threat of unrest or invasion had receded, most of the Volunteer companies were wound up. The last record of the Whitburn company that can be found is from 1809, when they presented a silver cup to James Waddell, their captain, 'in testimony of their esteem' and possibly on the occasion of their being disbanded.

CHAPTER 8

Coaching Days

The turnpike road

TURNPIKE ROADS WERE the solution to the age-old problem of bad roads. Local landowners and other interested parties would club together to have a private act of Parliament passed, which enabled them to borrow money to build or upgrade a road, then maintain it through the income from toll bars. The Shotts Turnpike Trust was formed in 1753 to build a toll road between Glasgow and Edinburgh, via Kirk o' Shotts and Whitburn. Some stretches were built from scratch but most were formed by widening and upgrading existing roads. The act which established the Shotts Turnpike Trust stipulated that no building was to be allowed within 30 feet of the centre of the road, providing a minimum width of 60 feet. In fact, the road widens out to over 90 feet (excluding the footpaths) at Whitburn Cross and copes with a volume of traffic its builders could never have foreseen.

The Trust advertised in 1754 for contractors to build 'the road betwixt Muiriehall [near Shotts] and Polkemmet'. By 1761, the road west of Whitburn as far as Newhouse was in operation and tolls were being charged at Polkemmet Toll (later Murraysgate Toll) and others along the length of the road.

Every six miles or so, the traveller's way was barred by a gate or 'pike' across the road, which was 'turned' once the toll had been paid, allowing the traveller to proceed. The toll varied according to the weight and size of the load that was passing along the road; pedestrians and certain other categories of travellers were exempt. Beside the gate or toll bar was a toll-house for the toll keeper and his family. The only surviving 18th century tollhouse in West Lothian is the one at Long Livingston – on the stretch of road now blocked to traffic near the Toll Roundabout in Livingston. There was a toll bar on the new road at Murraysgate, where in 1782 the toll keeper was Jean Lawson. She also sold drink from her tollhouse – no laws against drunk driving in those days! The kirk session records of 1789 record that John Edmistone and Margaret Weir, both servants at Polkemmet, met one evening at the toll house, 'and after taking a glass together', they discussed whether or not he was the father of Margaret's child. Jean Lawson the toll keeper was summoned to appear before the kirk session as a witness to this but her son was indisposed and 'could not attend the toll bar', so she was unable to come and give evidence.

Stagecoaches and mail coaches

The improvement of roads allowed heavy goods to be transported long distances, opening up markets in Edinburgh and Glasgow to traders in Whitburn for the first time. Coach travel became swift and reasonably safe and comfortable. The first coach service between Edinburgh and Glasgow (via Falkirk) began in 1749 and took two days to do the 48 miles, with an overnight halt at Falkirk. After the road was upgraded to a turnpike, the journey time was reduced to some 12 hours but passengers were warned that they would be 'called on to dismount at the rougher ascents'.

The increasing number of coach passengers and carters needed refreshment stops along the way where teams of horses could be changed, so inns were established along the routes. Whitburn Inn, a substantial two-storey house, was just east of the Cross, where it could benefit from travellers on both the east-west and north-south routes. By 1782, several different coach companies were offering services in each direction every day (except Sundays); most broke their journey at Whitburn Inn, halfway between the two cities. Whitburn's innkeeper in the early 1800s, Thomas Gourlie, combined the business with running a brewery and presumably supplied his own beer to his customers. The brewery with its malt barn, brew house, kiln and steep (where barley was soaked) did not survive for long, but was sold c.1806, and ceased to operate.

By 1805, the coach journey time had been reduced to some five hours, and 'mercantile people and travellers may depend upon the utmost punctuality'. The break for dining at Whitburn Inn was restricted to half an hour or less. Coaches, drawn by teams of four horses and with names suggestive of speed and bravado, dashed through the village many times a day in each direction. At various periods, they included 'the Commercial Traveller, 4.00pm from Edinburgh, driver Robert Scott and guard David Keith'; the Enterprise, the Rocket, the Royal Eagle, the Defence and the Royal Mail. A team of horses could pull a coach at four or five miles an hour for a couple of hours, so the original coaching inns were placed at roughly ten-mile intervals. Ten miles east of the Cross Keys at Newhouse was the Whitburn Inn, and eight and a half miles further east was the Red Lion Inn at Mid Calder. Coaches on the Edinburgh-Hamilton-Ayr road also passed through Whitburn and used the inn.

Poorer passengers sat on the top of the coach and paid a reduced rate. In August 1836, the Commercial Traveller coach overturned a few miles east of Whitburn, throwing the 11 outside passengers to the ground. Fortunately, they 'escaped more frightened than hurt'. The Commercial Traveller had been involved in another incident in February 1829, when three Whitburn weavers, James Walker, Thomas Walker and James Russell

> got upon the Stage Coach named the Commercial Traveller when it was proceeding along the said High Way westwards and did cling to the said Coach to the great annoyance of the Passengers theron, and in being ordered off and at last compelled to drop from it, did then... at a place called Gateside, from revenge and malice throw one or more stones with great violence at the Passengers on the said Coach, wherby one of them,... [the] wife of John Gowans... of Argyle Street, Glasgow... was thereby severely bruised and injured in her forehead.

At their trial, they admitted they had clung to the coach but denied they had thrown stones. They were sentenced to 14 days in the tolbooth of Linlithgow.

Until 1804, the post was carried between Edinburgh and Glasgow in the saddlebags of a post boy mounted on a pony. Royal Mail coaches were introduced on the Whitburn route in June 1805, the driver clad in a blue greatcoat with red lapels and the guard armed with a cutlass and two pistols. Soon, mail coaches carried passengers as well – four inside and up to a dozen on top – and some reached average speeds of nearly ten miles an hour.

New services were regularly introduced as companies tried to get a share of the profits of the route, and so busy was it that, by 1818, Whitburn Inn had stabling for 40 horses. The coach companies advertised widely in the newspapers, each promoting the comfort, elegance and speed of its coaches and services, and decrying those of its rivals. As early as 1781, the Edinburgh-Glasgow Diligence by Falkirk claimed that 'the road by Falkirk is greatly superior to that by Whitburn, and the country much more agreeable.' And in 1828, it was falsely alleged that the route by Bathgate and Uphall could be completed in three hours and 40 minutes or even less, while the Whitburn route still took five hours. In 1832, a coach company on the Bathgate-Airdrie road spread a rumour that the Whitburn Inn had closed down and claimed that its route was several miles shorter than that by Whitburn. The Shotts Road Trustees had the three routes measured and published their findings in the newspapers: the Linlithgow route was the longest at 48 miles; the Whitburn route was 43 miles, 1,639 yards; by Airdrie and Bathgate was 43 miles, 1,408 yards – a difference, the clerk to the Trustees pointed out, equivalent to a two-minute walk!

The stagecoaches and mail coaches brought unprecedented bustle and excitement to the quiet community, with the blare of their post horns to warn the toll keepers and inn keepers of their approach, and the swirls of dust or mud that the sweating horses threw up. But the heyday of coaching was over by 1840, killed off almost overnight by railways.

Halfway House and the Burns' connection

A public house was operating at Halfway House – exactly halfway between Edinburgh and Glasgow – by 1774. It still stands, much altered, at the south gateway to Polkemmet House and has an interesting connection with Robert Burns.

In 1784, Burns got his mother's maidservant Elizabeth Paton pregnant. His mother was keen that Burns should marry her and the poet himself was not averse to the idea but was persuaded by his brother and sisters that she was too coarse and ill-educated to be a suitable match.

The birth of the child (named Elizabeth) in May 1785 was greeted by Burns with two poems: 'A Poet's Welcome to his Love-Begotten Daughter':

> Welcome! my bonie, sweet, wee dochter,
> Tho' ye come here a wee unsought for,
> And tho' your comin' I hae fought for,
>   Baith kirk and quier;
> Yet, by my faith, ye're no unwrought for –
>   That I shall swear!...

and 'The Inventory' – a witty reply to a tax demand that he submit a list of all his horses, servants, carriages and dependants:

> Wi' weans I'm mair than weel contented,
> Heav'n sent me ane mae than I wanted:
> My sonsie, smirking, dear-bought Bess,
> She stares the daddy in her face,
> Enough of ought ye like but grace:
> But her, my bonnie sweet wee lady,
> I've paid enough for her already;
> An' gin ye tax her or her mither,
> B' the L--d, ye'se get them a' thegither!

Although he did not marry her mother, Burns made financial provision for the child. The young Elizabeth was brought up first by Burns' mother, then by her own mother, then by Burns' brother, Gilbert. In 1807, while living in Ayrshire with her stepfather, she married John Bishop, a Whitburn man, who was working on the estate of Auchenskeoch in Ayrshire. Although remembered by a school friend as being 'dark and swarthy, and strongly resembled her father', Elizabeth was probably an attractive marriage prospect, as two years earlier at the age of 21 she had received £200 from a public fund set up after his death to support Burns' family.

The young couple settled in Whitburn, where John was a small tenant farmer on the Polkemmet estate. Elizabeth gave birth to five or possibly six children but died in January 1817 at the age of 32, followed by her youngest child, Mary Lyon, just a few months later. Her cousin Isabella Begg wrote that Elizabeth 'was a good upright creature, and when she died, the minister of the parish wrote a beautiful character of her to my grandfather.' After her death, John took up the tenancy of the inn at Halfway House, 'a decent two-storey slated house with outhouses and a garden, all in good repair'. There, from at least 1831 until the early 1850s, John Bishop was the inn-keeper. He also farmed the 40-acre farm of Halfway House and became overseer of the whole Polkemmet estate. He re-married, had several more children, and died at Halfway House in 1857, aged 75.

Elizabeth Bishop's grave is one of the few surviving cast iron gravestones in the churchyard. The fame of her father has ensured that Burns' admirers have kept the grave in good repair. Though Burns was famous enough in the early 1800s for his daughter to have been something of a celebrity when she settled in Whitburn, it seems unlikely that when first erected the gravestone had any reference to her famous father. The reminder that she was 'love-begotten' was surely added by Burns' enthusiasts after the death of her husband: a respectable Victorian husband was unlikely to have inscribed a permanent reminder that his wife was illegitimate.

CHAPTER 9

The Weavers – From Riches to Rags

Working conditions

WHITBURN'S WEAVERS WORKED for the great cotton manufacturers of Glasgow and the west of Scotland, through agents in the local area. The weaver might hire his loom through the agent and set it up in his own home or share a workshop with others. The loom worked best with an earthen floor to keep it stable; moist, warm conditions to prevent the yarn becoming brittle; and sufficient light for the weaver to see what he was doing. The atmosphere would have been damp, oily and fibrous – unhealthy, particularly for children. The weaver sat at a handloom operated by his feet on a treadle. Having received his yarn, the weaver then had to tie several thousand threads from a beam at one end of the loom, through wire eyelets, and attach them at the far end. Then the warp (long) threads were moistened with a dressing of potato starch or similar paste to prevent their breaking. His children would wind the yarn onto pirns (bobbins) and place them into the shuttle which moved across and between the long threads, forming the weft of the cloth.

The cloths woven in Whitburn were probably similar to those woven in Bathgate – ginghams and pullicates. Gingham was woven from dyed yarn, often in spots or checked designs. Pullicates, too, were woven from dyed cotton yarn and mainly used for making handkerchiefs and neckerchiefs. They were cheap cotton goods, requiring of the weaver only a basic level of skill or training. Once the cloth was finished, the agent collected and checked it, paid the weaver and delivered the new web.

One elderly Whitburn man, James Gilbert, recalled that in the 1820s and 1830s:

> Mr John Calder was employed by the weavers to convey the material from and to Glasgow. Mr Calder was a kind of middle-man between the manufacturers and the weavers, and it would have done the latter no good to have got their work direct, as Calder was paid by the manufacturers.'

James Gilbert was 'put to the loom' by his father in 1832 at the age of ten and began a four-year apprenticeship with William Bryce.

The whole of Whitburn's Main Street was composed of weavers' [work]shops and there would be from 180 to 200 hand-loom weavers in the town. The shops were mostly all four-loomed ones, but there was one ten-loomed shop and one eight-loomed one.

The decline of weaving

By the 1820s and 1830s, the early requirement to serve an apprenticeship was breaking down. The rudiments of all but the fine work could be learned within the family, so new recruits flooded into the trade, especially after 1815, when the wartime boom in industries came to an end. The invention of steam-powered looms began to make an impact on the industry. Unknown to them, the handloom weavers were the first victims of the economic restructurings that were a result of the industrial era and would cause such suffering to working people. Within the first 20 or 30 years of the 19th century, the weavers went from the richest of artisans to the poorest.

However, demand from Scotland's fast-growing population for cotton cloth grew and for a while provided enough work for the ever-increasing number of weavers. People continued to enter the trade, convinced that the good times would return. Older weavers may have stayed in the trade because they were too old to learn a new trade or had their whole savings invested in their looms. Despite the difficulties, by 1831 the number of looms in the village had reached 218. Many families would have hired more than one loom, so the likely number of weaving *families* in Whitburn in 1828 was 83; and in 1838, 121 (out of a total of 186). In most families, sons would also have become weavers in an attempt to bring the family income up to a viable amount; wives and daughters were employed on embroidering the woven cotton and children as pirn-winders. At its height in 1851, some 62 per cent of Whitburn's population was dependent on weaving and related trades: flowering, tambouring and pirn winding.

Being a cottage industry, weavers had no trade union to protect them and no political power – none in Whitburn had the vote. Between 1810 and 1837, their wages fell by two thirds from £1 a week to 6s 6d – barely enough to survive on. Low wages meant that weavers worked longer hours, which led to over-production and a further fall in wages. The trade was subject to periodic slumps during which the once proudly independent weavers were reduced to asking for help. In 1826, Sir William Baillie chaired a meeting of local Justices of the Peace to set up a subscription fund for the relief of the 'distress and suffering of the operatives' (ie the weavers), and there were further slumps in 1829, 1837, 1842 and 1847.

The Scottish poor law did not permit the paying of poor relief to the able-bodied poor. There was no recognition of the fact that these men were thrown out of work, not by their own fecklessness but by structural changes in the economy. Some relief was provided by charitable donations from wealthy individuals, and some out-of-work Bathgate weavers were employed by the town council on building Academy Street – but there was no town council in Whitburn to assist them. With so many weavers reduced to poverty, other trades and shops in Whitburn suffered. A government report on hand loom weavers in 1839 pointed out the:

> bitterness of the contrast between past and present times: the income which formerly raised them as high, if not higher in social rank, than any other class of Scottish artisans, is gone from them; but the intelligence and education... remain now to embitter their poverty.

But they were not just downtrodden victims; they struggled against their lot, for in 1834, the Whitburn weavers were among those who sent a petition to Parliament calling for regulation of weavers' wages (ie a minimum wage). They petitioned again for relief in 1852 and 1853 but the government would not intervene and the relief of starving weavers' families was left to the parochial boards and to piecemeal charitable action.

David Pringle of West Main Street entered the weaving industry at the age of eleven in 1832 and was bound as an apprentice to pay his master half his earnings for three years. He left the trade around 1841 'when the trade was in its death-struggle in the competition with machinery' and became an assistant teacher in a Whitburn school. By 1851, two thirds of Whitburn's weavers were idle. James Gilbert, the former weaver, recalled:

> When the crash finally came and when it was generally understood that the weaving machinery had supplanted hand labour, many felt that it was a good thing that the hand-loom weaving trade went down, as it was just misery working away on the old conditions.

Looking back on that period from 1901, Robert Bain recalled that:

> the town was filled with unemployed weavers, who were debating with themselves the question what they should do to keep life in.

Fortunately, salvation was at hand in the form of the mining industry. Nearly two thirds of Whitburn's weavers gave up in the 1850s, and took work at the new mines at Cappers, Boghead and Torbanehill, or at the Bathgate Chemical Works. Ebenezer Steel, the son and grandson of weavers, was set to the trade at the age of eight in 1851 but left weaving as soon as alternative work was available. At 15, he became an ironstone miner at Cult mine, while his father got a pithead job at Boghead near Bathgate. 'Work was pretty constant, and wages, compared with those earned at the loom, were larger.' It was generally the younger men who deserted weaving, leaving the older ones, unfit for heavy labour, 'in a very destitute condition'.

Figures refer to the village of Whitburn, except where otherwise stated	Weavers	Flowerers and tambourers	Pirn and cotton winders	Other weaving-related jobs	Total weaving-related jobs
1774 (parish)	c.27				27 looms
1793 (parish)	20	50			70
1828					150 looms
1838					218 looms
1841	95	28	5	3	131
1851	151	92	53	1	297
1861	45	70	18	3	136
1871	29	31	5	2	67
1881	11				33
1891	3				11
1901	2				7

A handful of Whitburn's handloom weavers survived into the 20th century. The last of them, and probably the last in the whole of West Lothian, was John Leggat (72) of Park Lane (formerly Shuttle Row), West Main Street, who died in 1908. 'Practically up till the last he sat at his loom, in what was known to [have been] one of the largest workshops of its kind in Whitburn...'.

CHAPTER 10

The Baillies Acquire Whitburn

THE ESTATE OF Whitburn had been acquired by the Cunynghames in 1725 and was administered for the next 70 years from their mansion house at Livingston. In 1795, however, Sir William Augustus Cunynghame advertised in the newspapers the sale at auction of

> the land and estate of Whitburn, including the Town, Inn, and Mill of Whitburn... together with the lands of Yeathouses, Gateside, Townhead, Cults... The lands are all arable and inclosed, and consist, including the town of Whitburn, of about 531 acres Scots, of which ten acres and a half are planted.

The estate brought in an annual income of some £350. Evidently it did not find a buyer at that time, for it was not until the early years of the 19th century that the Cunynghame ownership came to an end and Whitburn got new lairds.

In 1803, William Baillie, Lord Polkemmet, bought the western end of the estate of Whitburn – including the 'market place of the town of Whitburn and ground around the same, Miln of Whitburn and part of the Miln lands thereof', Yeathouses and Gateside. He used these new lands as security for a liferent annuity of £250 per year to be settled on his wife and the purchase extended his ownership as far east as Whitburn Cross.

Thomas Gordon

The east end of the estate remained in the Cunynghames' hands until 1806 when it was bought by Thomas Gordon, a lawyer and Sheriff Substitute of Sutherland. His purchase comprised half of East Whitburn, as well as Townhead of Whitburn, the Inn, the Old Inn Farm, Whitburn Mill lands east of the drove road and Blaeberryhill.

When he bought Whitburn, he was a man of 51. He did not live in Whitburn and did not take any interest in it. Instead, he was using it as security for money that he was borrowing, and as a means of entitling him to a vote in parliamentary elections. His purchase had made him the patron of the parish, but not knowing the people, his choice of the Rev James Watson as Whitburn's new minister in 1809 was deeply unpopular and reviled.

Thomas Gordon's finances fell into disorder: in mid-1816, he went bankrupt and his property was handed over to trustees to administer on behalf of his creditors. His Whitburn estate was sold in August 1819 and was purchased by William Baillie of Polkemmet. So the Baillies added the east end of Whitburn estate to their existing lands and thus owned a great tract of land from Greenrigg in the west to the far end of East Whitburn. After two centuries as lairds of Polkemmet, the Baillies had also become the lairds of Whitburn.

Lord Polkemmet, the judge

Lord Polkemmet, who bought the west end of Whitburn estate in 1803, resigned as a judge in 1811 because the Tory administration wanted to appoint a more effective member of their party in his place. His wife had the temerity to write to Robert Dundas (who had recently succeeded his father Henry Dundas as Lord Advocate and 'the uncrowned king of Scotland') asking for her husband to be created a baronet in view of

> his great fidelity and uprightness as a judge, his uniform, steady and zealous support of your Lordship's party and his ready and unconditional compliance with their request to resign.

Some six weeks later, Dundas sent an equivocal reply, claiming that he would have to confer with 'Mr Perceval' (ie Spencer Perceval, who, the following year, 1812, had the distinction of being the only British Prime Minister ever to be assassinated – shot in the lobby of the House of Commons). Dundas also claimed to be unaware of any request to Lord Polkemmet to resign his judgeship. In the end, neither his resignation nor his wife's begging letter produced a baronetcy for him and he died with no reward for giving up his seat on the bench.

Smallpox and peaches

Lord Polkemmet's son, William Baillie, was the purchaser of the east end of Whitburn estate in 1819. He was born in 1782 and by the age of 25 was a Lieutenant in the 4th Regiment of Native Cavalry in Bengal. After his father's death in 1816, he left the Indian army to take up his new role as laird of Polkemmet. The year before inheriting the estate, he had married Mary Lyon Dennistoun, one of four heiresses to their wealthy uncle. It was in her honour that Elizabeth Burns Bishop's youngest daughter was named – the child who died in infancy early in 1817 – and it was probably her money which enabled the purchase of the east end of the Whitburn estate.

What William Baillie did to deserve a baronetcy (a hereditary knighthood) is not clear but he was created Sir William Baillie of Polkemmet, Bart. on 14 November 1823. One account states that the baronetcy had been intended for his father (perhaps Lady's Baillie plea had not fallen on deaf ears after all) but when he died, it was conferred on his son. Since it was seven years after the father's death before the honour was given, this sounds unlikely. It was more probably political – he may have supported the Tory government of the time in some way or contributed to the success of George IV's visit to Edinburgh in 1822.

Letters written by the first baronet's wife to her sister provide a gossipy glimpse of their life at Polkemmet in the 1820s and 1830s – full of visits to and from friends and family, with Sir William busy about church and county business:

> William has been going about a good deal... He was at Glasgow one night attending a Road Meeting [ie a meeting of the Shotts Turnpike Trust], and on Thursday went to the Hunt dinner at Linlithgow.

He frequently attended meetings in Glasgow and Edinburgh, travelling by the mail coach or occasionally in one of the commercial coaches.

> I believe we are to have some peaches today – the gardiner thought them ripe at least two days ago and begged to pull them. The grapes will soon be ready, no strawberries yet and the birds are eating the cherries as they color.

It was a life in sharp contrast to that of their tenants. The Baillies were not unaware of the poverty around them, living as they did within a mile of the village of Whitburn and in close proximity to their tenants:

> The small pox, I am sorry to hear, are very prevalent... a very fine looking young man – one of our tenants' sons – of about 27, died of them eight or ten days ago. They were of a most virulent kind – his brother continued all the time driving our stones to the door, past our house half a dozen times a day and our children following him and talking to him, and we knew nothing of it until his brother died... I spoke to his Father yesterday, poor body, he was saying... looking at my three Boys, that we should 'haud a loose grasp for

we had them today and didna ken how soon we might lose
them, for he had three as strong Bairns as onybody could
see in the Kirk yard.'

The Baillies had a large family, seven boys and six girls, and were clearly
fond of them. The mention of stones being brought to the house indicates
that building work was underway on Polkemmet House in 1824. When
they acquired the estate in the early 1600s, the Baillies had built or inherited a mansion house at Polkemmet. In the 1820s, presumably thanks to
the money which Mary Dennistoun brought to the marriage, the house
was rebuilt to match its owner's enhanced status as a baronet and large
landowner. Its later appearance dated substantially from this time, with
enlargements in 1878 and again in 1912. Sir William was also responsible for building the new entrance to the grounds at Halfway House.

The first baronet was much involved in the local militia, as a major in
the Royal Linlithgowshire Yeomanry Cavalry, and by 1827 in command
of it. He served as a Justice of the Peace, and as a Commissioner of Supply of the county of Linlithgow – the local government body of the time.
He was actively involved in the church, and in several business ventures.
In his leisure time, he kept coursing greyhounds which he raced with the
Winchburgh Coursing Club and, as a member of Whitburn Curling Club,
he attended the founding meeting of the Grand Caledonian Curling Club.

He took no obvious steps to assist the economic or industrial development of Whitburn, though he continued to feu land for the building
of new houses. In fact, there are no mentions of him in public life after
1842, because by then his mental health had begun to break down and
his affairs were put into the hands of a legal agent. He was probably confined in Murray's Royal Asylum for Lunatics which acquired the mansion
of Pitcullen near Perth in 1850 for

> a select number of patients of the Highest Class, whose friends
> may wish them to enjoy the comforts and luxuries of a Private
> Residence... and at the same time have the benefit of the High-
> est Medical skill in the treatment of mental disease...

He died in Perth in 1854, aged 71, without 'recovering his mental
faculties'. His younger brother, Robert, an army officer, also died in a
mental asylum.

One memory of the first baronet remained for long in folk memory:

> the sight of the old baronet with his six stalwart sons, all
> of them over six feet, walking to the parish church. For the
> Baillies of Polkemmet were Presbyterian to the core.

CHAPTER 11

Mining, 1750–1850

THE NEW VILLAGE of Whitburn was not an immediate success and probably did not bring the significant increase in income which its founder had hoped for. Whitburn failed to attract the variety of employment that Blackburn, founded at the same time, could boast by the early 1800s. Other than agriculture, the small mining venture in the west of the parish and the cotton jeanie workshop, it had no industry at all. No wonder the locals thankfully took to the weaving trade. But the large profits to be made in the cotton industry were made by the businessmen of Glasgow and the west, while the weavers earned only their piece wages.

By 1800, Sir William Augustus Cunynghame was getting on in years and perhaps losing interest in Whitburn. Thomas Gordon, the absentee landlord, took no interest in the village, nor are the Baillies known to have made any effort to attract industry. Therefore, it grew only gradually: from 500 inhabitants in 1800 to almost 800 in 1841 and scarcely larger in 1851. The village spread slowly along the turnpike road, mainly to the west. By the 1850s, it extended on the east almost to Whitdalehead school; on the west, as far as Lady Baillie's school (the Gospel Hall), then after a gap came a cluster of houses at Gateside, then another gap before Murraysgate Toll.

In his *Statistical Account* of Whitburn parish in 1793, the minister records that 'Coals abound in the parish, and are to be had both in it, and the east part of Shotts almost adjoining to it...' In addition, a start was about to be made on working a valuable seam of coal below the moorland at the west end of the parish. The minister who wrote the Whitburn entry for the second *Statistical Account* in 1843 claimed that the local seam of coal had been wrought for more than a century. No information as to the location of these early mines is to be found but they would have been small-scale, shallow mines, employing only a dozen or so.

Edinburgh suffered a shortage of coal at the beginning of the 19th century, making coal prices high. The hope of good returns made viable the expensive business of sinking a pit, buying steam engines and equipment and building housing for colliers. James Trotter's 1808 *Account of Lord Polkemmet's coal* states that a new pit was sunk on Polkemmet estate in June 1806, called

> Green-rigg Colliery, on a rising moor near the Cult... out of which the coal is now taken at the depth of 14 fathoms [c.26 metres] from the surface... The seam worked is four feet seven inches of clean coal. The quality is uncommonly good. It is so much in request that it is sometimes sent even to Edinburgh; and all the country as far as Ratho is principally supplied from it... It is worked by a common gin [steam engine]... Last year there were sold... about 10,666 single horse carts.

The pit employed 13 men and two boys, besides some labourers. When colliery serfdom was abolished by the act of 1799, the colliers' wages were increased in order to retain their labour: in the early 1800s, ordinary labourers earned 2s per day, while colliers earned 4s 6d a day. As Trotter remarks of the Greenrigg miners: 'The colliers have remarkably good appetites, are very healthy, and from their great earnings are enabled to live very comfortably.'

> **Colliery slaves**
>
> Until 1799, colliers were still serfs – bound for life to the mine where they worked. If the mine was sold to a new owner, they were sold along with it, and if a son or daughter went down the pit, then they too became bound.

A horse-drawn railway

With the increasing demand for coal in the 19th century, there was great incentive for landowners and entrepreneurs to exploit coal reserves but a major problem was how to transport the coal. When the Union Canal was being planned, one of the routes under consideration would have brought it close to Whitburn. Although the more northerly route by Linlithgow was chosen, landowners in the south of the county still wanted an easy connection to the canal in order to send coal and other heavy goods by water to Edinburgh and Glasgow. A West-Lothian Railway Company proposed in 1825 to build a horse-drawn railway line from Shotts, via Whitburn (just north of Main Street), to the canal at Broxburn. To ensure that the venture was financially worthwhile, the company commissioned from Robert Bald, the leading Scottish mining engineer and surveyor, a report into the Whitburn coal field. He reported favourably, calling it 'one of the most valuable Coal Fields in Scotland' but, despite this, the horse-drawn railway scheme came to nothing.

Child labour and the first Polkemmet colliery

Bald's report described William Baillie's small colliery, sunk in 1806–8, and by then known as Polkemmet. It was one of the collieries at which evidence was taken in 1842 by a Royal Commission into the employment of women and children below ground. The Polkemmet mine manager, Thomas Bishop, gave evidence:

> Boys never descend till ten years of age, and that is much too early, as they are not strong enough for the labour. Coal working being sore heavy labour, lads of 14 years of age, if strong, are more fitted, and are enabled to form themselves well, as also to become better workers.

In his evidence, Sir William Baillie stated that boys ought not to start work until they were 13, so that they had some years of schooling first. He did not, however, ban young boys from his pit, as an 11-year-old coal-putter at Polkemmet colliery, Peter Andrew, also gave evidence:

> Works about 12 hours daily, three or four morning till three or four afternoon. Gets porridge or tea sent, as live just convenient to the engine; work sometimes all night... Father and three brothers work below: two of my brothers write very well; I am not the length of writing yet; do not go to school at present, shall do as summer advances; the moor is not good to cross, and the teacher lives far away. [Reads and repeats his Catechism; is not very far advanced in Scripture knowledge.]

Another local lad, Robert Beveridge, just 15, was already a coal-hewer and had worked below ground at Polkemmet since he was ten:

> [I] work 11 and 12 hours, sometimes longer. I hew coal... and then I push the hurlies [wagons]....have not much to stoop, as the coal is not less than four to five feet thick; the work is guid sair and requires strength as well as to be used to it. Mother was a farmer's daughter, and she had nine of us; she never wrought below, nor have any women here; the lassies go into the fields or to service. [Reads and writes well; very well informed.]

Coal-hewers were obliged to employ their own coal-bearers. If wives and children did the work, it saved paying another wage, hence the miners'

willingness to subject their family to heavy labour and vile conditions. Of
14 West Lothian mines investigated, ten still employed women and young
children underground – 154 in total. Sir William Baillie and his manager
seem to have been among the more enlightened: of the 48 employed at
Polkemmet pit, none were female.

The publication of the report so shocked public opinion that an Act
was passed that same year, 1842, banning the underground employment
of boys under the age of ten and all females – the first ever legislation to
improve safety and conditions in the mining industry.

The quarrelling brothers-in-law: Polkemmet Coal Company, 1840s and 1850s

In 1846, the Baillies leased Polkemmet colliery to John White, a
Harthill farmer who already leased Cult pit (probably also part
of the Baillies' coalfield near Greenrigg), and his brother-in-law,
Alexander Geddes, a Stirlingshire coal company manager. They paid
the Baillies an annual rent of three hundred pounds, plus a royalty
on the amount of coal raised, and also supplied them with free coal
for Polkemmet House.

The miners were accommodated at Greenrigg in 12 houses with
thatched roofs, box beds and beaten earth floors. Despite the houses being
mainly of one or two rooms, one was occupied by the Kinghorns with
their six children and two lodgers and one by Robert and Jane Beveridge
with their eight children (one of them the child Robert who gave evidence
to the Royal Commission). Only the mine manager Thomas Bishop and
his wife were native to the parish; all the other families had come from
outside the county.

The Polkemmet/Cult colliery did not prosper under Geddes and
White and relations between the partners began to break down: 'Dear
Sandy,' writes White to Geddes:

> I have your note and am very much hurt at the tone of it. You
> know very well that whatever the state of colliery affairs might
> have been – although it had been £1,000 in my debt, I never
> would ask 1/- from you if you had it not to spare... I have
> plenty of effects to pay both my own debts and [the mine's
> debts], and am perfectly willing to stand up and do so...

Their argument seemed to centre on allegations by Geddes that White
was failing to keep proper accounts or to produce them when asked.
In 1857:

> As to the Colliery, it is paying its way, but little or nothing more, nor never will, unless a different system of working is adopted.

In fact, the company was wound up at the end of 1857. In a typical year it had produced nearly 6,000 tons of coal, for which Sir William Baillie got at least 4d per ton. This would have produced for him an annual income of £100; it was still his agricultural estate which was providing most of his income.

After the departure of Geddes and White, Polkemmet/Cult colliery passed through the hands of the Monkland Iron Company, then the Shotts Iron Company, but by 1895, belonged to James Wood, the coalmaster who is more closely associated with Armadale (where Wood Park is named after him). At this time, 300 miners were employed below ground and 40 above ground. A few years later, Wood sold it to John Nimmo & Son, who also owned extensive collieries in Lanarkshire and Stirlingshire. The workforce reduced from 350 in 1896 to just 80 in 1908, and it closed c.1912 after almost a century of working – the end of the first Polkemmet colliery.

Mining post-1850s: Ironstone

Within Whitburn parish, a major development of ironstone mining took place in the 1840s on the Fauldhouse moors at Crofthead and Greenburn. As the Rev Graham Mitchell described it:

> The change which this discovery has made upon this district is very remarkable: what was, till within the last three years a solitary moorland scene, has now become one of enterprise and industry. Tall chimneys are seen in all directions, and clouds of smoke rolling along from huge burning masses, show the extensive nature of the operations which are now carried on.

The next mining activity in the area took place between Whitburn and Armadale, where in the 1850s the Shotts Iron Company began to develop Cappers Pit: No. 1 (mainly ironstone) and No. 2 (mainly coal). No. 2 mine was the deeper at 33 fathoms (60 metres) and each was kept free of water by a small steam engine. Some of the miners were accommodated in miners' rows at Cappers (originally called Polkemmet Rows as they were on Polkemmet estate) and several dozen more lived in the village of Whitburn. The ironstone mine was in operation from the 1850s to the 1880s, the coal mine until c.1908.

The Torbanehill pits (coal and ironstone) to the north-east of the village would also have provided work for Whitburn miners. And from the 1870s, mining was developing in the Harthill area, again, within walking distance for the Whitburn men.

The processing of ironstone by burning produced smoke and fumes. Polluted water run-off from mine working killed off fish and vegetation in the burns and ended up in the River Almond, which became increasingly polluted in the 19th century.

Despite all this activity, however, mining was insignificant as an employer of Whitburn people until the middle of the 19th century. It was not until the 1850s that Whitburn was transformed from a weaving to a mining village.

	Number employed in weaving & related jobs	Number employed in mining & related jobs	Population of Whitburn village
1841	131	14	798
1851	297	25	808
1861	136	170	1362

CHAPTER 12

The New Polkemmet Pit

The Dardanelles

WORK BEGAN ON the new Polkemmet in 1913 when the coal industry was at its all-time peak in Scotland, producing over 42 million tons a year and employing nearly 150,000 men. In West Lothian alone, 31 coal mines were being operated by 19 different coal companies. William Dixon and Co were sufficiently confident of the industry's future to undertake the expense of sinking a shaft through hundreds of metres of rock – work that would take several years to reach the coal – just south-west of the burgh on Polkemmet estate. Test bores had revealed that the Main Coal was in workable thickness at a depth of 475 metres. Coal lying as far down as this had only become accessible in recent years as technology improved sufficiently to be able to sink and drain so deep a pit.

Work on sinking the first shaft continued through the outbreak of the First World War in 1914. Most pits were given a nickname; Polkemmet's two shafts, 'having been started at the time that great events were happening at the Dardanelles last year... were locally named "The Dardanelles"' reported the *Linlithgowshire Gazette*, 'a name that will stick to them as long as the pits continue to be a landmark, and a name that will register the tragic time of their birth to future generations.' The Dardanelles campaign of 1915 was a heavy defeat for British and Australian/New Zealand forces.

Work had to be halted in late 1915 and again in 1917 because so many of the pit sinkers were being called up to the army. Work resumed early in 1919 on sinking the shafts down to the Jewel and Wilsontown Main seams of coal. By then, the coal industry was in difficulty because of foreign competition and lack of investment during the First World War. Although output was falling in the 1920s, more coal was still being produced than could be sold. When the coal-owners took back control from the government in 1921, they resolved to reduce costs and output by cutting wages and jobs.

The miners fought back with a strike from 1 April to early July 1921 but it ended in defeat. One of the shafts at Polkemmet flooded during the strike and had to be drained again. In December and again in February

1922, there was an inrush of water and work was suspended yet again while the flooded shafts were pumped out. Polkemmet was finally 'coaled' (ie reached the coal seams) in February 1922 and, by the end of the year, its workforce had reached 245.

Strikes and soup kitchens

In late 1925, the miners' shift was increased from seven to eight hours and the coal-owners announced further cuts in wages. After long negotiations had failed to resolve the dispute, the miners responded by calling a strike. Supported by the Trades Union Congress which called out other unions, the General Strike began on 4 May 1926. In West Lothian, the centre of operations was Bathgate Co-operative Halls in Jarvey Street, where the railwaymen's union met daily to give orders to union members and hand out permit cards to bus or lorry drivers for essential transport. A few incidents of disorder occurred – stones thrown at 'illegal' bus and lorry movements, a barricade set up on the Bathgate-Armadale road and other roads blocked by trees felled so that pickets could prevent traffic moving, a scuffle with the police at Westrigg and some telephone wires cut near Blackburn – but the *Linlithgowshire Gazette* reported that in Whitburn, 'peace reigned supreme'.

The general strike of railwaymen, bus drivers, dockers, printers, etc lasted nine days but the miners stayed out from May until December, holding out for 'Not a minute on the day, not a penny off the pay.' The miners' union paid a small sum in strike pay and miners actively raised funds locally to supplement this. Soup kitchens were set up in Whitburn and surrounding villages to ensure that miners and their families got at least one nourishing meal a day. Despite this, towards the end of the year, the hardships of the striking miners were severe. Several Whitburn miners were fined for stealing coal from the railway embankment near Polkemmet colliery and another for cutting down a tree at Quarry Farm for firewood. Anger against those miners who had gone back to work very occasionally turned into violence, and eight Bents miners were found guilty of 'mobbing and theft' after a violent disturbance at the boycotted shop of a widow whose two miner sons had gone back to work.

In the end, despite all the tenacity and privations of the miners, the coal owners forced the union to accept longer hours and reduced wages – a bitter blow. Further mine closures followed, until by 1932 a third of British miners were out of work. Indeed, the 1920s and 1930s were decades of cuts, lockouts, hardship and bitter industrial relations. It was not until the start of the Second World War that the depression in the coal industry came to an end, by which time output from the central coalfield in Scotland had declined to half of its 1910 level. Mechanisation, while causing job losses, increased the proportion of coal cut by machine to nearly 80 per cent but these improvements were outstripped by several European countries, ensuring that British coal would lose out to cheaper foreign imported coal. The Second World War brought foreign competition to a halt and increased demand for home-produced coal. But, as in the First World War, too many miners were allowed to go into the forces, leading to a fall in output. In response, the Bevin Boys' scheme was introduced (by minister of Labour, Ernest Bevin). By this scheme, young men who had been called up could be directed into the mines instead of the forces. It was deeply unpopular with the young conscripts sent into the mines, as mining lacked the kudos of soldiering and most had no experience of mining or mining communities. Bevin Boys worked in Polkemmet Pit where they were obliged to join the local branch of the miners' union.

Nationalisation

After the war, the Labour government of Clement Attlee turned its attention to nationalising the nation's industries, starting with coalmining. On Vesting Day, 1 January 1947, signs were erected at all nationalised pits: 'This Colliery is now managed by The National Coal Board on behalf of the people'. On the same day, the National Union of Mineworkers (NUM) was created through the merger of the two largest mining unions. In Scotland, the National Coal Board (NCB) took over some 200 collieries (16 in West Lothian) plus brickworks and other ancillary industries, 21,000 miners' houses and 50,000 acres of land. The Scottish Division was divided into five areas and 13 sub-areas; Polkemmet was the HQ of the Central East sub-area and the offices were adjacent to the pit.

Nationalisation was expected to lead to improvements: instead of the many private companies competing against each other, there would be unified strategy and control. The NCB tried to reverse the wartime decline in output and investment by opening 30 temporary shallow drift mines, sinking new super-mines and reconstructing pits deemed to have a future of 20 years or more. In West Lothian, Kinneil and Polkemmet were given major upgrades in the 1950s and as a result, Polkemmet's output increased from 950 tons to 3,000 tons a day. In 1957, it employed 1,804 men (of whom 1,030 were West Lothian residents and most of the rest from Lanarkshire). Polkemmet's mine-workings lie below the west half of Whitburn and extend south-west almost to Fauldhouse and north-east almost to Armadale. As in many pits, some Polkemmet miners spent as much as two hours a shift walking to and from their working places. Upgrading of the underground transport system helped reduce this non-productive time.

Scottish output peaked in 1950 but thereafter, demand for coal declined due to foreign imports, clean air legislation and industries changing over to alternative fuels like nuclear power, natural gas and North Sea oil. More pit closures followed; the 16 collieries in West Lothian in 1947 had reduced to only five by 1968, employing fewer than 4,000 men.

By the 1970s, coalmining was widely perceived as a dying industry which young men were reluctant to enter. The average age of coalminers was higher than in other industries and their wages were not felt to compensate for the hardness and danger of their working lives. The miners' unions fought to maintain or improve their members' pay and conditions. The miners' strikes of 1972 and 1974 brought power cuts to the nation, the three-day week (because of interruptions to the power supplies) – older readers will remember shops and offices lit by candles – and petrol shortages. The 1974 strike brought down the Conservative government of Ted Heath and won a weekly wage of £4 for coal-face workers.

The OPEC price rises in oil in 1973–4 made coal more competitive again and the NCB briefly looked ahead more confidently. But the upturn was short-lived. Some of the largest of the new super-mines encountered unexpected geological difficulties and never achieved their hoped for output, becoming costly failures.

Miners' strike of 1984–5

In 1979, a Conservative government was elected, led by Prime Minister Margaret Thatcher. The 1980s were a sad decade for the mining industry, with a government not just indifferent but actively hostile to coal mining and determined to break the power of the unions. Mrs Thatcher favoured deregulation and a sink or swim policy for declining industries. She gave no protection to home-produced coal, yet continued subsidies for the nuclear industry. The last-ditch attempt by the miners' union to protect their jobs and their industry led to a year-long strike which divided communities and aroused political and personal bitterness which lingers to this day.

Polkemmet was at the forefront of the 1984–5 miners' strike in Scotland. In 1979, Polkemmet's workforce of 1,470 miners produced 500,000 tons of coking coal per year, most of which went to the Ravenscraig steel works near Motherwell. By 1982, output at Polkemmet had declined to 380,000 tons, perhaps due to investment well below the Scottish average. Working in the last surviving coal mine in West Lothian, the Polkemmet miners knew that their jobs were under threat. In March 1984, Arthur Scargill, president of the National Union of Mineworkers, called a national strike against proposed pit closures. He did not hold a national ballot and, in not doing so, allowed the NCB to claim that it was not a legal or democratic strike. The strike played into Mrs Thatcher's hands; she welcomed it as an opportunity to break the power of the miners' union – indeed, of trade unions in general. At Polkemmet, only 60 men out of 1,400 turned up for work on the first day of the strike but all refused to cross the picket line. This was the beginning of a year-long strike.

When the miners' strike is mentioned nowadays, most people remember the television images of violent clashes between police and miners on the picket lines and recall it as a political battle between Thatcher and Scargill. In Scotland, however, the main players were Albert Wheeler, NCB's Scottish area director, and Mick McGahey, the president of the NUM in Scotland. The strength of feeling in West Lothian was less concerned with trade union power versus the Tories than with a practical desire to prevent more pit closures, and particularly that of Polkemmet, the county's second largest employer, at a time when its largest employer, British Leyland, was also under threat of closure and local unemployment was already high.

One of the five Scottish regional strike centres was in Whitburn. The centre sent pickets not just to Polkemmet but to Bilston Glen, Ravenscraig, even down to England. For the first five months, no miner crossed the picket lines at Polkemmet, picketing was peaceful and relations with police were amicable. Then on 20 August, five months into the strike, six men crossed the picket line and returned to work at Polkemmet. The following day, the number of pickets soared as did the number of police, and in some violent incidents, 27 men were arrested and charged with breaches of the peace and other minor offences. There was never the level of violence at Polkemmet that was experienced at some other pits but relations between police and miners soured. The longer the strike lasted, the more the men suffered and the more their cause mattered to them. Attitudes on both sides became entrenched.

The NUM warned that if the strike-breaking continued at Polkemmet, they would withdraw the safety cover team – the essential workers who maintained the pumps and other measures to keep the mine free of water and gas. The NCB responded the next day by switching off the underground pumps at the pit. The situation quickly became serious, so the NUM offered to reinstate emergency cover to ensure that no lasting damage was done to the pit. There was a week's delay before the safety cover workers were allowed by management to go underground, by which time serious flooding had begun. The miners believed that the local managers were put under pressure by the NCB and perhaps by government to allow the pit to flood. Although this was denied at the time, it's widely believed that this was the case.

By mid-December 1984, the *West Lothian Courier* reported that just over 100 Polkemmet miners had returned to work and the number slowly increased during the early months of 1985. On 6 March, the miners conceded and went back to work. A moral victory may have been won by the men but politically the defeat was a death blow to the mining industry. In April 1985, Albert Wheeler announced that the still-flooded Polkemmet would not re-open – it was 'a dead pit'. Some 840 of the 1,365 miners took voluntary redundancy; 333 were redeployed, mostly to Bilston Glen colliery in Midlothian.

The Aftermath and the Enquiry

The strike created strong bonds among the miners and with the communities which supported them. Strike pay was limited by recent government legislation, so as the strike continued, miners' savings ran out; miners' families were in financial straits, anxious as to whether they could keep a roof over their head, put a meal on the table, clothe their children or buy them Christmas presents. The miners became dependent on family, friends and supporters to pay for rent, fuel and food. Door-to-door collections were undertaken throughout West Lothian and the regional strike centre in Whitburn made up a weekly food parcel for each striking miner. The Miners' Welfare committee ran soup kitchens to feed pickets and strikers through morning, noon and night. It collected food from local businesses and individuals to give out to striking miners' families and organised wood-cutting expeditions to supply fuel to miners deprived of their wages and their concessionary coal.

The strike was also important in the politicisation of women, who were not just cooking and feeding but raising funds, picketing, making speeches, organising, taking part in the Scottish Women's Support group and its local branch – learning that they had a political voice and skills that could be powerful and effective. Women's support made a vital contribution to the strength and longevity of the strike.

But the strike also created bitterness against the national press and television for their partisan reporting of the strike; and still more so against those who went back to work early, no matter what their economic hardship – a resentment and distrust that lingered long. Among the first six, Bob Marshall, an Armadale father of four who was interviewed by the *West Lothian Courier* at the time, believed that the strike leaders were not acting in the best interests of the men, that after 26 weeks a settlement was no nearer and that he would never have crossed a picket line if a national ballot of miners had been held before the strike began. Those who still held out regarded the returners as 'scabs'. The injustice of wrongful arrests and convictions against some pickets, leading in most cases to sacking, loss of pension rights and redundancy money, is still an issue some 30 years later, their cases having been recently taken up by local MSP, Neil Findlay. An independent review into the impact of policing during the miners' strike was ordered by the Scottish Government in 2018 (due in 2020), though it will not specifically review the conviction of individual miners.

Throughout the strike, West Lothian District Council had been supportive of the Polkemmet miners, had set up and donated to an appeal fund to assist striking miners' families and had lobbied Albert Wheeler at the NCB to keep the pit open. When the NCB announced that the pit was not recoverable and the government refused local MP Tam Dalyell's call for an independent enquiry, the council set up a public enquiry (the only such local authority enquiry to be held in the wake of the miners' strike) to determine whether or not the pit could still be saved. The enquiry was held in June 1985 and was chaired by an academic at the University of Manchester, the Rev John Bird (minister of Bathgate High Church) and Bill Sharp of Lockart Engineering in Livingston. The purpose of the enquiry was to determine whether the pit was still viable and what the social and economic consequences were of closing it. The enquiry's report concluded that without doubt it was technically feasible to recover Polkemmet colliery; and that 'a considerable body of sufficiently disquieting evidence' existed with regard to the NCB's activity after the pit began to flood and the delay in the subsequent attempt to prevent further flooding, to justify a public enquiry into the matter – but that did not happen. Of the 43 individuals and organisations invited to give evidence, only the NCB failed to send a representative or provide detailed information, despite being a nationalised industry accountable to its shareholders, the public. Its refusal to engage with the enquiry fuelled the belief that the NCB was not interested in whether Polkemmet was recoverable or not: their decision to close it had been a political one.

The enquiry also looked at the social effects of closure – £2 million in redundancy payments alone, the loss of many hundreds of wages to local shops and businesses, not to mention the resulting demoralisation, poverty, isolation, mental and physical ill-health. Their very cautious estimate was that the loss of Polkemmet would cost local and national government £6 million and probably more; and that closure made no economic sense. Unemployment in the Bathgate-Whitburn-Fauldhouse area soared from 9 per cent to over 25 per cent: more than one in four adults of working age was unemployed. The town's population declined by more than 10 per cent.

Polkemmet was Scotland's most important pit in terms of longevity combined with numbers employed: it provided the highest man-years of employment of any Scottish colliery during the post-1947 period, providing high-quality coking coal for the steel industry for nearly 40 years after nationalisation, with an average workforce of 1,500.

Mining accidents

Beginning with the 1842 legislation which banned women and children underground, the government sought to regulate the mining industry and force the coalmasters to operate more safely. Conditions underground were foul in the early days – dark, dirty, and dangerous. As mines went deeper, the temperature below ground rose approximately 1° Fahrenheit for every 46 feet in depth, making working conditions difficult and exhausting. Mechanisation came late to coalmining: in 1914, four-fifths of all coal was still being cut by miners' toil. Most of the hewers, those who actually cut the coal, were young men – such strenuous work wore them out before they were old.

Injury or death had been an accepted part of a miner's lot since the earliest days of the industry and at first were not even recorded. Thomas Bishop, miner and overseer at Polkemmet mine for more than 30 years, declared in 1842 that:

> **Just four of many**
>
> In 1872, William Stafford (15) fell down the shaft at Polkemmet and was killed. Patrick Cadden Jr, 108 Glebe Road, died on 19 March 1937 when a large piece of stone fell on him. Alexander Forrest, 31 Dixon Terrace, died on 1 November 1945 after being crushed between a descending cage and the landing. Walter Douglas Robertson, 11 Gilchrist Crescent, died on 26 January 1975 at Bangour Hospital, from injuries sustained when coal fell from the roof and crushed him.

Few accidents have occurred; lately two boys were injured by a stone falling from the roof – one had his leg shattered and suffered its loss, this other the leg broken, from which he is fast recovering. We have no kind of record of accidents: it is the only serious accident I recollect occurring during 30 years.

In 1850, the government introduced a legal requirement to record deaths and serious accidents, making it possible to identify and ameliorate the various dangers which threatened both underground and surface workers.

The Whitburn area has been mercifully free of major mining disasters – the sort which brings publicity and relief funds; but during the last 100 years of the industry, the toll of recorded deaths at Polkemmet in ones and twos adds up to somewhere near 80. The most common causes were falls of coal or stone from the roof or being crushed by hutches or other machinery. Other dangers included falling down the shaft, falling from the cage, explosions, shot-firing accidents and the slower death brought about by lung diseases such as emphysema and pneumoconiosis.

Mining safety improved slowly throughout the 20th century and more rapidly after the nationalisation of coal mines in 1947. Rescue brigades were made obligatory in 1913 for mines with over 100 men. One was established at Polkemmet and there was also a central rescue station in Bathgate. By 1950, the Mines and Quarries Act contained no fewer than 600 regulations and, after nationalisation, the NCB and mining unions gave safety a higher priority and, through technical improvements, regulations and training, reduced the number of accidents still further. However, it remained one of the most dangerous occupations and this helps to explain the close nature of mining communities.

Social conditions for the miners' families also gradually improved. The poor quality accommodation provided by the coal companies was replaced by decent council housing. The Miners' Welfare Fund, set up in 1920 and funded by a levy on the coal-owners of 1d per ton of coal, provided facilities for mining areas. With a grant from the Fund, Whitburn Miners' Welfare committee built a hall in 1932 which they hoped would be 'a source of social, moral and intellectual benefit to the community'. In 1937, miners' baths and a canteen were built at Polkemmet for the 1,000-strong workforce.

Whitburn's other mines

Whitburn miners worked in surrounding mines, including Easton at Bathgate, Riddochhill at Blackburn and many more in the Whitburn area.

Greenrigg began production under the Loganlea Coal Company in 1905 and was later acquired by United Collieries. It produced coking coal in addition to gas and house coal and supplied fireclay to the Etna brickworks in Armadale. It was a substantial pit, a mile west of Polkemmet, employing 500 to 600 men, with baths and a canteen. After its peak year in 1952, it swiftly declined in workforce and output and was closed in 1960.

Cultrigg (adjacent to Polkemmet pit on the west) was opened c.1900 by local coalmasters Barr and Thornton; it closed after its pithead gear was destroyed by a fire in 1929.

Whitrigg (also known as the Lady or the Dales) was sunk by Robert Forrester & Co and came into production in 1912. At its peak in 1952, it employed 1,200 men. It was closed by the NCB in 1972.

East Benhar Colliery, southwest of Harthill, operated from 1942 to 1957. The small mine at Dumback, east of Harthill, was opened by the NCB in 1954, employing no more than 30 men. One of the NCB's short-term pits, it was closed just five years later. Blairmuckhill and Southfield, north of Harthill, closed in 1960 and 1959 respectively and Northfield in 1961. Other small mines in the vicinity were Torbanehill, Torbane and Heads, and a small fireclay mine at Drum Farm that opened in 1913 and closed in 1960, replaced by Pottishaw.

Murraysgate, the 'wee mine', was a private mine (too small to be taken over at nationalisation) which opened as a drift mine to the Ball coal in 1934. In 1936, it was taken over by Thomas Greer and Sons who continued to operate it till its closure in 1957. It employed about 40 men.

Legacy

Weaving disappeared from Whitburn after 100 years and mining was lost after dominating Whitburn life for 130 years. So many jobs with their associated skills have been lost – brushers, roadsmen, bottomers, drawers, hewers, strippers, banksmen, reddsmen. And a whole vocabulary of mining – lype, cleading, snibbles, choke-damp, horseheads, dook; and types of coal – splint, soft, jewel, triping, dross – is now an unknown language to most of us. The mining landscape has also been changed, certainly for the better. Gone are the derelict buildings and gear, the damaged environment, bare and burning bings, dust and sulphurous fumes. West Lothian's councils have spent vast sums on rehabilitation of former mining sites and government bodies will have to continue for the foreseeable future to pay for the pumping and treating of contaminated water from abandoned mines before release into waterways.

And, not least, a way of life has been lost: a close-knit, communal life, in which people lived, worked and socialised together. Many men spent their whole lives in the pits – like Thomas Duncan of 26 Union Road, who started work at the age of eleven in Bathville Pit and, after some 64 years underground, the last 20 of them at Polkemmet, retired in 1947 with the British Empire medal and a letter from King George VI. Like weaving, mining is already fading into the past and may soon be as incomprehensible to young people as weaving. However, local people have recently established a memorial in Armadale Road to the mining industry, which will ensure that the many miners who died in the local pits will not be forgotten.

CHAPTER 13

'Shake off the Galling Chain' – More Whitburn Radicals

IN 1795, THERE were only 28 genuine voters in the whole of West Lothian, all of them landowners; plus 57 'fictitious' voters – those who held parcels of land feued off by landowners purely for the purpose of creating a new voter, whose vote was of course dictated by that landowner. The small number of voters made it easy for election candidates to bribe or threaten them; the more so as voting was by a show of hands, not by secret ballot. There was a desperate need to expand the electorate, to give the vote to the less well off and to prevent election corruption.

The Great Reform Act of 1832

In 1832, the Whig government brought forward the first Great Reform bill (pushed on by vast public demonstrations in its favour). Whitburn's weavers were eager for reform and made a banner which bore the message, 'Shake off, shake off the galling chain, And like our sires our rights maintain.' It was carried by the Whitburn contingent at the demonstrations in favour of the 1832 (and later) reform bills.

After the passing of the 1832 act, 77 men (no women, of course) became entitled to the vote in Whitburn parish – certainly a great increase on the handful of landowners who had the privilege of the vote before 1832. But suffrage was still restricted to those who owned or rented land of some value; therefore, the new voters were primarily farmers, landowners and prosperous farm tenants of the parish, plus a few of the better off tradesmen. They included John Bishop (Robert Burns' son-in-law); Whitburn's schoolmaster Samuel Greenshiels; the various clergymen; James Graham, the Whitburn clock and watch-maker (who owned houses and land in the village); John Dick, the merchant; Robert Calder, the weavers' agent; and one solitary labourer, William Milne of Blackburn, who owned 'a piece of ground and houses there'. For ordinary workers, nothing changed.

The failure of the 1832 Reform Act to produce real reform led to the rise of Chartism – the campaign for a People's Charter which demanded the vote for all adult males and five other radical reforms. Whitburn had no formal Chartist society but it had several political associations and many local individuals were politically informed and engaged – like the six local men who clubbed together to buy a newspaper and keep abreast of politics: John Shanks, the cooper; William Waterstone, the local roadman; James Flemington, the tailor and former soldier; Adam Pringle, the weaver; Dr Wilson; and Dr Mitchell, the minister. They gathered in Cooper Shanks' house and a schoolboy was paid a few pennies to read it to them. The first three were Liberals, the others Tories, but 'however furious were the debates, the six always remained good friends'– though of the six, only the minister had the vote. Several political associations existed in Whitburn during this time of reform agitation. In 1836, John Calder, John Wilson and William Auld, as committee members of the Whitburn Reform Association, wrote to the *Glasgow Argus*, protesting against the creation by Sir William Baillie of ten 'fictitious' votes by leasing small parts of his estate to friends and associates, none of them local. In addition, other proprietors had created 'paper votes', making a total of 22 in the parish of Whitburn alone. 'The County of Linlithgow is, we believe, fairly swamped by paper vote manufactories...' wrote the three radicals. 'It is evident that every Reformer ought to be up and doing' and they called for a new Reform bill to stamp out the abuse.

A Political Union of Whitburn was founded in 1837 and, at the hustings in 1838, the Hon Charles Hope made ironic reference to 'that respectable body', the 'Radical Association of Whitburn', which may have been a third political group in Whitburn. In February 1838, Whitburn Political Union sent to the Houses of Parliament a petition for repeal of the Corn Laws (which kept bread prices artificially high, to the benefit of farmers and landowners). That same month, the Political Union petitioned for a repeal of the poor law, for the withdrawal of the pension paid to the King of Hanover (a relative of the British royal family) and against government money going to the Church of Scotland for its schools, on the grounds that it was 'flagrantly unjust' to dissenters 'who received and asked nothing from the state...' It seems that radicalism in Whitburn was still partly influenced by its dissenting background; but certainly the disastrous decline of weaving encouraged the radical discontent of Whitburn's weavers.

Also in 1838, signatures were gathered for the first of the three national Chartist petitions demanding universal suffrage and they included some 4,000 names from the Bathgate and Whitburn area (though it should be borne in mind that petitions at that period were sometimes found to contain fictitious names). There were 43 Chartist associations in Scotland, including one in Bathgate (a weaving community) and one in Linlithgow (a town dependent on leather-tanning and shoemaking). Bathgate's association urged local people to buy goods only from Chartists and Chartist supporters. Whitburn's Political Union preferred 'total abstention' – ie not buying any goods which were subject to excise, with the intention of hitting the government by reducing its tax income. Chartism was never a coherent or well-organised movement: in the more prosperous 1850s, the Chartist movement folded and reformers became resigned to having to work within existing Liberal (and later, Socialist) politics.

In 1842 comes the first mention of organised political activism among the women of Whitburn, though doubtless they had long been active in support of various causes alongside their menfolk. Men's voices could be heard by Parliament but women's were of no account; instead, the custom for women was to send a memorial to Queen Victoria. Some 619 women in Whitburn parish signed a protest against the Corn Laws and sent it to the Queen in early 1842.

But Whitburn people were aware not only of British politics. The Political Union may have been responsible for the petition sent from the inhabitants of Whitburn in 1838 opposing a possible war with Canada, during a period of unrest and insurrection in that colony. And in the 1850s, much interest was aroused in Britain by the struggle to achieve independence from Austria and the unification of the various Italian states under their charismatic leader, Garibaldi. When Italian unification was achieved in 1859, the Whitburn Mutual Improvement Society, which had discussed his cause, wrote to Garibaldi, 'congratulating him… and assuring him of the keen interest with which they had watched his struggle from beginning to end.' They were delighted to receive a reply in Garibaldi's own hand, thanking them for their interest and for their good wishes: 'Wishing them all happiness, I honour my self to be G. GARIBALDI.' Another Whitburn parish link with the great man was the naming of a miners' row built in Fauldhouse c.1860 after him – Garibaldi Row, the stone cottages which still stand on the south side of Main Street.

The largest demonstration

Throughout the 19th century, the struggle continued to extend the franchise to working men. Whitburn petitioned the House of Commons in favour of the 1866 Franchise Bill. Agitation for the 1884 reform bill was particularly widespread and the *West Lothian Courier* printed a detailed report of the demonstration held in Bathgate in favour of the bill – probably the largest political event ever held in West Lothian. People from every town and village in the county took part, bringing decorated floats and banners with political slogans and their local pipe or brass bands:

About three thousand took part in the procession which walked through the principal streets of the town, and the vast crowd which gathered at the Muir has been estimated at between four and five thousand... The Whitburn contingent... numerically strong, made an exceeding good exhibition, and were also favoured with good music by the Whitburn Band, which accompanied them. At their head was proudly borne the flag... round which the Covenanters of the parish rallied and fought at Bothwell Brig... The place of honour behind this grand relic of other days was given to the old reformers of Whitburn, who ten in number, occupied a couple of machines [carriages], on the first of which was carried the flag borne by the Whitburn weavers in 1832...

The various trades – bakers, miners, tailors, shoemakers, etc – each had their own decorated floats; the Whitburn tailors' banner read:

Good my lords, we've ta'en your measure,
And, gin ye oppose our bill,
Shears and goose we'll clip and press ye,
Till ye answer to our Will.

Clearly, Whitburn was still politically aware and radically inclined. By the end of the century, however, its radicalism seemed to have softened into an attachment to the Liberal party and then to socialism and Labour. A letter writer to the local paper in 1903 remembered its radical reputation as a thing of the past: 'As a community, it was one of the most intelligent and progressive in the county. It had a good lending library. Many of its tradesmen were excellent debaters.' There were still possible glimpses of the radical streak: in 1913, as part of their militant campaign to win votes for women, it may have been suffragettes who cut telegraph wires on the Harthill Road but whether they were Whitburn women is not known. A branch of the Independent Labour Party with its socialist programme to benefit working people had been set up in Whitburn by July 1918 but struggled to expand in a burgh with a strong Labour following.

Labour councillors had already won a significant share of the town council seats by 1931. Labour-dominated, the town council continued to demonstrate sympathy with the communism of the Soviet Union, sending greetings annually to a mining town in the USSR under the auspices of the Scotland-USSR Friendship Society. That, however, came to an end with the Russian invasion of Hungary in 1956, when the council sent a letter to the Russian ambassador in London, 'expressing the Council's horror and grief at the reports of the terrible and terrifying punishment being suffered by the people of Hungary at the hands of Russian armed forces' and calling for withdrawal of the troops. The council shed its admiration for the Soviets but from the 1920s when political affiliation began to come in, right up to the abolition of the burgh in 1975, local electors continued to return Labour councillors – until the huge surge in SNP support in the 1980s and 1990s. Since the introduction of large multi-member wards in 2007, Whitburn and Blackburn have shared four councillors, always electing a mixture of the two main parties, Labour and SNP; but in 2017, for the first time in many decades, a Conservative councillor, Bruce Fairbairn, was elected for the ward, probably at least partly in protest against the present unpopular Tory Westminster government or the perception of Scottish Labour's ineffective opposition to the SNP.

Trade Unions

Whitburn's continuing tendency towards radicalism was also evident in the extent of union involvement, particularly in mining. The coalmining industry was highly unionised and Whitburn's miners adhered firmly to the major coal strikes of 1921, 1926 and 1984–5 in the face of tremendous hardships. The concentration of miners in small towns and villages such as Whitburn encouraged feelings of solidarity among miners and loyalty towards the mining union.

CHAPTER 14

Whitburn: Occupations, Incomers and Emigrants

IN THE MID 19th century, Whitburn was still a village, though the *Imperial Gazetteer* described it as having 'an appearance of more bustle than might be expected from the amount of its population.' The surveyors working on the first Ordnance Survey mapping of the village in the early 1850s noted that:

> The houses are one and two storeys high, thatched and slated, and generally in good repair, having vegetable gardens in rear. It contains some very good general shops with a number of small ones of various kinds, a few spirit shops and one very good inn, the Whitburn Inn.

After 80 years of very gradual increase, Whitburn made a sudden spurt of growth in the 1850s, when the surge in mining activity produced new jobs and drew many incomers to the village. In that decade, the population grew from 808 to 1,362.

Occupations	1841	1851	1861	1871	1881	1891	1901
Farming	28	77	14	25	21	23	17
Weaving & related trades	131	297	136	67	33	11	7
Total mining	14	25	170	142	146	172	191
Ironstone mining	3	5	68	53	72	18	-
Coal mining	11(all at Greenrigg)	11(all at Greenrigg)	74	54	19	112	129
Mining related	-	9	28	35	54	42	62
Trades	51	52	85	108	101	89	139
Shopwork	12	23	44	32	30	35	39
General Labouring	1	7	84	59	45	34	22
Dressmaking & millinery	6	20	12	30	21	21	25

Domestic service	15	9	26	44	40	59	62
Professional & clerical	5	7	18	19	25	23	26
Total Population	798	808	1362	1432	1200	1185	1442

The figures in the table make it clear that Whitburn was a weaving village until the 1850s. Only in that decade was weaving overtaken by mining and it was mining which caused the substantial growth in population. Mining dominated Whitburn's employment for some 130 years, from about 1855 until 1985. For the first 30 years or so of that period, ironstone mining predominated; thereafter, coal mining.

Trades and shopwork grew slowly in importance as the century went on, but, for women, the dressmaking trades and domestic service were the most common form of employment. In addition to those women employed as servants in Whitburn, many more would have gone into service elsewhere, particularly in prosperous, middle class Edinburgh. Most married women did not have paid work, of course; working women were generally young girls, spinsters or widows.

	Population of Whitburn	Percentage Irish-born, Whitburn (%)	Percentage Irish-born, Blackburn (%)	Percentage Irish-born, West Lothian (%)
1841	798	1.1	4	5
1851	808	4.5	20	9.2
1861	1,362	7.9	20.6	9.5
1871	1,432	4.7	14.6	8
1881	1,200	2.6	8.3	7.6
1891	1,185	1.8	8.2	6.8
1901	1,442	0.3	n/a	6.8

Irish Immigration

From its earliest days, Whitburn was a place of incomers. During its first half century, they came mainly from within West Lothian and the adjacent counties.

In the 1840s, the potato harvest failed in Ireland and millions were reduced to desperate hunger. Scotland was close and offered one of the shortest and cheapest crossings for the poor to leave the destitution of their own country; therefore, a large number of Irish came to Scotland.

The table compares the percentage of Irish-born in Whitburn with those in Blackburn and in West Lothian. In 1841, Whitburn had nine Irish-born residents. In 1851, after the famine, there were 36 – an increase certainly but small compared to Blackburn where a fifth of the population had been born in Ireland. But Blackburn had a large cotton mill offering plenty of unskilled jobs to the incomers, whereas Whitburn was still dependent on the dying trade of weaving and had yet to develop its mining industry.

By 1861, there had been a change. Whitburn had 107 Irish-born, practically all of them miners or labourers, and concentrated on the north side of West Main Street, around the old Malt Barns near Market Place, at Shuttle Row and Gateside. The 1850s were the peak decade of Irish immigration to Whitburn, which coincided with the rapid development of the ironstone and coal mines in the area where plenty of work was available. Thereafter, the Census returns show that the number of Irish-born declined to a negligible number, though there would have been a larger number of second- and third-generation Irish.

Why were the numbers for Whitburn so much lower than elsewhere in West Lothian? At first this was because of lack of work available to them. But as mines opened in the area, a great deal of work became available and yet the Irish did not settle in Whitburn in any numbers. One reason may have been the lack of miners' rows; the greater cost of private renting made Whitburn an unattractive destination for poor Irish immigrants. It's also possible that those recruiting workers were discriminating against the Irish and preferred to take on Scots. Racial or sectarian discrimination against Catholics was commonplace in Scotland until the 1950s and 1960s. These are not the sort of facts which are recorded in official records but given Whitburn's historic attachment to anti-'Papism' and to dissenting Protestant denominations, and the presence in the mid-19th century of a Whitburn branch of the Protestant Reformation Society, it seems likely that anti-Catholic feeling was present in the mid- to late 19th century and probably for much longer.

There were certainly tensions between the Irish incomers and the existing population. For example, at Whitburn Fair in 1861, police attempted to arrest an Irishman named McKenna on suspicion of assault but were confronted with 'a score or two of other Irish miners, who immediately assailed the constables with all sorts of missiles and weapons'. According to the newspaper report, the policemen were rescued by a 'strong party of the inhabitants' of Whitburn and several arrests were made.

Given the greater opportunities of the new country, however, many of the Irish newcomers rose rapidly out of poverty. One of them, William Gromley or Crumley, came to Whitburn in the late 1840s, married a Scottish girl, Grace Creech, and worked first as a labourer and later on the railways. He must have been a hard-working and thrifty man as his widow was able to buy a four-roomed house at 33–9 West Main Street. William Crumley's son William also worked on the railways, rising to be assistant stationmaster at Paisley. In his will of 1903, he left the residue of his estate to the town council of Whitburn 'for the purpose of erecting and maintaining a Marble, Granite or Bronze Drinking Fountain at or adjoining to Whitburn Cross, to my memory, and to be named the 'Crumley Fountain'; or failing this, to Tippethill Hospital.' Since no Crumley Fountain was ever built, it's to be assumed that the money went to Tippethill.

Orangeism

The period of overt anti-Irish feeling seems to have been of brief duration. Integration of the Irish was slow at first but rates of marriage between Scots and Irish were healthy in West Lothian. The presence of Orange Lodges, however, might be an indicator of continuing tensions between Catholic and Protestant. The Orange Order was founded in Ireland in 1795 to defend Protestantism and the Protestant ascendancy over Catholics in Ireland at that time. It spread to Scotland in the 1800s, mainly brought by Ulster Protestants, so was usually strongest where Irish Protestant immigration was highest. This was not the case in Whitburn, where the spur seems to have been a long-standing veneration of the Protestant tradition, and its Covenanting history, but probably exacerbated by dislike of Catholicism and Catholic Irish immigration. Whitburn certainly had an Orange Lodge by 1875, when it and some six other local lodges organised 'One of the largest processions seen in Whitburn... [which] perambulated through the streets' before convening in the grounds of Polkemmet by permission of Sir William Baillie.

After 1921, when at Irish partition Protestant Ulster remained part of the UK, the number of Scottish lodges declined. By the 1930s, there were only 15 left in the East of Scotland but still some 250 in the West of Scotland. In Whitburn, however, the Order seemed to grow in strength: LOL 81 was founded in 1947, the flute band in 1962, LOL 203 in 1969 and LOL 403 in 1977; LOL 555 has disbanded; there is also a Ladies LOL 150. With so many lodges, Whitburn became District 60 County Grand Lodge of the East in 1994. In 2006, West Lothian had the highest concentration of Orange membership in Scotland and Whitburn probably the highest concentration in West Lothian. Each of the Lodges, the two Royal Black Preceptories and the two flute bands holds a march through Whitburn during the year and most raise funds for local good causes. The continuing popularity of the Order in Whitburn perhaps owes most to the influx of Glasgow people who came to Whitburn post-war and particularly during the overspill, as well as to family traditions of membership.

During the Irish Troubles, Orange fundraising for Protestant paramilitary organisations made it controversial. The leadership of the Order tried to distance it from the violence: in 2002, when the Grand Master of the Orange Lodge in Scotland was Whitburn man, Ian Wilson, he criticised the appearance of UVF slogans on walls in the town, attributing them, however, to vandalism rather than sectarianism, and condemning the paramilitaries on both sides of the Troubles. In 1998, Whitburn South minister, the Rev Gordon McCracken, a Depute Grand Master of the Order in Scotland, resigned from the order following an incident at an Orange walk in Drumcree, Northern Ireland, in which police came under attack. He warned that the Order had 'provided a platform for sinister elements' in the Troubles and criticised it for its focus on Irish politics instead of the Reformation and Covenanting tradition in Scotland.

Other incomers

The population of Whitburn grew slowly during the second half of the 19th century. When local mines contracted in the 1870s and 1880s, the population declined, despite high fertility and large families. As always, newcomers tended to come from the other parishes in West Lothian or from the surrounding counties. Immigration from other countries was almost unknown until late in the 20th century – with a couple of exceptions.

Italian immigration to Scotland began in the 1890s, when families, mainly from the Barga area of northern Italy, began to arrive, opening ice cream parlours, chip shops and barbers' shops. Notable Italian families in Whitburn have been the Morettas, who had a hairdressing business at 41 West Main Street, and the Boni family, ice cream merchants and café owners, both of whom were in Whitburn before the First World War; and the Franchittis, café and stationery shop owners, now more famous for their racing driver sons, Dario and Marino.

The second significant group of incomers were the Poles. During the Second World War, tens of thousands of Polish troops were stationed in Scotland, several hundred of them at Polkemmet. At the end of the war, Polkemmet estate was used as a re-settlement camp and some of the 10,000 Polish soldiers who chose to stay and settle in Scotland took up mining jobs in the Whitburn area. As with the Irish, there was some initial friction as two unfamiliar cultures rubbed up against each other. The Polkemmet miners had even voted that Poles should not be allowed to work in the pit: Scottish trade unions wanted the Poles to be sent back to their Soviet-dominated homeland – many of the union leaders were communist and saw no problem with Soviet dictatorship. This period of friction, however, was short-lived and their integration was swift. Some took British nationality and changed their names – for example, Tadeusz Dziegiel of Whitburn managed to keep close to his own name though adopting a Scottish one – James Dalziel – and became a prominent businessman, owner of the garage in Armadale Road.

In 1972, Whitburn received three of the thousands of Ugandan Asian families expelled from Uganda in 1972 by the dictator Idi Amin; in contrast to Bathgate, whose Councillor Cameron declared 'While sympathising with these poor Asians, our first responsibility is to our own people.' In February 1973, the three families were welcomed to Whitburn by Provost Alex Bell and his fellow councillors with a meal in the Roadhouse and then taken to their new homes: the Carrascos in Whitdalehead Road, the D'Souzas in Empire Street and the Kotakias in Dean Street.

A more significant number of Polish and other Eastern Europeans have settled in Whitburn in the last decade or so, making up about 1 per cent of the population of the Whitburn and Longridge area according to the 2011 Census. The largest 'ethnic' group, however, remains the English at 2 per cent. Other figures are tiny: Irish 0.4 per cent; Asian 0.5 per cent; Chinese 0.15 per cent; Afro-Caribbean 0.3 per cent. Ethnic diversity in Whitburn remains very low but each wave of incomers, whether from elsewhere in Britain or further afield, has enriched and enlivened the local population.

Emigration

'At no time have any considerable number emigrated from this Parish and only two within the last six months', reads a handwritten note in the 1841 Census of Whitburn. Whitburn experienced no mass movement overseas of population such as afflicted the Highlands during the 19th century but it had its share of adventurous or ambitious men and women who emigrated to various parts of the British Empire. The most common destination for Scottish emigrants was America. One Whitburn man who sailed there was Robert Hamilton Bishop, born at Cult on 26 July 1777. A cousin of John Bishop of Halfway House, he attended the Rev John Brown's church at Longridge, studied at the University of Edinburgh and became a minister of the Associate Burgher Church. In 1802, he set off for the United States at the invitation of an American church. There his work brought him into contact with African American slaves and persuaded him of the need to abolish slavery. In 1824, he helped set up and became the first president of Miami University in Oxford, Ohio, a frontier town at that time no larger than Whitburn. His views on theology, slavery and student freedoms were considered alarmingly liberal: in his most significant book, *Elements of the Science of Government*, he taught that civil and religious liberties were even more important than obedience to government. He wished his university to be open to all – to all *men*, at least; perhaps he had imbibed the radical strand of Whitburn thinking in his youth. He died in 1855.

The regular depressions in trade and agriculture in the 19th century led many to seek a better life in the colonies. Often an emigrant would write home encouraging friends and relatives to follow him. A letter survives from William Morton in America to Thomas Bishop of Midseat of Foulshiels farm, urging him to come to the States, offering advice for the voyage and requesting he bring certain items with him:

> You must lay in provisions for 8 weeks, oatmeal and [oat] cakes baked thick and well-fired, potatoes, butter, tea, sugar, a currant loaf or two... Thomas Graham's wife wants a blanket shawl; brother George wants a german flute with some sets of music for it... You might bring a good number of sacks... and some moleskin trousers... Brother Andrew would like to have a light iron plow.... I am mutch obliged to you for your kind offer to bring me one of my old sweethearts, it would be very acceptable but I doubt it would be a harder task for you than all the other articles.

The Midseat farmer must have been relieved to read the second thoughts in the postscript: 'Don't bring the plow'. In 1837, Thomas Bishop did in fact emigrate to the 'Scotch Settlement' in Indiana and became a naturalised citizen of the United States five years later.

The peak years for emigration were just before and after the First World War. Emigration was cheap and easy in the early 1900s – shipping companies like the Anchor Line and the Allan Line advertised fast and regular services to Canada and the United States and tickets could be bought through local agents in Bathgate and Armadale. In the depression years of the 1920s, 80 out of every 1,000 Scots emigrated (the equivalent figure for England was only five), Scotland had the third highest rate of emigration of European nations and West Lothian had the fifth highest rate of all the Scottish counties. However, the outflow from Whitburn was offset by the natural increase in population and the number of miners and families arriving to take up work at the new Polkemmet Pit. Emigration continued after the war, though on a much lesser scale.

CHAPTER 15

Whitburn becomes a Burgh

IT WAS NOT until the second Baillie baronet and his wife settled at Polkemmet in the late 1850s that active lairdly interest was brought to bear on the town; but it was philanthropic activity for the poor, the church, schooling and welfare – useful indeed but not directly contributing to the economic development of the town or to the improvement of its housing conditions.

By the late 1850s, the lack of facilities spurred seven of Whitburn's leading citizens into action. They were the Rev Graham Mitchell, parish minister, and Robert Gardner, the bank agent and draper, (these two the *Falkirk Herald* later referred to as 'the aristocracy of the new burgh of Whitburn'), together with Dr Thomas Clark, farmer and carrier Thomas Geddes, nurseryman John Ramsay and two others whose names are not known. Together they petitioned the Sheriff of Linlithgowshire to have the village declared a 'populous place' under the terms of the Police of Towns (Scotland) Act of 1850. With a population of 1,362, Whitburn was only just large enough to qualify. Police acts had nothing to do with police in the modern sense but conferred the legal power to raise money for paving, draining, lighting and otherwise improving towns.

The Sheriff drew up the boundaries of the new burgh and at a public meeting of male householders on 4 January 1862, the scheme was laid before them to ensure that they wanted civic improvement enough to pay the increased rates that would be the price of them. As more than three-quarters voted in favour, Whitburn became a burgh. Then the 'respectable company of electors' sat down to dinner at the Inn in celebration. The whole process had taken just eight months.

Why become a burgh?

The main problem which induced the seven men to seek burgh status was the lack of an adequate water supply. As a burgh, the commissioners would gain the power to levy rates on each property holder and tenant and also to borrow money, in order to build a reservoir and put public wells in the street. The new police commissioners (town council) comprised at least four of the seven men who had achieved burgh status for Whitburn, plus five others. Robert Gardner was chosen to be senior magistrate (Provost) and the very first meeting was held in Whitburn Inn on 10 February 1862. A list of those liable to pay rates was ordered to be made and some of their number were requested to find out where a 'copious supply of water' could be got. Matters moved on swiftly and by June they had settled on a site at Blaeberryhill Farm owned by Sir William Baillie. In late September, he was asked to cut the first sod: 'filling a neat little barrow with a few spadefuls of soil, which her Ladyship wheeled off to some distance and emptied as a commencement of the embankment'. The barrow and spade were then presented to Lady Baillie as a memento of the occasion. Less than a year later, Lady Baillie was back again to turn the key letting the water into the town's pipes, this time collecting 'a handsome silver cup and salver'. Six wells were erected along the Main Street for the residents to access the new water supply and the commissioners also saw to the erection of street lamps along the Main Street and the appointment of Thomas Kelly as lamplighter. These lamps, however, were the target of the first act of vandalism in the new burgh; the council offered a reward of £1 for information leading to the conviction of the culprits.

Whitburn Burgh in the late 19th century

After such a swift and successful start to burgh business, the commissioners seemed to run out of steam. They levelled the kerb stones of the pavements and ordered property owners to repair their gutters and other minor work but no major projects were undertaken in the rest of the 1860s or the 1870s. In fact, it was not uncommon for the minutes to record 'as there was no business, the meeting separated'.

Upon Mr Gardner's retirement in 1882, the new Provost was the parish minister, the Rev JA Ireland – an energetic but not altogether popular figure. Mr Anderson of Fauldhouse said:

> he was the rudest man he ever met. While giving evidence before Commissioners in Edinburgh regarding Wilson's Trust, the Rev Mr Ireland impressed upon them that the [Whitburn] School Board was a pack of ignorant men, and that the inhabitants were still worse.

But ordinary men were beginning to take a greater role in local government: the occupations of the councillors elected in 1882, in addition to the parish minister, were clothier, registrar, innkeeper, carrier, joiner, grocer, mason and baker. However, they hesitated to tackle large problems, knowing how unpopular they would be if they raised the rates to pay for them – the rate-payers were also the electors. The council's total

Whitburn Parish Church, now Whitburn South Parish Church. © MS Cavanagh

'This given by William Wardrope, Apothry, to Wheitburn Parrish, Edr Nov. 1727' – though it was to be another four years before Whitburn was officially disjoined from Livingston parish. © West Lothian Local History Library

A chaise. © Author's collection

Sir William Augustus Cunynghame as a young man. © *History of the Linlithgow and Stirlingshire Hunt, 1775–1910* by JH Rutherford (Blackwood, 1911)

The new village of Whitburn, located at the crossroads of the Great Road and the north-south drove loan, 21 miles from Edinburgh. On the left, Polkemmet Toll. © Armstrong's Map of the Three Lothians (1773), detail.

The spinning jenny was invented by James Hargreaves and patented in 1770. John Dick's 'cotton jeanie house' would have contained several of these machines, worked by turning the wheel by hand. Later and larger versions were powered by water or by steam. © *The cotton manufacture of Great Britain investigated and illustrated* by Andrew Ure and Peter Lund Simmonds (HG Bohn, 1861)

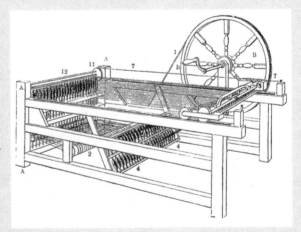

Some women as well as men worked as weavers. © Internet Book Archive on Flickr

The Barracks. The lower storey was Archibald Bruce's Antiburgher Church and the upper floor was the barracks accommodation for his divinity students. © West Lothian Local History Library

The Rev John Brown of Whitburn. © *Dr John Brown and his sisters Isabella and Jane* by ET McLaren (1902)

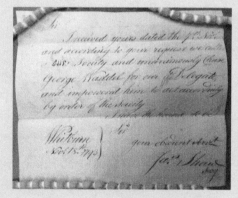

From the title page of one of Archibald Bruce's books. © New College Library, University of Edinburgh

Letter from the Whitburn branch of the Friends of the People, dated 1793. © National Records of Scotland, JC26/1793/1/67

East Main Street, looking east from the Cross. The wide street outside Whitburn Inn (third building on right) makes an impressive centre to the village. © Almond Valley Heritage Centre

The two-storey building was the Whitburn Inn, seen here in the 1950s, long after it had ceased to function as an inn. © West Lothian Local History Library

Halfway House, c.1910.
© Almond Valley Heritage Centre

The gravestone of Elizabeth Burns Bishop in Whitburn South churchyard. © Brian Cavanagh

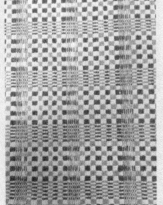

A blanket woven in Whitburn around 1850 in the 'overshot' weft weaving style, a Scottish speciality at the time. The main fabric is woven cotton, with a geometric pattern woven in contrasting wool. © West Lothian Council Museums

Lord Polkemmet, an eccentric judge, in whom 'caution took the place of lucidity of intellect'. He spoke broad Scots.
© William Kay

The second last of the Whitburn weavers, William Melvin, at his loom in East Main Street. The son of a weaver, he was already working as a weaver by the age of 15 and probably earlier. He died in 1907 aged 82.
© West Lothian Local History Library

Polkemmet House.
© Robert Braid

Boys as young as 11 laboured below ground for 12 hours a day. © *Condition and Treatment of the children employed in the Mines and Collieries of the United Kingdom...* by William Strange (1842)

Polkemmet Colliery in 1979, with a colliery pug engine in the foreground. © Stephen JG Hall

Soup kitchen at Greenrigg Colliery during the 1921 miners' strike. © West Lothian Local History Library

Police arrest pickets at Polkemmet during the miners' strike of 1984–5. © Herald & Times Group

Polkemmet after closure in 1985. The site has been cleared and rehabilitated. © West Lothian Council Museums

Miners underground at Polkemmet pit, c.1950s. © The Colliery Hub

The Whitburn weavers' banner of 1832. The leopard with a shuttle in its mouth is an old heraldic symbol for weaving. Now faded, the banner was originally blue with red lettering. © West Lothian Council Museums

Garibaldi. © Internet Book Archive on Flickr

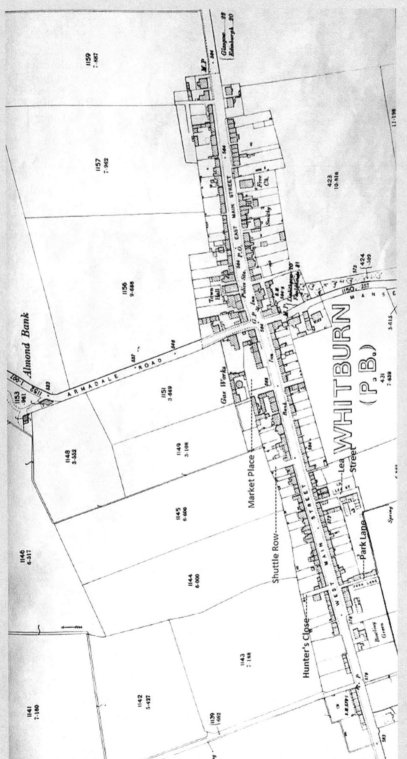

Whitburn in 1897. © Ordnance Survey

West Main Street, looking west. On the right, the entry to Hunter's Close and to Park Lane on the left. © West Lothian Local History Library

Alex Mitchell, tailor and town councillor. © West Lothian Local History Library

Women workers at the National Fire Training School at Townhead Gardens, 1946–7. They include Lena Adamson, Maggie Topping, Ann Gibson, Pearl Graham, Isa Cleland, Martha Neally, Elsie Aitken and Jean Boyd. © West Lothian Local History Library

'The Sir': Sir William Baillie, 2nd baronet, dominated local government in West Lothian, and also chaired the Whitburn heritors, Whitburn parochial board and Whitburn school board. © West Lothian Local History Library

The Baillie Institute. The original building is on the left and one of several extensions is on the right. © Almond Valley Heritage Centre

Sir Gawaine Baillie was killed in the 5th week of the Great War, aged 21. © Internet Book Archive on Flickr

Polkemmet Auxiliary Red Cross Hospital – staff and patients in the grounds. Commandant Lady Baillie is in uniform, looking to the left. © *Red Cross Work in the East of Scotland* (T & A Constable, 1918)

Sir Adrian Baillie. © West Lothian Local History Library

Staff of Polkemmet House in the 1930s. Back, L-R: Nan Easton (née McNeil), Belle Stirling, James –. Front, L-R: Lizzy Morrison, Mary Mazs, Duncan –, Mary Page. © Mrs Nan Easton

Trefoil School at Polkemmet House, 1945–51. © West Lothian Local History Library

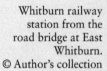

Whitburn railway station from the road bridge at East Whitburn. © Author's collection

West Main Street, looking east from close to Gateside. © Almond Valley Heritage Centre

Brucefield Parish Church. © MS Cavanagh

Gospel Hall, built as Lady Baillie's Sabbath school. © MS Cavanagh

One of the last thatched houses stood about where the Clachan pub is now. Robert Bain, who settled in Whitburn about 1859, recalled that at that time: 'The cottages were mostly all thatched'. The very last thatched house was pulled down about 1922. © West Lothian Local History Library

Children in Union Drive, 1930s. Council houses provided decent housing, gardens, and safe places for children to play. © West Lothian Local History Library

Overspill housing in Polkemmet Road, with the headgear of Polkemmet Pit in the distance (1960s). © National Library of Scotland

Working on a cutting machine at Levi's jeans factory. © West Lothian Local History Library

The Heartlands development from the air, looking south. New housing is being built to the south and west of Whitburn, with industrial development to the north. © Green Town Heartlands Ltd

Whitdalehead School in 2008 before demolition. The two-storey centre portion was built in the early 1820s as Wilson's school. © Brian Cavanagh

John Dick's house, shop and post office is on the left, built by him in 1813 – the date still visible on the scrolled skew putts on the chimney gable. Beyond the Baillie Institute, the single storey Town Hall can be seen, before the Masonic temple was added above. © Almond Valley Heritage Centre

Part of the town centre redevelopment of the 1960s, looking north-east towards the Cross. Market Inn on the left. © West Lothian Local History Library

Whitburn Miners' Welfare (burnt down in 2011) stood immediately east of where Weavers' Court sheltered housing now stands. © Richard Webb (CC BY-SA 2.0).

Dr JB Michie, Whitburn GP, killed in action, North Russia, December 1918. © West Lothian Local History Library

Whitburn Juniors Football Club won the Scottish Junior Cup in 2000. © David McNie

Whitburn Gala, 1912. The procession passes the Cross and moves west along West Main Street. © Dr John Thomson

Leon Jackson, *X Factor* winner, 2007. © West Lothian Local History Library

John Lambie, playing for Whitburn Junior Secondary School football team. He became one of Scotland's best-known football managers. © West Lothian Local History Library

Alex Bell, last Provost of Whitburn. © West Lothian Local History Library

Margaret K. Dean came to teach at Whitdalehead in 1902. 'At the singing lessons, she had a most ardent penchant for two songs – 'The Harp that once thru' Tara's Halls' and 'The Minstrel Boy'. I see her standing there, less than five feet of animation, wielding the baton...' During the First World War, she was a VAD nurse at Polkemmet Auxiliary Red Cross Hospital in her spare time. © West Lothian Local History Library

Bert Gamble, long-serving councillor.
© West Lothian Local History Library

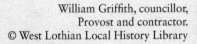

William Griffith, councillor, Provost and contractor.
© West Lothian Local History Library

expenditure in the early 1880s never reached £200 and several council meetings were abandoned because a quorum of three was not present. Nor were the electors particularly interested: on several occasions, not enough new councillors were elected and the retiring ones had to serve again. Until 1918, the right to vote depended on being male and owning or renting property valued at £10 or over – though from 1869, single women who were ratepayers could vote in local government elections.

The burgh commissioners fell out with Robert Gardner in 1886 over his refusal to pay water rates for the water supply to his farm at Whitdalehead. Thereafter relations deteriorated. The commissioners then quarrelled with Gardner's Whitburn Gas Company over various unreasonable increases in gas costs and its using too much water. And in 1889, the commissioners demanded that Mr Gardner repair the unsatisfactory footpath at one of his properties. Mr Gardner was probably by now regretting ever having Whitburn erected into a burgh! He moved to Edinburgh and died there in 1905, aged 89; but he was buried in Whitburn Cemetery.

> **Gas works**
>
> Whitburn had its own gas works from 1851, erected by a company of local businessmen: 'The building contains the usual Gas Apparatus and the Gasometer contains 5000 Cubic feet of Gas which is consumed in the interiors of the dwellings, there being no street lamps. Mr R. Gardner, Banking Agent, is Chairman of the Company.' Perhaps there was a conflict of interest ten years later, when the burgh commissioners, headed by Mr Gardner, purchased the gas for the new street lamps from Mr Gardner's gas company! Whitburn Gas Company was taken over by Armadale Gas Company in 1925 and was nationalised in 1949.

In 1892, the streets were officially named and numbered for the first time. The name Lea Street was given to the 'the entrance at Peter Murray's' (87 West Main Street) and Shuttle Row was changed to Park Lane. Each house had its number painted beside the door.

The Local Government Board, which oversaw the work of local authorities, began to press for a more professional approach by councils large and small. The average population of a burgh c.1901 was 4,000; Whitburn's population of 1,442, meant that its income from the rates was almost too small for burgh status to be viable. However, the board continued to press local authorities to improve the health and housing of the population and, in 1893, ordered Whitburn to look at the drainage of the burgh, which flowed unpurified into the Almond. The commissioners replied complacently that things were not as bad as they seemed, for 'there are only three WCs in the burgh... practically speaking there is no sewage by the time it reaches the river'. The rest of the population, presumably, were not relieving themselves.

Whitburn Burgh in the 20th century

Under new legislation in 1901, the Whitburn burgh commissioners became Whitburn town council, and the magistrates became the Provost and bailies. The focus of the council during the first decade of the new century was the improvement of the town's drainage and sewage system, as required by new national legislation which obliged all house owners to connect to the public water supply and sewers. During the few years before the First World War, the councillors were much occupied with upgrading the street lighting, as well as a shameful amount of in-fighting, rowdy and disorderly meetings – 'pandemonium let loose' – culminating in discussion in the council and the town as to whether burgh status ought to be dissolved. Meanwhile Councillor Alex Mitchell's repeated calls for the council to build decent working-class housing failed even to find a seconder.

After the First World War, however, the focus of the council was firmly on council housing (see chapter on housing), clearing away substandard properties, and continuing to improve the drainage and water supply of the burgh. From 1920 or so, Whitburn town council was a Labour-dominated, high-spending, high-borrowing council, which by the 1960s was counting its expenditure in millions of pounds. 'The magnitude of Whitburn's plans is staggering for a small burgh', observed the *West Lothian Courier* of its overspill scheme but they had huge social and housing problems to solve, which could only be done by high public expenditure. They were not irresponsible and did not borrow above their ability to repay; and as Provost Alex Bell observed in 1973: 'We are [£8.5] million in debt. But that £8.5 million is solid asset. If we liquidated that asset, we could all leave this room very rich people. But we would have no houses, no schools, no factories, no community facilities.' However, by the time Whitburn town council was wound up in mid-1975, Provost Bell

> ### The bellman
>
> The town council employed a town crier or bellman who announced council and public meetings by ringing a handbell in the streets. It was still in use when town crier, John Newton, died in 1925 while out with his bell in Murraysgate Crescent. One of 'Johnnie Nitten's' regular jobs was advertising filmshows in the Town Hall: he would ring his hand bell vigorously, then shout 'Picters! A guid yin!' The council did not finally dispense with the services of a bellman until 1958.

claimed, they would hand on no deficit to the new West Lothian District Council.

Councillors were elected for a three-year term and annual elections were held in November to fill the places of the three councillors who retired each year. The Provosts and bailies were chosen by the councillors, usually on the basis of seniority. Women were almost unknown in elected posts in Whitburn. The appointment of a woman to the School Board in 1917 caused 'some adverse criticism'. The only woman previously to stand for election had received little support and 'it is argued from that, that Whitburn people do not want lady members on their public boards'. The only two women who served on the town council were co-opted, not elected. Whitburn's radicalism did not extend to equality for women.

The freedom of Whitburn burgh was awarded to only three people. The first was Provost David Drysdale in 1953. In 1967, Miss Margaret Allan retired from Whitburn Junior Secondary School after 40 years and was presented with the freedom of the burgh for her teaching and her work for the gala day and the community. The third and last was Robert Mickel, the respected burgh chamberlain (treasurer) and town clerk of Whitburn from 1957 to 1975, who helped to implement the huge growth and development of Whitburn.

Whitburn's Provosts

1862–82	Robert Gardner, banker and draper
1882–91	Rev John Ireland, minister
1891–1905	James Flemington, draper
1905–06	Dr Hugh MacPherson, GP
1906–09	Alexander Craig, draper
1909–11	James Wood, baker
1911–6	John Hunter, butcher
1916–29	William Shanks, blacksmith
1929–30	Robert Lambie, miner, then Singer Sewing Machine Co employee
1930–5	James Cleland, miner
1935–44	William Aitken, newsagent and tobacconist
1944–53	David Drysdale, trade union official
1953–6	William Griffith, contractor
1956–9	James Dick, miner
1959–62	James Brown, miner then Co-op Insurance employee
1962–5	Henry Stewart, miner then fish merchant
1965–8	William Brown, miner
1968–71	John Boyle, miner
1971–5	Alex Bell, plumber, Leyland worker, salesman

The end of Whitburn Burgh –
local government reorganisations

Town councillors had a close knowledge of their town and its inhabitants but, despite this, the system of small burghs and county councils was becoming less efficient. Conflict occurred over the differing priorities of the county and the burghs and, as the responsibilities of local government grew, costs increased and small, independent burghs ceased to be viable.

In May 1975, a major reorganisation of Scottish local government took place. Burgh councils and county councils were swept away and replaced by a two-tier system. Whitburn became part of West Lothian District, which together with Midlothian, East Lothian and Edinburgh formed Lothian Region. The town council feared that 'a great deal of authority and autonomy is being taken away from the people...' Under the old system, Whitburn people had nine town councillors and four county councillors to represent them. After 1975, they had one regional councillor and two district councillors, whose differing responsibilities were not always clear to the public. In 1996, under a further reform of local government, the two-tier system was replaced by a system of single-tier local authorities. In 2007, Whitburn became part of a larger ward (together with Blackburn and surrounding villages) of West Lothian Council, represented by three councillors.

Fire Service

In the early days of the burgh, the council acquired a hose pipe and handbarrow and trained some of its employees in their use against fires. Over the years, the equipment improved but there was no fire station. At the outbreak of the Second World War, an Auxiliary Fire Service unit was formed in Whitburn of local volunteers equipped with a light pump towed by car. Their duty was to fight fires caused by enemy action only; normal cover was provided by Bathgate or West Calder fire stations. Later, the demands of wartime resulted in the setting up of a National Fire Service (NFS) and, after the war, the NFS set up a training school at Whitburn to train professional firemen. It took over the premises to the south of Townhead Gardens which had been built (but not used) for Bevin Boys during the war. The college accommodated staff and lecture rooms etc, while the trainees (mostly ex-servicemen) slept in Nissen huts during their six- to eight-week courses. To gain practical experience, the trainees attended local fires along with the local retained firemen and in this capacity helped fight the underground fire at Burngrange Pit in January 1947 in which 15 men died – a baptism of fire for trainees. Just a couple of months later, the training school moved to Paisley, after only a year in Whitburn.

By 1970, Whitburn's population had grown to some 10,000 and a dedicated fire station was opened in 1974 at Murraysgate industrial estate to cover the south-west of the county. The two largest fires in recent years destroyed two public buildings within a matter of weeks: in June 2011, the Miners' Welfare Club was gutted by fire and, just four weeks later, Whitburn swimming pool was burned down. Fortunately, no one was injured and, though many believed that the Welfare fire was a case of fire-raising, no one was charged.

CHAPTER 16

The Later Baillies, the Baillie Institute and Polkemmet Estate

The second baronet

AFTER HER HUSBAND'S death without recovering his sanity, the widow of the first baronet of Polkemmet and her family went to live at Manuel House near Linlithgow Bridge, leaving Polkemmet House to the second baronet, her son William. Eton and Oxford-educated, he became an advocate and was MP for the burgh of Linlithgow from 1845–7. His parliamentary career was cut short when his father's mental incapacity required him to run the Polkemmet estate. Thereafter, he concentrated on local government, becoming the chairman of every committee and board. Known locally as 'the Sir', 'he was a man of commanding presence, resolute courage, and great business capacity'... 'of that genial bonhomie disposition... in expressing his opinions he was always straightforward and convincing – there never being any difficulty in knowing what his mind was on any question...'

The second baronet married a Wigtownshire laird's daughter, a highly educated and artistic young woman. It was a happy marriage, though they had no children:

> She and Sir William travelled extensively, and each was interested in the other's special hobbies; her Ladyship's leaning towards philanthropic work had her husband's entire approval.

Polkemmet estate

By the 1870s, Polkemmet estate comprised over 4,000 acres, bringing in an annual rent from its farms of nearly £3,000. In addition, the Baillies enjoyed an increasing income from the mineral wealth below their lands. Their mansion was surrounded by kitchen and flower gardens, hothouses and a vinery, which the Baillies were happy to open to 'respectable parties who wish to have a few hours relaxation'. Lady Baillie outlived her husband by 20 years, during which she continued her philanthropic work and her generosity to good causes, particularly those associated with education, foreign missions, the poor and local sports clubs. She gave a substantial sum for the building of a large extension to Bathgate Academy, which was named the Lady Baillie Wing in her honour. For many years, she employed Christina Sangster as a 'Biblewoman', whose task it was to ascertain cases of poverty and sickness in Whitburn and assist them with advice, clothing and bedding, etc funded by Lady Baillie (but presumably only if they were the 'deserving' poor). She dispensed not just fruit from the hothouses at Polkemmet but substantial sums of money to charitable causes. Possessing a sharp business brain, she was much involved in the running of the Polkemmet estate, working closely with the long-serving estate factor Robert Allan to modernise the 23 farms on the estate. Such a model of dairy farming did the estate become that it was visited by several parties of agricultural students and agriculturalists.

The Baillie Institute

It was Lady Baillie who provided Whitburn's best-known facility, the Baillie Institute. She took a lease on premises at 4 West Main Street and turned them into a Coffee House and Reading Rooms for 'the promotion of the social and moral well-being of the district', opening in January 1879. They were of course strictly alcohol-free and consisted of a library, games room and coffee room, together with a flat for the manager. When the lease expired in 1881, she decided to buy the building at 7 East Main Street, probably built in the late 1850s or early 1860s as a private house but which at that time also housed two shops. The front of the building was slightly altered to enlarge the windows and the main doorway, which, oddly, is not quite centred.

The Coffee and Reading Rooms in their fine new premises continued to be administered by a local committee but failed to gain as much use as Lady Baillie had hoped. In 1896, she gifted the building to the burgh of Whitburn, on condition that the new committee of trustees continued to ban 'intoxicating liquors', to be non-political, non-denominational and to offer 'friendship and kindness... to outsiders'. In honour of her gift, which was accompanied by an endowment to assure its future, the building was renamed the Baillie Public Institute.

Following this, she provided four more Baillie Institutes: in Blackburn, Harthill, Longridge and Fauldhouse. They were intended as a counter-attraction to the pubs, providing recreation and education and 'a safe and pleasant resort for the young men and lads of our village and district'.

The clock and tower were added by the town council in 1897 to mark the Diamond Jubilee of Queen Victoria. As use of the institute increased, a first extension was built in 1902 and a second in 1910 to the rear, containing a hall for the use of the local friendly societies and two public bathrooms with large enamel baths – a boon at a time when few houses had bathrooms. Both extensions were built at Lady Baillie's expense, though she did not live to see the opening of the second. The Institute continued to operate as a community centre and a suite of halls for hire and was run by a committee of local people until sold to the town council in 1960. It was converted into the Burgh Chambers but Lady Baillie would have been horrified to read reports in the national press of drunkenness at the official opening. The building still functions today as council offices and is being converted into a partnership centre, containing the library, museum and other council services.

Though a childless widow, Lady Baillie continued to live very comfortably at Polkemmet House with the aid of a butler, a coachman, six domestic servants and two gardeners, until her death in 1910 at the age of 88. Her style of 'Lady Bountiful' benevolence now seems patronising and intrusive but she seems to have been remarkably generous and was respected in the village. The reputation of the Baillies as the paternal lairds of Whitburn is owed mainly to this Lady Baillie and her husband, who between them had the leadership of Whitburn in their hands – he in parish and county government and she in domestic and cultural life. Fortunately, none of the Baillies stood in burgh elections, so the town council at least was able to retain its independence.

The income of the Baillies had been substantially increased by the coal on their estate, so their generosity might be seen as no more than restitution of some of their wealth to those who had actually earned it.

The three Australian baronets

Since there were no children of the second baronet's marriage, the baronetcy passed to the son of Sir William's brother Thomas who had emigrated to Australia. The new baronet, George Baillie, continued to live on his sheep station at Benerembah, is not known to have visited Polkemmet and died of typhoid fever at Melbourne in 1896. So little was he known in Whitburn that there was not even a mention of his death in the local papers. As he was unmarried, the title passed to his younger brother. Robert Baillie, the fourth baronet, was born and brought up in Australia. After inheriting the title, he appears to have come back to Britain but lived the life of a wealthy businessman in London. By the time of his death in 1907, he was still virtually unknown to the people of Whitburn.

His elder son, Gawaine, the third of the 'Australian' Baillies, became the youngest baronet in Britain when he inherited the title at the age of 13 in 1896. He was educated at Eton and Sandhurst and was commissioned as a lieutenant in the Scots Greys. He allowed the previous Lady Baillie (widow of the second baronet) to live at Polkemmet until her death, then two months later he and his mother came to take possession. An extensive reconstruction of the house interior was carried out from 1912–3; evidently Sir Gawaine was fond of sports, for a nine-hole golf course was created, an artificial curling pond, lawn tennis courts, croquet lawn and billiard room.

However, the young baronet was destined never to live at Polkemmet. On 4 August 1914, Britain entered the First World War; battalions of the regular army, including the Scots Greys, were sent out to stop the German advance through Belgium and France; and on 7 September Sir Gawaine Baillie was killed.

Polkemmet House Hospital

At the outbreak of war, Sir Gawaine had offered the use of Polkemmet House as a hospital for wounded troops. After his death, his bereaved mother honoured his wish, and began the work of adapting the main rooms of the house. At first Lady Baillie seems to have envisaged a local scheme, organised by her, staffed and maintained by volunteers from the community. She appealed for help in the local newspapers:

> a hospital is a very costly affair, so I trust you will all give me a helping hand. I was hoping that each one of you would help in taking in part of the very large washing which must be sent out every week, but I am told that no one will volunteer to do any part of it. As this is the case I am again appealing to you to ask if every one of you will subscribe 2d a week to a washing fund, and this will help to send the large hospital washing to a laundry... I would feel very proud of Whitburn if you would all come forward and help in this appeal. Will you all send me a post card to let me know if you will give 2d a week, and I will then arrange for a box to be put at some convenient place where all can deposit the money every week.

Donations arrived in kind more than in cash: from a billiard table to a promise from Kay the baker of 'buns every week' and weekly pennies from the children of Whitburn Public School. Presumably, however, she realised that this amateurish set-up was unsustainable and handed it over to the Red Cross as an Auxiliary Hospital. The main expense of setting it up, however, was borne by Lady Baillie and when it opened in late 1915, she carried on as administrator. An auxiliary hospital tended convalescent soldiers, therefore only the senior nursing staff were fully trained nurses; the local GP Dr Michie acted as medical officer, and the rest of the staff were VADs – part-trained voluntary nurses.

Forty beds were squeezed into the house – 20 in the music room, 11 in the dining room and nine in the drawing room. Local people tirelessly raised funds for 'comforts' and treats for the troops and Dr Michie ran first aid classes to train the VADs. The hospital continued to operate until the end of the war and closed in January 1919, having cared for several hundred wounded soldiers in its three years of operation.

Sir Adrian Baillie, and a racing driver

After the First World War, the new baronet Sir Adrian Baillie made a career in the diplomatic service. Despite the crippling taxes levied by the government on great estates, the Baillies substantially increased their wealth when Sir Adrian married an immensely rich American widow, co-heir of both the Whitney brewery fortune and Standard Oil (later Esso). They preferred to live at their English property, Leeds Castle in Kent, where they moved in wealthy, fashionable circles. During the 1930s, the Leeds Castle 'set' included British and foreign royalty, Hollywood film stars and senior politicians and gained a reputation for right-wing leanings. Certainly, Sir Adrian was a member of the January Club, founded by Oswald Mosley in 1934 as a discussion group for those in sympathy with fascism, and a speech reported in the *West Lothian Courier* which he gave to the Linlithgow Unionist Association in January 1934, discussing 'Herr Hitler', makes uneasy reading today. Although an appeaser, there is no evidence that he was an outright Nazi sympathiser.

He became Unionist (Conservative) MP for West Lothian in 1931; he occasionally visited his constituents and stayed at Polkemmet. But his mother was the real laird of Polkemmet and continued the same sort of benevolent maternalism as the earlier Lady Baillie, though 'she didn't endear herself as readily' as the previous one. But she lived comfortably with her sister and niece and a large staff of domestic servants and gardeners. Nan Easton was head housemaid in the 1920s and, 70 years later, recalled that the staff consisted of a butler, cook, housekeeper, four housemaids, kitchen maid, scullery maid, footman, ladies' maid, pantrymaid and tablemaid – as well as gardeners and outdoor staff: all this for three ladies who 'lived very quietly' except when Sir Adrian and his society friends came to stay. The servants were treated relatively well: 'we all had lovely coal fires in our bedrooms, and rugs'. Despite being addressed by her surname, Nan Easton enjoyed the work and 'really liked' the ladies.

Perhaps planning to spend more time at Polkemmet, Sir Adrian bought Howden House and moved his mother and aunt there but he was defeated at the 1935 election by George Mathers, the Labour candidate. He later served as an English MP, was divorced in 1945 and died two years later.

His wife and son Gawaine continued to live at Leeds Castle. Gawaine (whose godfather was King George VI's brother, the Duke of Kent) became an engineer and a racing driver, competing in the 1950s and 1960s as a wealthy amateur against the greatest drivers of the day such as Stirling Moss and Jack Brabham. A proposal in 1963 to build a racing track at Polkemmet, however, came to nothing. Sir Gawaine sold Polkemmet estate to the National Coal Board in 1956 and died in 2003, leaving an outstanding stamp collection which sold for over £16 million.

Polkemmet House during and after the war

On the outbreak of the Second World War, West Lothian was judged not to be at risk of bombing, a safe area for receiving evacuee children. To avoid pressure on local schools, Polkemmet House was requisitioned as a residential school for evacuee girls. It opened at the very start of the war in September 1939 with 13 pupils and five teachers. Towards the end of the year, the roll reached 80 – its highest number. The education on offer was primary level only. Older girls continued to live at Polkemmet but went to the Lindsay High School in Bathgate. By 1942, the risk of air raids was low and many of the children were taken home by their parents. The role declined steeply from October 1942 and the head teacher was notified that the school would not re-open after the Christmas holiday.

Trefoil School

The next occupant of Polkemmet House was another school. At the outbreak of the Second World War, the Guide movement in Edinburgh had been asked to take charge of some physically handicapped children being evacuated from the city. Their first two locations proved temporary and at the end of the war they sought premises for a permanent residential home and school for the children. Sir Adrian Baillie offered the use of Polkemmet rent-free and the school moved there in 1945. The school was supported by a grant from the Scottish Education Department and the guide staff gave their services free.

> Make do and mend was the order of the day, as house-mothers mended their charges' clothes after a hard day's work... But the kindness of the people in Whitburn was heart-warming.

The Trefoil School (the trefoil being the symbol of the guide movement) was officially opened by Princess Elizabeth (the present Queen) on 25 September 1945. The premises were far from ideal – vast distances between kitchen and dining room and between dormitories and bathroom; leaking roofs, dry rot, poor public transport and a long dark drive for staff to walk up on winter evenings. Some 28 children aged five to 14 were educated and cared for, some of them even during the holidays. Gifts for the school were received from far and near, including two canaries in cages from Field Marshall Montgomery of Alamein! A Whitburn boy who had been badly injured in a pit accident, Jimmy McIntyre, helped organise various activities for the children and became assistant scoutmaster of the school's own scout troop.

When the lease ran out after six years, the school found more suitable premises at Hermiston and left Polkemmet in 1951.

The Polish at Polkemmet

After the German invasion of Poland in 1939, thousands of Polish troops made their way to France, from where they were evacuated to Britain. Some 30,000 or more were stationed in Scotland to defend the east coast from invasion. From late 1943 till spring 1944, the artillery of the 1st Armoured Division was stationed in a hutted camp on Polkemmet estate. Later that year, the camp became a reception centre for processing recruits to the Polish forces and was also the headquarters of some infantry units undergoing training. It's believed that some officers were accommodated in the mansion house and some were in households in Whitburn. Ian Tennant recalls that a Captain (or Lieutenant) Agapi was among the officers billeted on their house in West Main Street. The other ranks were accommodated in the huts, grouped into East and West Camps.

At the end of the war, the soldiers were given the option of returning to Poland (by then under Soviet rule) or staying in Scotland. In the autumn of 1945, Polkemmet became No. 94 Polish Repatriation Camp for soldiers who wanted to return to Poland. The first contingent left for Poland in May 1946 and another 1,200 in August. In September 1946, with the demobilisation of the Polish army, the Polish Resettlement Corps was formed of those who wished to stay on in Britain (some 10,000 chose to settle in Scotland) and Polkemmet camp served as one of the re-settlement camps for processing these troops. The men were required to take up whatever jobs were offered by the Ministry of Labour and at least 70 were sent into the mines in the Whitburn area.

Squatters' Camp

The Polish Resettlement Camp emptied gradually in 1947–8 and, as the soldiers moved out, squatters moved in, the first families in August 1947. Desperate for a home at a time of severe housing shortage, young couples and families occupied the army huts and made their homes there. The take-over was organised by the local branch of the Communist Party and there was general sympathy in the district for the squatters: 'these people have come from rooms after years of waiting on houses, trying to rear a family under impossible conditions' reported a letter to the *West Lothian Courier*. 'Others have come from places where it wouldn't be fair to keep pigs. Don't you understand, these people are desperate.'

Conditions in the camp at first were primitive: the squatters' council had to ask the county council to partition the huts into rooms, install two wash-hand basins in each hut and even provide doors on the communal lavatory cubicles. A month after the first squatters moved in, there were 120 adults and 98 children in the camp, still with no electricity.

The Department of Health took over the camp from the War Office early in 1949 and a visiting official said 'Don't call them squatters. The work they had done to make homes for themselves is simply marvellous.' There were over 100 habitable huts in the camp and the tenants had set up their own employment committee and drawn up camp rules. 'Mr Walker has turned his hut into a beautifully furnished 3-apartment home – far better and more comfortable than many Council houses.' From 1949, the squatters were concentrated into Polkemmet West Camp, the East Camp closed down and no new families were accepted. Rent of 6s per week was charged and former army sergeant 'Alastair Walker, the camp leader, has been appointed factor, with full control of the camp'.

Polkemmet being outside the burgh boundaries, Whitburn town council took no responsibility for the squatters' camp but some of the squatters were on its housing list. In 1953, the Scottish Office asked the town council to rehouse the remaining tenants and, after six years, the camp finally closed.

Police College

When the Trefoil School left Polkemmet, the house and grounds became a Scottish police training school. The training school had moved into the former National Fire Services training centre in Townhead Gardens in spring 1947, where an intensive one- or two-month training course was provided for all Lowland Scottish police forces. In 1951, the training school also took over Polkemmet House, and thereafter some 30 civilian staff trained an average of 150 students. On the opening of Tulliallan Police College in 1954, Polkemmet gradually became redundant and ceased to be used in 1959. As a memento of their time in Whitburn, the College donated a Provost's chair for the new Burgh Chambers in 1960.

The Country Park

The National Coal Board had purchased Polkemmet House and estate in 1956 in order to acquire the coal reserves. After 1959, the empty house deteriorated and was demolished by the NCB, leaving only the stables and staff houses which now form the visitors' centre. In 1978, the estate was purchased by West Lothian District Council and, after upgrading, was officially opened as a country park by Councillor Bert Gamble in 1981. Nowadays it offers riverside and woodland walks, bowling green, golf course and golf range, a children's play area – and a horn sculpture by young sculptors Matthew Dalziel and Louise Scullion, set up in 1997. Since 2012, Polkemmet has also been the home of the Scottish Owl Centre, one of the largest collections of owls in the world and a valuable tourist attraction.

CHAPTER 17

Railways and Roads

THE FIRST EDINBURGH-GLASGOW railway line opened via Linlithgow in 1842; and the Bathgate-Edinburgh line in 1849. Railways provided a quicker and cheaper alternative to coach travel and rapidly put coach services out of business. Although there was no station in the village, Whitburn people still preferred to walk to the nearest station rather than continue to travel by coach. The Ordnance Survey, at work in Whitburn in the early 1850s, noted that the Whitburn Inn was 'in a flourishing way previous to the formation of the railway, but is now much reduced'.

For a while, coach companies tried to compete with the comfort and cheapness of rail travel, and advertised widely:

> Messrs Mein & Croall beg to offer to the Public... Two Splendid New Four-horse COACHES...with every comfort and convenience equal... to any Railway Carriage, and... exceedingly Low Fares... The First Class... is handsomely fitted up with divisions and arm-rests, similar to the First-class Railway Carriages....

The fares started at 4s from Glasgow to Edinburgh, set at a level to compete with the third-class rail fares; but there was no way to compete on journey times: four or five hours by coach but only two and half by train.

When the mania for railway building was at its height, Whitburn was a weaving village rather than a mining or industrial centre of any importance and so no railway company thought it worthwhile to build a line to it, whereas mining and foundry centres like Bathgate and Shotts were connected to the rail network. However, in 1853, a two and a half mile branch line was built by the local coalmasters to connect the Polkemmet area to the main line just south of Bathgate. Mining couldn't develop on a large scale without railway access but equally, railways were able to develop more quickly because the ironstone mining and foundry industries increased the production of iron.

A Railway to Whitburn?

In 1845, at the height of the railway-building boom, there were three abortive proposals to build railways that would have brought a line through Whitburn but each was abandoned. That same year, however, a line from the Wilsontown, Morningside and Coltness (WMC) Railway was built to bring ironstone from Crofthead to Morningside (near Wishaw) and thence to Glasgow. At first it terminated at Longridge but was extended in 1850 to Bathgate, with new stations at Bents and Whitburn. Unfortunately for Whitburn folk, the station was a mile's walk away at East Whitburn and getting to Edinburgh or Glasgow required a change at Bathgate or Morningside or a walk to the station at Armadale.

The WMC line was mainly intended for mineral traffic and its passenger trade was so slight that passenger services ceased in 1852. A few horse-drawn services survived: Mr Dykes ran a horse omnibus service for many years, leaving Whitburn Inn each morning to carry passengers to Edinburgh or to the station at Holytown, from where they could travel on to Glasgow. It's likely that this, the last of Whitburn's horse-drawn coach services, closed when the line through Whitburn re-opened to passenger services in 1864. However, with only two or three passenger trains each way per day, a *West Lothian Courier* writer noted in 1877 that the station had a 'dull and depressed look'. Whitburn, along with the four other stations on the line, closed to passengers on 1 May 1930, though freight services continued until 1963 when the line finally closed. The route has been turned into a footpath.

Although its pits were all eventually connected by mineral sidings to a railway line, Whitburn undoubtedly suffered from lack of easy access to passenger services – almost the only community of any size in West Lothian without a station.

The end of the toll roads

In addition to the toll bar at Murraysgate, another bar was set up in 1851 in East Main Street, at its junction with what is now Shanks Road. There was widespread resentment but it was not challenged until Bathgate sheriff's officer Roberts refused to pay the toll in 1868. The resulting court case turned up an old legal document which stated that where the Cleugh Road coincided with the Shotts turnpike road, no tolls should be erected. The East Main Street toll had to be taken down, much to the satisfaction of local people.

By this time, toll incomes were falling significantly due to competition from the railways, and were finally abolished in 1883. Responsibility for the upkeep of main roads passed to county road trustees (later the county council), so that small burghs like Whitburn with few resources did not have the expense of keeping up these main roads where they passed through their towns.

Roads after 1900

One consequence of the coming of the railways was the decline in Whitburn's carrier trade: several local men had made a living by carrying agricultural produce into Edinburgh for sale there and bringing manufactured goods back in return but that trade was soon diverted to the railway and the carriers had to survive on local trade only.

With most long journeys undertaken by rail after 1850, the main road system deteriorated and it was not until the rise of the motor car from c.1900 that major improvements to the roads were made. The town council was already concerned that the speed of motor cars was causing danger to children going to school at Whitdalehead and throwing dust over pedestrians as they roared by. They asked the county council to put up signs for a 10mph speed limit and for the tarring of roads whose surfaces were being cut up by motor vehicles. Despite repeated requests, the roads in the burgh were not tarred until during the First World War.

Buses and carriers

As motor traffic increased, carrier services revived, and bus services began. The first motor bus services to Whitburn were offered by the Scottish Motor Traction (SMT) company in 1913, then were suspended briefly during the war because of fuel shortages but resumed in 1920. Robert Sangster of Whitburn recalled Lothian Bus Company's Commer vehicle which offered four services a day between Whitburn and Bathgate in the 1920s:

> The risk of injury from such was practically non-existent, as the petrol-driven contraption snorted and reverberated its approach long before its visibility, at about 20 miles an hour.

SMT expanded throughout the Lothians and Borders, buying up local bus operators. Whitburn bus company James Scott was taken over in 1924 and JS Dewar & Sons in 1931. In the 1900s, James Browning had started operations from the old Inn in East Main Street but soon abandoned horse-drawn for motorised transport and claimed to have owned the first motor car in West Lothian. Just after the First World War, he set up a bus service around Whitburn, Armadale and Bathgate, building up his business until he had some 40 vehicles. After SMT took over his bus routes in 1935, he continued with the hire of coaches, lorries and wedding cars. Another Whitburn firm, Campbell Bros, operated a bus service from Whitburn to Glasgow from 1935 until it was taken over by SMT in 1945. The firm continued as coach-hirers.

Bus services have gradually lost custom because of the increase in car ownership – from 40 per cent of Whitburn households in 1971 to 70 per cent today.

New roads and motorways

Traffic increased significantly between the two World Wars and, in response a new Edinburgh-Glasgow trunk road, the A8, was built in the 1920s and 1930s. It skirted the north of Whitburn, crossing the Armadale road at Almondbank, taking some of the through traffic away from the town centre. The Roadhouse with its distinctive art deco style was built in 1934 to cater for traffic on the new road.

Whitburn's road pattern remained that of the 18th century loan and causeway. Despite the setting up of traffic lights at the Cross in 1964, there was congestion in the town centre and, as part of the town's redevelopment plan, Blaeberryhill Road was built to take traffic from the south away from the Cross.

By the late 1960s, the A8 had become inadequate for the volume of traffic it was carrying and the government began work on the M8 motorway. The Whitburn to Dechmont section opened in 1970, the last but one section to be completed. The design of the bridge carrying the motorway over the A706 allowed for jacking up any individual footing in the event of mining subsidence and a short stretch of the Almond had to be diverted a few yards north in order to be clear of the new bridge. The old A8 was realigned slightly to the south but the abandoned bridge that carried it over the Almond still stands just west of the roundabout.

CHAPTER 18

The Churches After 1820

Church of Scotland

THE FIRST MINISTER who was presented to the parish by Sir William Baillie as patron was the Rev Graham Mitchell, appointed in 1823 on the death of the Rev James Watson. We catch two glimpses of him in the letters of Lady Baillie in 1823:

> We drank tea at the manse where the children's pockets were stuffed with oranges, fruit and sweeties and their shoes crammed with mountains of shortbread and plum cake, and had I not put my foot upon it, James [one of her many children] would have brought home an old Scloss watch in a marble stand.

> Church was overflowing yesterday... there was a Public rebuke and the Regular Dissenting minister was sick. Mr Mitchell's opinion was decidedly against a Public Rebuke and Baillie also expressed himself strongly against it but the Parish had set their hearts upon it. I should scarcely have understood it however, it was so gently touched upon, so short & spoken in so low a tone of voice, had I not expected it.

During Mitchell's ministry, adulterers were required to appear twice for rebuke before the congregation, fornicators once; other churches imposed harsher and more frequent rebukes. As a Moderate, Mitchell remained in the Church of Scotland after the Disruption in 1843, when over a third of the ministers and members left to form the Free Church of Scotland over that very issue of patronage which had so long irritated the people of Whitburn. Because Whitburn's opponents of patronage had for many years had a choice of two Seceding churches to join, both free of patronage, the Disruption produced no split in the Whitburn congregation.

In 1843, Mitchell wrote the report on Whitburn parish for the *New Statistical Account of Scotland*. Since more than half of it is devoted to geology and mining, presumably these were among his particular interests. And in 1848, he published a book entitled *The Young Man's Guide against Infidelity* – of the spiritual rather than the marital kind. He died in 1869 after a ministry of 45 years.

He was followed by a number of ministers who served for shorter periods and left little mark – with the exception of the Rev John Ireland. He was the first minister to be chosen by the congregation after the abolition of patronage in 1874. An energetic man, as interested in the social as the spiritual condition of the local people, he served on the school board, as both a county and a town councillor, and as Provost from 1882 to 1891, and as his own session clerk for the last six years of his ministry. He was strongly built, high-handed, forthright to the point of rudeness, and made enemies as well as friends. His farewell sermon revealed something of the man:

> I have no apology to offer for the work I have done outside
> of the ordinary work of the ministry... I soon came to see
> that if I did not do it, nobody would do it. It required a man
> independent of business connections, and this small place
> did not supply such a person.

But his self-regard was accompanied by regret that he had been unable to do more to improve the lot of the villagers: 'I could not make wages better in dull times; I could not bring work nearer your homes; I could not give you better houses...' During his time in Whitburn, however, the debt of the burgh was fully paid off; he promoted the Whitburn Public Band, introduced the first church organ and started classes for young people in elocution and other subjects. He was minister from 1876 to 1891 and is remembered in the street name, Ireland Avenue.

In 1898, the Rev JL Buchanan was inducted and followed his predecessor by serving on the town council. In 1909, he resigned from his charge and went south to join the Anglican Church. In 1912, another long-serving minister was inducted, Robert Bruce MacKinnon, who stayed for 43 years. A scholarly and retiring man, Mr MacKinnon did not make the impression on the townspeople which others achieved.

He was succeeded by the Rev Bill Hume, minister from 1956 to 1983. Apparently he had agreed to join the shortleet of applicants only to oblige a friend, but when called by the congregation, he felt unable to refuse because of the disastrous fire which had burnt out the church a couple of weeks earlier. He stayed for 28 years and was well respected in the town. He oversaw the fundraising and rebuilding of the South Church, which was re-dedicated in November 1959. His particular interests were chaplaincy – he served 30 years as a Territorial Army chaplain and at Bangour

Village Hospital – and freemasonry, serving as both a Grand Chaplain and Provincial Grand Master of Linlithgowshire. He was also a town councillor from 1957–60 and Dean of Guild.

Following the brief ministry of the Rev Gavin Forrest, the Rev Gordon McCracken came to Whitburn South in 1988. An engineer before entering the ministry, he was a popular and effective minister. Controversy enveloped him in 1998 when he resigned from the Orange Order in Scotland and criticised it for being hijacked by hardline elements. In Whitburn, he encouraged his congregation to reach out to the wider community and himself took part in public life by serving on schools boards and the council's education committee, as well as on various local projects and wrote an excellent history of the South Parish Church. He moved from Whitburn in 2002.

He was followed by Whitburn's first woman minister, the Rev Christine Houghton, from 2004 to 2010. The Rev Dr Angus Kerr came in January 2013 and commends his congregation for their community-mindedness, their willingness to give both their time and money, and their support of one other and of the community. The South Kirk continues in good heart, with Boys' Brigade and Girls' Brigade companies, a Bible study group, Sunday School and a Friday coffee morning open to the community. The church has a good working relationship with Polkemmet Primary School, with members assisting various groups in the school. It is financially self-supporting, contributes to outside organisations and regularly makes it halls available to community groups. Dr Kerr retired in 2019.

The Seceders, the Free Church and Brucefield

The Anti-burgher minister, Archibald Bruce, was succeeded by another long-serving minister, Dr Robert Shaw. Unlike Bruce who twice broke away into ever smaller denominations, Shaw helped to reunite denominations. Bruce's Auld Licht Antiburghers had rejoined the Original Secession Church, which, led by Dr Shaw and others, united with the Free Church of Scotland in 1852. Bruce's Barracks church became Whitburn Free Church. Thus Whitburn gained a Free Church congregation as a result of a union rather than a division, and it promptly began to raise funds to build a new church on the Main Street. It opened in 1857, a simple rectangular design with a belfry; today the building is known as the Shaw Hall. The minister's chair still in use in Brucefield Church was the chair used by Thomas Chalmers as moderator of the first General Assembly of the Free Church of Scotland after the Disruption in 1843 – though how it comes to be at Brucefield is not known.

No longer needed by the Free Church, the Barracks building became briefly Dr Gillespie's School for Boys, then housing for miners – said to be popularly known as the Devil's Barracks. It was pulled down in 1930 and the stone used as road metal. Some of its stones were found during landscaping work and were set into a cairn in Brucefield Church garden. Another stone was sent to Canada in 1992 in response to a request that each parish in Scotland donate a stone for the Cairn of Tears at Winnipeg, a memorial to Scottish settlers in Canada.

Shaw was followed by Dr John McKnight, a much-loved man who spent 40 years in Whitburn. During his ministry, he was instrumental in establishing a Free Church in Harthill, of which he was also minister for a year until it was able to call its own minister. Dr McKnight retired in 1903. It's remarkable that just

> ### A sad end
>
> Dr Shaw, the first Free Church minister, came to a sad end in 1863. While getting off a train at Holytown to catch 'the omnibus for Whitburn', he 'fell among the wheels. His daughter shrieked out for assistance, and on being lifted up, it was found that his left arm was broken... and several other injuries received.' Two doctors who happened to be on the same train attended him and he was taken to a local manse where his arm was amputated, but he succumbed to his injuries.

three Antiburgher/Free Church ministers spanned the 135 years from 1768 to 1903 – Bruce, Shaw and McKnight.

In 1929, the Free Church of Scotland and the Church of Scotland reunited nationally. Whitburn Free Church chose as its new name Brucefield Parish Church in honour of its first minister. Whitburn Parish Church became Whitburn South Parish Church.

After Dr McKnight, half a dozen ministers served for short periods of ten years or fewer, until the coming of the Rev JB McMartin in 1935. He was a tireless worker, ensuring first of all that the congregation became self-supporting. He was particularly interested in young people and founded the 7th West Lothian (Brucefield) Scout group, later receiving the medal of merit for 35 years of service to the Scout movement.

Under Mr McMartin's leadership, the congregation grew greatly and a new church, hall and manse were built and the old church was turned into hall accommodation. Half of the £32,000 cost came from the Church of Scotland and the other half from the members – a substantial sum for the congregation to raise. For the design, the church approached a former member, architect Tom Duncan, son of a Whitburn miner. His design was clean and bold in white concrete, 'with a theme of movement, the curved walls and ceilings directed inwards and the roofs over the main entrance, the sanctuary and the vestry reaching upwards'. More than 50 years after it opened in 1966, it still looks uncompromisingly modern. The quality of the whole complex – old and new churches and connecting courtyard – was recognised by its being A-listed in 2008.

Mr McMartin was succeeded by the Rev Robin Brough, who served from 1977 until 2002. A more reserved man than his predecessor, his priority was developing congregational worship rather than community involvement. The briefer ministry of Richard Darroch was followed by a year under a transition minister charged with regrouping the congregation after a period of difficulty. The present minister, the Rev Dr Sandy Roger, was inducted in 2013 and the church is now growing, with a revived Sunday School, choir and Guild, as well as Beavers, Cubs, Scouts and Explorers, Guides, Brownies and Rainbows.

Roman Catholic Church

During the second half of the 19th century, there were few Catholics in Whitburn and they had to make their way to one of the surrounding communities – Fauldhouse, Bathgate, Armadale or Blackburn – in order to hear Mass. Fauldhouse became the first independent Roman Catholic parish in West Lothian in 1865, and a chapel was opened in 1873. The Fauldhouse priest was given responsibility for Whitburn's Catholic population as well.

In 1905, however, Father Bernard Eardley moved into 54 West Main Street, Whitburn, from where he also looked after the parishes of Armadale and Blackburn. Armadale and Whitburn continued to share the same priest for the next 50 years or so. In 1913, Father Edward Miley moved to no. 59, and his successor, Father Robert Rattray, who came in 1917, moved into Almondbank House at the end of Armadale Road. The first RC church in Whitburn opened in March 1939 on a site adjacent to Almondbank House.

In 1953, Whitburn became a separate Catholic parish under Father Thomas McGregor. A much-loved priest was Father John McCallum who served during a decade of great change between 1962 and 1972. During the time of Father Daniel McGuinness, the Catholic population of the parish reached nearly 2,000 and the old church in Armadale Road became inadequate. The present much larger church was built in Raeburn Crescent, with a new presbytery attached and the dedication was carried out by Cardinal Gray in May 1979.

As part of a wider restructuring of parishes in the archdiocese to cope with shortage of priests and funds, St Joseph's church in Whitburn and Sacred Heart and St Anthony's in Armadale were united in September 2018 as a new parish, St Barbara's – an apt name, as St Barbara is the patron saint of miners. The Catholic Church has long been a church of ethnic diversity and Whitburn's Catholic community has welcomed successive waves of incomers – the Irish in the 19th century, the Italians, the Poles, Latvians and Lithuanian miners at Stoneyburn and Fauldhouse in the early 20th century, the Polish troops who settled here after the war, the Ugandan Asians refugees; more recently, the young newcomers from Poland and other Eastern European countries and, not least, the present parish priest, Father Sebastian Thuruthipillil, from Kerala in south-west India. Under his fresh and energetic leadership, the new parish of St Barbara's is thriving, with lively, welcoming worship, a healthy proportion of young families and children, good relationships with its local RC primary schools, and with the other denominations. Special efforts have been made to integrate this ethnically diverse parish and help parishioners learn more about fellow worshippers' cultures through social and educational events.

Pentecostal and Evangelical

The Pentecostal Church in Whitburn was established in 1977 and was successful from the start in attracting children and young people, so much so that a new building to seat 200 was erected in 1984. A full-time pastor, Andrew Smith, affiliated to the Assemblies of God Churches of Great Britain, was appointed in 1991 and the church went from strength to strength. It first offered dementia care in the community through a volunteer respite service in 1994 and, realising a growing need, it began fundraising for a major project. 'Addressing the Needs and Serving Whitburn Elderly Residents' – the Answer project – offers care and support for dementia sufferers and their carers in a purpose-built centre at the church in Reveston Lane, Croftmalloch. After some six years of hard work, some £400,000 was raised, the centre was built and opened in June 2006. The centre with its paid staff and 50 volunteers is now open Tuesday to Friday and offers an invaluable service to those affected by dementia. The project was led by church member Robert Cook whose work was recognised by the award of the MBE in 2012.

The Pentecostal Church was also the moving force behind the West Lothian Foodbank, set up under franchise from the Trussell Trust in 2012. Now partnered by other local churches, the foodbank operates throughout West Lothian, has four paid staff, 150 volunteers, ten distribution centres, two warehouses and a charity shop and plays a vital role in assisting disadvantaged families in crisis. Under pastor Stephen Roy, the church also supports overseas work, in particular a community in south Bulgaria; and it provides school, workplace, prison and hospital chaplaincy services.

Whitburn Gospel Hall is the former Lady Baillie's School. An independent congregation of the Christian Brethren worships there, a small but active congregation with a Sunday School and weekday Kids' Club, which reaches out to the community through involvement in the gala day and a monthly family tea open to all. Whitburn Christian Fellowship, an independent congregation, took over a disused industrial unit at the west end of the town and converted it to a church in 1997.

Since the 1960s, the numbers of church adherents in Scotland have been in decline and all denominations are struggling to attract and retain the young. All the Whitburn churches have been through recent periods of discouragement but all are currently in good heart with active leadership. Several projects, such as gaining Fairtrade status for the town, have pooled the efforts of all the congregations, strengthening their effectiveness in the community as well as their own fellowships. The churches continue to do much good work among their own members and the wider community. Of all the organisations in Whitburn, they have the longest uninterrupted thread connecting them with the past and, not least, by their efforts they keep up the fabric of some of the town's most important public buildings.

CHAPTER 19

Housing

A VISITOR TO the new village of Whitburn in the late 18th century would have seen a long street of mainly single-storey cottages opening onto the street, stone-built, with beaten-earth floors, each with a yard behind in which the residents could grow vegetables or keep poultry or a pig. Houses built by the better-off might be two-storey with a slated roof and perhaps as many as four rooms and a pend giving access to the back yard. In the cottages occupied by weavers, room might be made in the attic space for the handloom, lit by a dormer window; but in most cases, one of the two downstairs rooms was sacrificed to the loom, or the family lived with it in their midst.

As the population grew, how were the people to be housed? There was no public body or local authority to build housing for the poor. By 1841, there were 186 houses in the village, housing a population of 798 – an average of 4.3 persons per household. The better-off villagers might buy or build one or two extra houses for let, in order to bring in some rental income for themselves. However, private housing provision did not meet the need and many older houses were subdivided or tenants took lodgers into already overcrowded homes. Marital fertility in mining areas was high and mining families in Whitburn tended to be large – over six children was common – and yet most houses were small. The population of Whitburn almost doubled between 1850 and 1900, yet the number of houses did not greatly increase. The resulting overcrowding, together with lack of water supply or sewerage, was a serious problem by the end of the 19th century.

Until the 1890s, councils had no powers to build decent housing. Their medical officer of health could declare a house unfit for habitation but doing so might make the shortage worse since the council could not provide a replacement. New legislation in the 1890s empowered local authorities to draw up an 'improvement scheme' to provide working class housing at an economic rent but Whitburn was too small a burgh to have the resources to do this.

Housing for miners

Another problem was the lack of miners' housing. Perhaps because there were no mines with large workforces around Whitburn in the

19th century, none of the mining companies built the traditional type of single-storey miners' rows in the town. There were several abortive attempts to provide miners' housing: the West Lothian Housing Society built 'ideal homes for the worker' at Garden City, Bents, and Greenrigg Cottages but none in Whitburn. In 1917, William Dixon and Co planned to build 300 miners' houses in the town for its new Polkemmet pit. A curving, spacious layout was planned but unfortunately the only part of it which was built was 24 houses in Dixon Terrace, first occupied in 1918 and demolished 40 years later. Another plan of Dixon's in 1925 for good quality semi-detached housing for its miners also came to nothing, presumably because of the economic difficulties of the decade.

Nimmo's and United Collieries built several blocks of two storey housing for their miners in West Main Street and Armadale Road, with an outside stair at the rear giving access to the upstairs house. The sanitary quality of these tenement blocks was poor and all were demolished in the mid-20th century. In general, however, the lack of housing in the burgh meant that many miners were obliged to find housing elsewhere and travel daily to Polkemmet.

Council housing

At the end of the First World War, the government passed a series of housing acts, whereby local councils were forced to draw up 'schemes' to tackle the housing problems in their areas. In Whitburn, council housing was desperately needed, as in 1921, 68 per cent of its residents lived in just one or two rooms. The result was serious over-crowding: nearly two thirds of Whitburn residents were living more than two to a room (worse even than Glasgow with just over half) and a quarter were living more than four per room. However, Whitburn burgh had one advantage – it was by far the largest burgh in West Lothian in acreage (though being by far the smallest in population, it was long known as the Wee Burgh), so it had space for house-building.

In 1921, Whitburn town council embarked on its first housing scheme, fixing upon land at Murraysgate. It was planned as a 'garden village', with a curving layout and grass verges with trees separating the pavements from the roads. The local MP James Kidd congratulated the councillors on their 'courage' (which must have alarmed them) in spending something like £80,000 (over £1,000 per house). Difficulty was encountered because of the post-war shortage of building materials and the tight control exercised by the Department of Health Scotland (DHS) but the first of the houses in Murraysgate Crescent were occupied in 1922 and the rest in 1923.

The houses were of such high quality that the council felt they were too good to let to the poorest tenants most in need of rehousing; therefore, they were let to the respectable and well-doing in the town. However, the high rents meant that some of them proved difficult to let, so for its second scheme, the council opted for 120 smaller, mainly two-apartment houses on land at Whitdalehead Farm. The first of these new houses (at Townhead Gardens) were occupied in late 1928.

The council would always have preferred to build smaller houses but was told by the DHS to reduce the number of two-apartments: 'Although many children remain uncorrupted under these conditions, it is safe to prophesy that much of the crime that springs from early and unnatural sex depravity will not be eradicated until the conditions are altered', ie until fathers sleep separately from children and boys separately from girls.

With the 1930 Housing Act, government subsidies were restricted mainly to slum clearance schemes – removing the worst properties and building new houses for the displaced tenants – and this at last forced councils to rehouse the worst-housed residents. Whitburn's slum clearance area included the infamous Park Lane (formerly Shuttle Row) and Lea Street, and plans were drawn up for 100 three- and four-roomed houses to be built – the Manse Road scheme. The houses (Union Road and Drive) were let mainly to Whitburn people and were completed in 1933.

> ### Council incompetence?
>
> Not everyone was delighted with the council's house-building schemes. The costs of building council houses were shared among the government, the tenants and the ratepayers. In 1931, Whitburn council received a letter of objection signed by 358 ratepayers. 'Through the Council's incompetence, the Burgh has been saddled with a debt of several thousand pounds on Townhead Housing Scheme which will fall to be liquidated from the rates... With our high rates, nearly double those of Edinburgh, any unnecessary expenditure which would add even a fraction to the rates is unjustified.'

The next developments were Jubilee Road (99 houses) and Armadale Road (70) in 1935. Manse Avenue (23) and Glebe Road (147) were ready by 1936, Empire Street (55), Bank Street (28) and Baillie Street (24) by 1940 – a grand total of 722 new council houses in the 20 years between the wars. There's no doubt that it was Polkemmet colliery which allowed (or forced) Whitburn to expand at such a swift rate. No matter how many newcomers came to the town, the pit with its huge workforce could provide jobs for them; and no matter how many houses the council built, there was always a demand for more.

The war and after

Work on housing was curtailed by the Second World War. It resumed in 1945 but councils were hampered by a severe shortage of building materials. To share resources as fairly as possible, the DHS gave each council an 'allocation' of houses to be built; for Whitburn council in 1950 it was fewer than 30 houses. With several hundred people on the waiting list and more in the Polkemmet squatters' camp, the council protested but to no avail. The site chosen was the Manse Avenue area, the new roads built being The Avenue and White Street (named after Captain White whose bequest to the town's poor was received by the council in 1948).

To assist local councils with the housing problem, the government in 1937 had set up the Scottish Special Housing Association (SSHA), which began to build houses for public rent in Whitburn in the late 1940s; its first streets were Burns Crescent and Kings Road. Over the next 50 years, it built several hundred houses in Whitburn but in the 1990s and early 2000s its housing stock was transferred to housing associations such as Weslo.

Bricks and timber continued to be in short supply, so the government promoted types of non-traditional housing – Weir, Cruden, timber and temporary aluminium houses (better known as pre-fabs). Cruden houses were built to the east of Armadale Road, and named Ellen Street. After the police college moved from Townhead Gardens, its site was cleared to make way for the first timber housing scheme. In the early 1950s, the Millbank 2nd scheme was developed with 120 houses and the streets named after recent Provosts – Aitken, Cleland, Lambie, Shanks, Drysdale.

The council's policy was to borrow money to build, let their houses at below the economic rent and make up the difference from the rates and by further borrowing. There was not complete local agreement with this: council treasurer Christie Barras resigned in protest at the council's high borrowing and spending. However, they had the permission of the Scottish Office for their policy and carried on.

By 1960, Whitburn town council and the SSHA together had built 1,376 houses, thereby increasing the burgh population to nearly 6,000. Another huge increase, the largest in its history, was about to happen in the 1960s.

Glasgow overspill

Of all the cities in Britain, Glasgow had the worst housing problems. Despite building huge housing scheme round the edges of the city and the creation of two new towns (East Kilbride and Cumbernauld), there were still 112,000 on the Glasgow corporation housing list in 1958. The city corporation looked to other areas to take part of its 'overspill' of population. Agreements were signed with various county councils (including West Lothian) and with various burghs, as far apart as Selkirk and Wick. In 1959, Whitburn town council decided to sign an agreement with Glasgow corporation – one of 60 local authorities to make overspill agreements with the city – and it was formally ratified in 1960.

Why should they have done so when they were already struggling to build sufficient houses for local people? By signing up, the council was not undertaking the whole financial outlay: it would receive a subsidy for part of the cost of building the new houses. And the overspill families were not to be rehoused at the expense of Whitburn ratepayers – no additional rates burden was to be imposed. But what actual benefit would Whitburn receive? The lure was that some 2,500 industrial and commercial firms were expected to move out of Glasgow to the receiving areas. Eager as ever to diversify its economy and bring in new industry, the Whitburn town council wanted its share of these firms and was given assurances that it would not be asked to build houses until enough new industry was established in the area to provide work for the incomers.

However, by 1960, Whitburn lacked sufficient land for new housing development. Large areas of ground within the existing burgh were rendered useless because the NCB was reluctant to declare ground safe for building in case it later wanted to mine beneath it. Therefore, the council looked to extend its burgh boundaries to acquire more land for housing both the overspill and those on its own waiting lists. As if all this was not enough, the council accepted the DHS' recommendation that a town development scheme be implemented along with an overspill agreement. It was an ambitious council under Provost Dick which was willing to take on the three major schemes – burgh extension, overspill and town redevelopment – all at once.

In the event, the incentives offered to Glasgow firms failed to persuade many of them to move. But Whitburn was not being asked to accept a large number of families being moved out of Glasgow against their will, with no jobs to come to: the overspill scheme ensured that the newcomers came voluntarily and already had jobs. Firms in the receiving areas could recruit their own workers from Glasgow and ask Glasgow corporation to add them to its overspill list. Only three conditions were set – the overspill tenants must be married, be good tenants and have lived in Glasgow for ten years or more. Often the overspill tenants were not in fact those living in the slums of Glasgow and 'a lengthy chain of decanting' was necessary before slum families benefited.

Under the agreement signed by Whitburn town council, 500 houses were to be built for overspill tenants: three quarters by the council and the rest by the SSHA (later amended to half and half). In 1971, the council agreed to build another 100 overspill houses. Glasgow corporation paid Whitburn council an annual £14 per house for ten years. Whitburn was able to take in the new population without having to insist on the arrival of dispersed Glasgow businesses, for it was about to benefit from two major industrial developments: in 1961, the British Motor Corporation (BMC) set up its new truck and tractor plant at Bathgate and in 1962 Livingston was designated Scotland's fourth new town. (Whitburn council had suggested to the Secretary of State that Whitburn should be the site of the new town but its letter was merely 'noted'.) BMC would provide some 6,000 new jobs and Livingston tens of thousands more. Despite getting no Glasgow firms, Whitburn was able to house, employ and absorb these incoming workers without difficulty.

Housing the overspill

The new housing for the overspill was built at Gateside at the west end of the town. The first four families arrived in May 1962 and the very first to move in were James and Anne Hazelton from Springburn. Mrs Hazelton was delighted with her new house at 23 Polkemmet Road and her daughter Annemarie (2) was 'seldom indoors nowadays... she can get out to play. I didn't dare risk letting her out like that in Glasgow.' The other three families, Mr and Mrs Godfrey McCabe, Mr and Mrs Joseph McKenna and Mr and Mrs Cameron Crozier, were also from Glasgow and the men all had jobs at the BMC. Provost Harry Stewart welcomed each of the ladies with a bouquet and remarked that it wasn't intended that all the Glasgow people should be housed in one area of the town. 'We don't want a separate community... Although this is the main area, we hope that by spreading them round the town, they will be more rapidly integrated'. In practice, however, the overspill families were concentrated in the Gateside/Murraysgate scheme. Allan Road, Gardner Crescent and Welsh Road were occupied the following year and the other houses by 1964. The houses were good quality, two- and three-storey flats and terraced houses.

In the mid-1960s, a survey was undertaken of overspill tenants in Blackburn and Whitburn, the towns with the largest overspill population in the county. The overspill people came voluntarily, from all parts of Glasgow so there was little sense of grievance at the break-up of an old community. For most, the prime reason for moving was to get a better house. Secondly, they came because the breadwinner of the family (almost invariably the husband) had got a job at BMC (later British Leyland). And thirdly, they wanted to make a better, healthier life for their children.

The majority professed themselves pleased with their new surroundings, except for the shortage of play areas and the distance to the town centre (only 40 per cent owned a car). Most were satisfied with their new houses, with the exception of some of those who had been allocated a flat but would rather have had a house. When asked whether they were glad they had moved, 90 per cent of Whitburn tenants agreed.

Housewives in both Whitburn and Blackburn organised a social club which provided a support and advice network for newcomers. Over two thirds of overspill women joined it – membership of the Murraysgate Women's Social Club in Whitburn had to be capped at 200 as it was growing too big to be manageable. The club also functioned as their representative body in negotiations with the council. Joining local organ-isations like the churches, the WRI, a sports or social club helped the new-comers feel at home and accepted. The effort towards integration was perhaps made more by the incomers but on the whole, it was managed with remarkably little friction and served as a positive model of overspill.

1960s and 1970s

The efforts of Whitburn town council to expand the town, its housing and industries were not universally admired: West Lothian County Council (WLCC) convener, James Boyle, complained that Whitburn kept on build-ing houses, then demanding that WLCC put up schools, libraries and other facilities, at the expense of other parts of county. In the 1970s, concern was voiced that Whitburn's continuing growth was hindering the full development of Livingston New Town, therefore 'for the betterment of the sub-region', the county council decided that any further growth of Whitburn should be limited to natural increase from 1971 onwards. At that point, 96 per cent of Whitburn's housing was publicly rented.

In response, the town council began to encourage the building of private houses by providing sites for speculative builders: south-east of Mansewood and three more sites south east of the town, to be reached by the new distributor road, Blaeberryhill Road.

The great days of council house building were coming to a close. Governments had been reducing housing subsidies and applying greater controls over council spending, a process much accelerated by Mrs Thatcher's government after 1979. New council house building virtually came to an end, except for housing for particular needs – for example, the first sheltered housing complex, built by the Help the Aged (now Bield) Housing Association in Mansewood Crescent and opened in 1977.

Right to buy

The right of sitting tenants to buy their council houses and later their housing association houses was promoted by Mrs Thatcher's

Conservative government from 1980. At that time, there were 3,560 council and SSHA houses in Whitburn. Some 1,758 – half the stock – were sold between 1980 and 2016, when the Scottish Government ended the right to buy. Governments had been gradually withdrawing subsidies for new house-building, forcing councils to charge full economic rent, and higher rents persuaded tenants that it made economic sense to buy their council houses. The scheme was clearly popular, allowing tenants to acquire and bequeath a major capital asset to their families. However, the scheme was criticised for selling houses at a price below their replacement value, and because councils were not permitted to use the money from sales to build new council housing. For the first time in 60 years, the proportion of publicly rented houses in Whitburn began to decline.

Private housing

There has been an enormous change in the proportion of private housing over the last few decades. In 1971, only 3 per cent of Whitburn houses were owner-occupied; in 2018, the figure is probably about 60 per cent. With the Heartlands development well underway to the west and south-west of the town, that proportion is going to rise considerably over the next few years. At the moment, no new council or social housing in Whitburn is being built or planned, so council house waiting lists are unlikely to shrink. But a more balanced housing situation has emerged and, although Whitburn still has the highest number of publicly rented houses in West Lothian, the change to a large proportion of home ownership in so short a time is remarkable.

Whitburn Housing

	Total Households	Publicly rented	Privately rented	Owner Occupied	Households with one or more cars
1921	414	18 4%	330 78% (incl. 56 colliery houses)	73 18%	
1931	533	194 36%	272 51% (incl. 51 colliery houses)	69 13%	
1941	1039 (est.)	700(est.) 67%	255 25% (incl. 68 colliery houses)	84 8%	

	Total Households	Publicly rented	Privately rented	Owner Occupied	Households with one or more cars
1951	1311	1000 76%	212 16% (incl. 66 colliery houses)	99 8%	
1961	1716	1517 88%	104 6% (incl. 29 colliery houses)	94 5%	
1971	3075	2955 96%	20 0.6%	100 3%	1214 39%
1981	4182	3560 85%	90 1%	532 13%	2149 51%
1991	4269	2745 64%	28 0.6%	1564 36%	2373 56%
2001	4942	2125 43%	212 4.5%	2570 52%	3212 65%
2018*	5482	1510 (council houses) & unknown number of housing associ-ation houses)	n/a	n/a	3159 66%

*2018 figures supplied by West Lothian Council

CHAPTER 20

Industry After 1945

SUCH WAS THE dominance of weaving and coalmining in Whitburn's past that other industries scarcely began to develop in Whitburn until the mid-20th century. Once it was clear that mining was in decline, the town council actively sought to attract other industries to the town. Its proactive energy was often commented on by local and national newspapers.

In 1936, the council purchased land and erected a factory for Campbell Brothers Ltd, a Harthill coachbuilders and bus company employing 25 men. They joined Harper's and Browning's in a longstanding road transport industry tradition in Whitburn, dating back to the carters and coaches of the 18th century. This was the first advance factory (built in advance to attract industry) in West Lothian.

In the immediate post-war years, the council's attention was mainly taken up with housing, but they recognised the pressing need to attract new industry to the town, to alleviate its absolute dependence on mining.

1950s and 1960s

The government was intent on dispersing new industries to areas of decaying heavy industry and, following the Distribution of Industry Act of 1945, West Lothian benefited from two major economic developments in the early 1960s: the establishment of the new BMC truck and tractor plant at Bathgate in 1961 and the designation of Livingston as a new town in 1962. Both were to provide thousands of new jobs for Whitburn men and women and contributed to its rapid growth post-1960. Whitburn, however, was not content just to be a dormitory town for BMC/British Leyland or Livingston new town; it wanted its own industries. As was seen in the previous chapter, the council tried to get its share of Glasgow firms along with the overspill but they also began to promote the burgh as a location for modern industry, producing and widely circulating promotional guides to the town in 1967 and 1972. The council persuaded the Board of Trade to build another advance factory close to the A8 road at the west end of the burgh. Seventeen acres of land were set aside for immediate industrial development with a further 40 in reserve. The town had nearly tripled in population since the war and with 800 of its men employed in the mines and unemployment already at some 5 per cent, the decline of mining was a huge concern. Women in particular had little work in the town and several hundred were obliged to commute to TCC in Bathgate or to Edinburgh for work.

In March 1965, Belmos, makers of electrical switchgear, moved into Whitburn's advance factory, promising up to 200 jobs eventually. An attempt in 1966 to provide several hundred jobs for women by bringing a women's underwear firm to Whitburn failed but other sites for industry were made available at Blaeberryhill, Croftmalloch and Burnhouse.

Meanwhile, a Whitburn entrepreneur and local councillor, William Griffith, had moved from road transport services into sand and gravel. Then, realising that the 150 coal and shale bings that scarred the local landscape formed great quarries of material for road bottoming, he began to buy a few of the larger ones. As a result, West Lothian's spent shale was used in construction of the M8 and M9, Forth Road Bridge approach roads and the BMC factory. In 1967, Griffith was removing the largest of the shale bings, Deans at Livingston, comprising some 20 million cubic yards of spent shale. With 160 trucks in operation, he claimed to be moving it at the rate of one truckload every 30 seconds.

Whitburn was located within the government's Central Redevelopment Area of Scotland so had access to funding and powers to lend any developer up to 90 per cent of the cost of new buildings. It also stressed its central location between the cities of Edinburgh and Glasgow, close to the motorways, to Grangemouth docks and Turnhouse airport. These advantages persuaded one of Europe's largest makers of semi-trailers, Crane Fruehauf, to open a new service depot in Whitburn in 1968. Another incentive was Whitburn's guarantee to new industries that housing would be available for incoming workers, earmarking for industrial needs 400 of the 2,000 new houses to be built by 1970.

It was not all good news, however: Whitburn was not within the Greater Livingston area, so was competing against New Town grants and subsidies to attract industry. And, as always, economic forces beyond local control affected the town: Belmos closed its Whitburn plant after only three years, blaming the downturn of its main customer, the coal industry. Negotiations in 1968 to bring a tyre firm to Whitburn as an ancillary industry to British Leyland fell through, but the following year, in the greatest coup of Whitburn's industrial campaign, jeans manufacturing firm, Levi Strauss, bought the former Belmos factory at Murraysgate industrial estate for its new British operation, creating 120 immediate jobs and later over 600. According to the *West Lothian Courier*, Levi's were 'fulsome' in their praise of the council's willingness to help in every way, 'especially Town Clerk, Mr Robert Mickel'.

Levi's

Men made up most of the management and the technical staff at Levi's but the vast majority of the workforce were women, some of whom had previous experience in the clothing industry, particularly in Bathgate and Armadale hosieries. Workers remembered that their first impression was the huge size of the place and the noise of the machinery. Training was on the job and all the spreading and cutting was done manually. By 1971, the workforce had reached 400. In 1984, the first automated equipment was installed in the factory and thereafter the workers were required continually to adapt to new technologies and constant change of work practices. Levi's recognised the General and Municipal Boilermakers union and negotiated with them on pay and conditions. Relations between management and workers seem to have been better than average but strikes and disputes were certainly not unknown.

The pay was good but workers were expected to work hard for it:

> Piecework meant ye made your own wage. You got your average, so ye built up yer average through how much per cent ye done... When ah left, ma average wis really quite high because o' all the money ye could make. Ye could make up tae £8, £10 per hour which was a lot o' money then. Ye were coming out with over £300 at the top... ah ended up making more money than ma man.

Workers were involved in various committees to assist the management. A subsidised canteen, subsidised bus and various incentives and bonuses helped to maintain workforce loyalty. The company also encouraged team spirit and cohesion through the social club which offered nights out, trips, cabarets, dances, fancy dress social nights, etc and a community involvement team which took an active part in raising funds for many local and national charities. For example, in 1996, its community involvement team was busy raising £10,000 for the Childline charity through various events including an open day at the factory. The money they raised was matched by contributions from Levi's. Substantial sums were raised by events like pram pub crawls and a bed push along Main Street – enough to buy dialysis machines for Bangour hospital and special beds for the burns unit.

> We actually got letters in from people who wanted our help. There was a committee of us – about eight to ten – who decided which projects we'd put forward. We tried to

be as fair as possible. The majority of money came from
Whitburn.

By 1996, Levi's was producing nearly five million pairs of jeans a year,
with a workforce of 630. But by 1999, there was a worldwide oversupply
of jeans as youth fashion changed and the European youth population
shrank. Sales declined and plant closures became necessary. The sudden-
ness of the closure of the Whitburn plant and the uncompromising way
in which the redundancy payments were decided left some bitterness in
the minds of the former workforce but most remember with fondness
the social side of Levi's, the friendships and laughs and the community
fundraising.

1970s and 1980s

In 1970, despite the best efforts of the council to bring industry to the
town, only one in three Whitburn workers worked within the burgh;
two thirds had to go elsewhere. Almost a third of them went to Bathgate
and probably most of those to British Leyland. The close economic ties
between the two communities had grown even stronger since the war.
With Levi's and British Leyland in addition to Polkemmet, unemployment
in the Bathgate/Whitburn area was down to about 3 per cent. Housing
and population continued to grow but the boom in public spending was
coming to an end and the most painful decade was about to begin.

In 1979 Margaret Thatcher came to power and her Conservative government set about restructuring British industry. There was to be no more
'propping up dying industries', the weak and inefficient were allowed to
go to the wall and resources were concentrated on growth sectors and
modern industries. Severe restrictions were placed on trade union powers, wage and price controls were introduced and public spending was
cut. Unemployment soared, manufacturing fell from a third to a quarter
of output in just two years and closures multiplied but the pain was not
equally shared across the whole country. The top 10 per cent of earners
(mostly in the south-east of England) actually increased their wages by 22
per cent in real terms, while elsewhere the traditional economies of whole
regions collapsed and the gap between rich and poor yawned ever wider.
Some 30 changes in the way unemployment was recorded obscured the
full extent of the tragedy, but male unemployment at least doubled during Mrs Thatcher's 15 years in power.

West Lothian's economy was based on declining heavy industries,
and the effects on it of Tory policies in the 1980s were dire. Whitburn had
already lost 30 jobs with the closure of the Volkswagen (GB) parts depot
on Murraysgate industrial estate in 1977. In 1981, the long-established

haulage contractors Hugh Harper & Sons closed their doors with the loss of 20 jobs. British Leyland closed its Bathgate plant in 1986 and, worst of all, Polkemmet Pit was never to re-open after the miners' strike of 1984–5: some 1,400 lost their jobs, a third of whom were West Lothian residents. The district and regional councils did what they could, setting up training and temporary employment and regeneration schemes and refurbishing small business units at Burnhouse in 1984, but these were sticking plasters for an arterial wound. Unemployment in West Lothian reached 22.6 per cent in 1982 and male unemployment peaked at 25 per cent in 1985. In the pages of the *West Lothian Courier*, the remorseless news of firms closing week in and week out – 7,000 in the first five years of the Thatcher government – induced a feeling of hopelessness in the community. The loss of so many jobs caused a knock-on effect on local shops and businesses, leading to further losses. In Whitburn, unemployment shot up and as just one marker of the damage done to Whitburn's jobless in the 1980s, the proportion of the town's unemployed who were 'permanently sick' rose from 12 per cent in 1981 to 21 per cent ten years later. Compare Whitburn with affluent Linlithgow in the north of the county: the 1991 Census records that 164 of Linlithgow's working-age residents were permanently sick; Whitburn, with nearly the same working-age population, had 610.

Year	Unemployment rate
1958	2.5% (Bathgate Travel to Work Area)
1971	7.5% (West Lothian
1981	12% (Whitburn)
1986	18.6% (Bathgate Travel to Work Area)
1991	13% (Whitburn)
1996	7.5% (Bathgate Travel to Work area)
2001	4.4% (Whitburn)
2011	c.5% (Whitburn)

The way unemployment was counted frequently changed, so it's difficult to compare like with like but the table gives some indication of the devastation caused by unemployment in the 1980s. Male unemployment was considerably higher.

Recovery

The 1980s represent a watershed in Whitburn's post-war history. Before then, the signs were positive – Whitburn was modern, progressive, developing, expanding. After that, all was negative – problems, closures, anger, despair. The process of recovery was long and slow. The Conservatives distrusted local government and tried to bypass it as much as possible by setting up national boards and initiatives to assist in regeneration but it was local initiatives that proved the most effective. What they could not do was create new jobs and many of the older employees at Polkemmet and Leyland never worked again. Unemployed people were retrained with the new skills they would need in service and electronic industries; and great efforts were made to change the old image of West Lothian and project it as a modern centre, attractive to new hi-tech industries. But it was not achieved overnight and, by the end of the 1980s, unemployment still stood at about 13 per cent.

Things looked better for Whitburn at the opening of the 1990s but the decade brought the closure of Crane Fruehauf in 1998 with the loss of 20 jobs and, in 1999, Levi's and its 600 jobs. It was particularly difficult for families where two members lost their jobs: 'everybody wis crying, we couldnae believe it. For the first time in my life I wis on job-seekers allowance... ah went frae £300 a week to £52 a week.'

West Lothian Council focused on upgrading the county's road and rail communications and providing sites and premises for new housing and industries, making it an attractive destination for house-builders, commuters and for city residents driven out by high property prices. Whitburn benefited eventually from this strategy when a very large development chose to come to West Lothian.

Heartlands

In 1997, Whitburn was West Lothian's fourth largest town, after Livingston, Bathgate and Linlithgow. Among the long-established communities like Whitburn, there was some resentment of Livingston for attracting all the new shopping and leisure facilities and taking the county's public buildings – West Lothian College, the Sheriff Court, the council HQ, Police HQ – away from the older towns. Yet the New Town brought many jobs for Whitburn residents and they are now within easy reach of its centre by car or bus and appreciate its shopping and leisure facilities.

In 2002, plans were announced for a major ten-year redevelopment, privately funded by Ecosse Regeneration Ltd, part of the Kelvin Homes group, to be located at Whitburn. It would involve the rehabilitation of the former Polkemmet pit site into two golf courses, some 1,500 houses and, on a second site to the north, a new motorway junction to connect to offices and factories to be built on Cowhill Farm. The figures were amazing – a £100 million investment and up to 4,000 new jobs. What caused initial concern in Whitburn was that the remaining coal at

Polkemmet was to be extracted via a vast opencast mine, followed by land restoration, and fears were expressed that the opencast would come but not the restoration or the redevelopment of the 1,500-acre site. However, supported by local councillors Jim Dickson and Bert Gamble and much of the community, only eight objections were received (at least for the initial part of the work), and the application was approved by West Lothian Council (despite the site cutting across the council's Countryside Belt around Bathgate and Whitburn).

By the time work began on extracting, clearing and decontaminating the site and putting in the drainage and roads, the developers were promising up to 7,700 jobs (later revised back to 4,000 jobs, plus a luxury hotel) and up to 2,000 new homes. The council imposed 79 conditions on the developers, including provision of a park-and-ride scheme at the new motorway junction linking to an express coach service, provision of some affordable housing, a new primary school and the appointment of a compliance officer to be paid for by Ecosse Regeneration but under council control. The company worked hard to publicise its development (now estimated at £500m), to refute criticisms and to keep community councils and other community groups in Fauldhouse and Whitburn informed of progress through consultation, information days and tours of the site. The removal of the burning Polkemmet bing (Bing 3) in 2006–7 was particularly welcome to local people who had endured its sulphurous fumes for years.

The first sod was cut by Provost Joe Thomas in 2007 and work on the business park at Cowhill, funded by Ecosse Regeneration, the Royal Bank of Scotland and West Lothian Council, with a large injection of European Regional Development Fund money, began that same year. By then, the development was being hailed as the UK's largest regeneration project, with over 2,500 acres under development. The motorway junction (J4A) opened in September 2013, by which time the investment figure had gone up to £650m and the development was being spoken of as 'one of Europe's largest regeneration projects'. It was no wonder that some local residents felt it was all too good to be true, suspecting that the development (if it was ever completed) was for the well-off and would bring no benefit to those in the town who were struggling financially.

The first 28 houses were completed (by Taylor Wimpey) in 2013. The developers were attempting the usual balancing act of providing houses and jobs at more or less the same time, so that each would attract the other. It was hoped that high quality housing would attract high quality jobs to the area, stimulate investment and support the economic growth and development of Whitburn and the whole depressed southwest corner of the county. The financial crash of 2007–8 was a major set-back and the golf courses were dropped from the plans but, in 2014, the first business tenant was secured for Heartlands – Oil States Industries (UK) Ltd, who already had a plant employing 80 at Bathgate specialising in offshore oil and gas industry equipment but wished to 'upscale' their operation and promised 100 new jobs. A commitment by Tesco to come to Heartlands, which would have acted as a draw to other businesses, was withdrawn after the recession and the firm's financial troubles in the 2010s.

By 2015, work was so far advanced that suspicions that the developers would fail to develop the main proposal were allayed. The Whitburn Community Development Trust and the community were wholly behind the project and looking to it to benefit all sections of the local population, not just the well-off incomers buying houses on the outskirts of the town. In 2016, Heartlands was sold to WElink, a developer specialising in energy efficient materials and modular construction, using renewable energies. The housing development work continued, with 207 houses completed by January 2018 and another 400 under construction or in planning. The housing developers are Bellway, Persimmon, Taylor Wimpey and Allanwater and the development is heavily promoting the advantage of home, work and leisure on the same site.

Both Whitburn people and West Lothian Council are concerned that the new developments should be integrated into the town, regenerate the town centre and benefit all residents, rather than create a shiny new and separate town to the west. This is a genuine concern, as it's obvious from the Heartlands website (which mentions Whitburn just once) that Whitburn is not part of their marketing strategy and (with the sole exception of Polkemmet country park) is considered to be off-putting to prospective businesses or house-buyers. A further concern is that, while the housing developments and house sales appear to be flourishing, as yet no new business or industry (other than Oil States and planning permission given for a filling station with shop) has come to Heartlands, despite the many advantages of its central location at the heart of Scotland. It remains to be seen whether Heartlands will be able to solve the perennial problem of attracting new industry to Whitburn.

Meanwhile the gap between the employed and the unemployed and in-work poor grows wider and Whitburn finds itself in the poorest third of Scotland's communities. Its recovery from the loss of heavy industries and those which replaced them is far from complete.

CHAPTER 21

Schools

UNTIL LATE IN the 19th century, education in Scotland was the joint responsibility of the Church of Scotland and the heritors – the heritors paid for the schoolmaster and premises, the kirk session ensured that the schoolmaster was properly qualified and provided his pupils with a good education.

After Whitburn became a separate parish in 1730, the heritors ignored their legal responsibility to provide a schoolmaster's salary and a schoolhouse but, despite this, the kirk session went ahead and appointed William Campbell as schoolmaster in 1733. With the fees from his pupils, he got just about enough money to live on, 'until Providence shall give some better fund'.

Teachers, good and bad

In 1735, Providence not yet having moved the heritors to pay up, the kirk session again took the initiative, raised money from the congregation and bought land for a school and schoolhouse; its location is not known. A simple rectangular building of stone and thatch was built, one room for the schoolroom, the other for the master's house. The fees of the poorest children were paid by the session; all others paid a few pence weekly. William Campbell was succeeded by Robert Brown who stayed in post for over 50 years (1747–1801), perhaps encouraged by the fact that in 1753, the heritors finally agreed to provide him with a proper salary.

By 1788, the establishment of the new village of Whitburn had caused a growth in school numbers and Robert Brown was growing old, so got permission to employ an assistant. However, he still had enough energy to help draw up Whitburn's declaration against slavery in 1792. After his death in 1801, the heritors advertised for a new schoolmaster, 'qualified to teach English, Latin, Arithmetic, Writing and Book-keeping'. The successful candidate was Samuel Greenshiels who was also appointed session clerk and clerk to the heritors. To accommodate the children in the growing village, the heritors built a new school and schoolhouse near Bridgend. Greenshiels continued in post for 42 years until his death in 1844. He was perhaps unusual (or less than honest) in declaring that his means of discipline was not corporal punishment but 'appeal to the judgment and feelings'. Years later, a former pupil recalled that 'Dominie Greenshiels... took little interest in the dull, backward scholar; give him the 'lad of parts', and he was in his glory. To prepare a boy for the university was his great delight.' Among his pupils were John Bishop, son of 'Dear-bought Bess' and grandson of Robert Burns; and the youngest son of Sir William Baillie of Polkemmet.

After two respected and long-serving school masters, Whitburn was not so lucky with its next teacher, George Davidson, who came from Torphichen school in 1844. Within a year, complaints were brought about him. 'I solemnly swear that I have often seen George Davidson tipsy, as almost all the Village of Whitburn must have seen, as something that's so often happened' was just one of many allegations. Davidson denied them but the evidence against him mounted: drunk one freezing winter's night, he locked his wife out of the house so that she had to be taken in by neighbours; he appeared drunk at school and inflicted brutal punishment on some of the children. Davidson was sacked but three months later was still living in the schoolhouse and teaching in the school! The Presbytery eventually resorted to Sheriff's officers to eject him.

Venture Schools

In a large parish, there was scope for private individuals to set up schools as a commercial venture, charging small fees for providing a very rudimentary education. One of these venture school teachers in Whitburn was John Adams who took up the attention of the kirk session for much of 1781. Adams was accused by Helen Brice of being the father of her illegitimate child. A witness claimed that 'John Adams had said to her that he would give any Body a twopence to tell him how he might act with a woman, and yet not get her with child.' Adams eventually confessed to adultery with Helen Brice, and seems to have left the parish in 1782.

An elderly Whitburn man, James Gilbert, left some memories of the venture school which he attended in the 1830s or 1840s:

> John Waterston was a working man, and he conducted the school for his own benefit. He was a pretty good age, and although he was not a great educationist, he had ability enough to impart... all the education that working folks' children generally required in those days. He had a common dwelling-house for a school; he taught from 9.00am till 5.00pm, and the fees were 2d per week. Reading, writing, and arithmetic were all the subjects he taught, and as those were not the days of steel pens, Mr Waterston supplied us with quills.

Another old man recalled the 'earthen floor, unplastered walls, and beasties and vermin of many kinds crawling on the floors and walls. Yet we learned our alphabet and were happy.'

Wilson's school

James Wilson was a Whitburn merchant, eccentric and miserly but an astute businessman. He came from a poor family: one anecdote claimed that his first business venture was finding a horseshoe on the road, which he took to a smithy and had made into tackets (nails for boot soles) then sold. Later he set up a shop selling grocery goods, cloth and hats – 'any Felt, or Wool, Stuff, or Beaver Hats or leather or japanned Hats', his licence specified. When fetching his goods from Glasgow, he is said to have walked there to save money.

In the early 1790s, he erected a memorial in the churchyard to his parents, 'humble Christians', and to his only two children. John died as an infant and James died in 1792 at the age of eight. The grieving parents inscribed on the gravestone:

> His Body was delicate but His mind active and cheerful. He took great delight in reading and painting. His proficiency in these and other acquisitions were great at his age.

James Wilson valued education. When he died in 1816 aged 74, having no direct heirs, he left legacies to about a dozen educational institutions and charities in various parts of Scotland, including the library at Whitburn and the Whitburn Penny-a-Week Bible Association. In addition, he left £4,250 (equivalent to hundreds of thousands of pounds today) for the building of four schools – at Whitburn and Fauldhouse and at Harthill and Stane in Lanarkshire. He also endowed each school with some £660 to provide the teachers' salaries in perpetuity. James Wilson did not stipulate that his schools must offer free education but he left money to each school to pay the school fees of poor children.

Each school was built to the same design, a plain two-storey rectangle. Whitburn's school was demolished c.2012 but the Almond Housing Association block of flats which replaced it is based on the original design. Wilson's school building in Fauldhouse survives and has been restored as a private house.

Wilson's schools were administered by the eight trustees of his bequest. They purchased half an acre of land at Whitdalehead farm in 1820 and built the school there. It was larger and more impressive than the parish school on the Longridge Road and rapidly gained higher status and greater popularity. By the early 1850s, the average attendance was some 90 boys and 79 girls. 'Beside a plain education, Latin, French, Geometry, Geography, [illegible word] Music and Stenography' [short-hand] were taught. Schoolmaster Mr Leggat had two assistant teachers whose salaries were paid by a government grant.

Lady's Baillie's School

An Infant and Sabbath School was built in 1851 by Lady Baillie – a plain, brick building at the west end of the village. On Sundays, children who were already working or whose parents could not afford school fees were taught religious education and basic literacy free of charge by volunteer teachers, using the Bible as their only textbook. During the week it oper-ated as an infant school, teaching literacy and also sewing and domestic skills to girls; its teachers were all women.

Lady Baillie's School continued to prosper, its annual outing to Polkemmet grounds attracting some 500 children. In 1872, the annual soirée featured 'an immense Christmas tree loaded with presents for the children' – perhaps the first ever Christmas tree in Whitburn. With the coming of compulsory state education, however, the children were trans-ferred to the Whitdalehead school and the daily infant school ceased in the 1880s. The Sabbath school continued until 1903, when Lady Baillie gave the building to the friendly societies of Whitburn. It continued to be known as Lady Baillie's school and was used as a public hall for meetings, talks, concerts and Sunday school. The building is now the West End Gospel Hall.

The Andrew Little case

Following Davidson's eviction from the parish school in 1849, Andrew Little was appointed in his place, so that by the 1850s, Whitburn had three good schools – Wilson's endowed school, the parish school and Lady Baillie's infant school.

As late as 1862, the parish school under Andrew Little was examined and found to be offering excellent education, including Latin and French; the school roll was so large that it was overcrowded. However, in the late 1860s something went wrong and in 1870, Little was told by the heritors to resign his post. A government inspector had made an unfavourable report on the school, but unfortunately failed to specify that its failings were the fault of the schoolmaster. Andrew Little claimed that they were due to 'the character of the population', went to court and won his case against dismissal – and was granted costs as well, much to the disgust of minister and heritors. The case dragged on but a second inspection found that 'Mr Andrew Little is inefficient, through fault on his part'. He was eventually removed in 1874, by which time the parish school and its school roll were at a low ebb.

School boards

By the 1860s, there were innumerable different bodies running Scottish schools – Church of Scotland, other denominations; schools built by mining companies and foundries, private endowed schools like Wilson's and venture and subscription schools set up and run by private individuals. Most were in receipt of some form of government grant but the difficulty of ensuring a good and uniform standard of education made the government decide to bring them all under unified state control. In 1872, the state took over most schools, together with the training and payment of teaching staff, acting through an elected school board in each parish. Education became compulsory from 5–13 and from 1890 it was free. That there was still a great deal to do, especially among girls, is shown by levels of literacy – in West Lothian in 1871, it was 83 per cent for males and 73 per cent for females.

In 1882–3 Wilson's school was sold to the School Board (ie to the state). A couple of years later the old parish school near the Dixon Terrace road end was closed, and Wilson's school became Whitburn Public School, usually known as Whitdalehead School.

The population of Whitburn was growing at such a rate that soon Whitdalehead was bursting at the seams. Several extensions were built and a new annex in 1912, by which time the role had reached nearly 650. Each of the new classrooms could seat 60 (though 'only 50' would be put in each), so no wonder teachers exerted strict discipline over their classes, with ready use of the tawse.

20th century

It was becoming clear that the health of children affected their ability to learn, so government began to improve child health by providing school meals and medical examinations for children. The school leaving age was raised to 14. Children with academic ability and better-off parents might go on to secondary education at Bathgate Academy or the Lindsay High School in Bathgate – but they were few in number. The rest would enter the advanced division of their public school for two or three years, before leaving school at 14. Provision was made for 'continuation classes' after this, teaching 'the crafts and industries practised in the district' – in Whitburn it was basic mining skills for the boys and domestic science for the girls.

In 1918, after more than 350 years, education ceased to be organised at parish level and schools were passed to the control of county educational authorities. The principle of free compulsory *secondary* education for all was introduced but the vast majority of Whitburn children continued to leave school and start work at 14. In the late 1940s, the advanced division of Whitburn public school became Whitburn Junior Secondary School (using the Whitdalehead school), with an emphasis on technical and commercial subjects; while children between the ages of five and 12 attended Whitdalehead Primary School (in the same building).

By the 1940s, the school roll had increased to such an extent that classes were being held in Brucefield Church Hall, the Masonic Hall and the Mission Hall. However, wartime and post-war shortages of building materials meant there was no possibility of building a further extension, far less a new school.

New schools at last

It was not until 1954 that a new school was opened – Polkemmet Primary School. With its 16 new classrooms it could accommodate 715 pupils, which helped but by no means solved the overcrowding. Eventually the government lifted its tight spending controls and the county council was able to build the many schools that had so long been needed. Whitburn's need being the most acute, it acquired three new schools in a remarkably short space of time, all opening in 1967. Whitdale Primary School was formally opened in November by Provost Brown, who had chosen its name. It was built to serve the new housing on the east side of Whitburn, and had places for 630 pupils under headmaster, James Gall. St Joseph's RC Primary and Whitburn Academy opened that same year, although the Academy was far from finished and work continued for another eight months. At this time, comprehensive education was being introduced, so the Academy was large enough to take all of Whitburn's secondary school pupils – those at the Junior Secondary as well as those who had previously gone to Bathgate for senior schooling. Its facilities included playing fields, two gyms, a swimming pool, an extensive library and even a potter's kiln. The Academy rector, Dr DK Sommerville, set out ambitious plans not just for academic achievement but for a school orchestra, annual operas, concerts and displays. A survey of the pupils was carried out in January 1967: they were happy with the range of subjects but wanted more sport and sex education and less French and religious education. Some 40 per cent wanted corporal punishment retained but 92 per cent criticised its being given for the most trivial of offences: 'I forgot my ruler'; 'I lost my pencil'. Catholic secondary children attended St Mary's Academy in Bathgate until the opening of St Kentigern's Academy in Blackburn in 1973.

Five years later, the fourth of Whitburn's primary schools, Croftmalloch, opened in 1973 to serve the south side of the town. As the population of Whitburn stabilised, school-building came to an end, and there were no more until Burnhouse was set up in 1997 in an annex at Polkemmet Primary, bringing together pupils with social, emotional and behavioural difficulties. A primary school at first, it was later extended to secondary education as well, and was designated a 'School of ambition' in 2005, a centre of excellence for pupils with special educational needs throughout West Lothian.

Catholic education

There was no Catholic school in 19th century Whitburn except for a Sunday school which operated around the 1860s and 1870s, teaching basic literacy as well as religious instruction. A few Whitburn Catholic children may have attended the Catholic schools in Blackburn or Fauldhouse, but most went to the non-denominational Public School in Whitburn.

The 1918 Education Act brought Roman Catholic schools into the national education system and provided them for the first time with government funding – to the anger of diehard Protestants who called it 'Rome on the Rates'. Catholic education, being underfunded till then, was far behind the non-denominational schools in terms of buildings and teaching standards and took some years to catch up.

For a time in the 1940s and 1950s, Whitburn's Catholic children attended St Anthony's RC Primary School in Armadale. Following a petition by parents in 1965, two huts were erected in the grounds of Whitdalehead as a school for the 65 Catholic children. The first purpose-built Catholic school – St Joseph's – opened in 1967. It was designed with plenty of natural light, an assembly hall with stage and toilets accessible from both inside and outside! Today it has a roll of 250, plus 60 in the nursery class.

CHAPTER 22

A Frozen Postman, a Bank Scandal and Some Shops and Pubs

Post Office

A POST OFFICE was opened in Whitburn in 1786, with deliveries on horseback from Edinburgh three times a week. Within a few years, however, the town lost its direct delivery and was served by a postal runner from Linlithgow. Since the cost of postage was high, the volume of letters was low and the job was a part-time one usually taken by the schoolmaster or some other respected local person. James Wilson, the merchant who left money for the founding of schools, was postmaster from 1800 till his death in 1816 and was succeeded by another merchant, John Dick (possibly a son of John Dick, the cotton jeanie owner), who sold groceries, linen and drapery.

> **Frozen to death**
>
> In March 1827, a short news item appeared in the *Edinburgh Advertiser* and other newspapers around the country: 'On Thursday the Post Office runner [postman] between Whitburn and Wilsontown was found standing upright in the snow, with the post-bag in his hand, and quite dead.' However, the archive at the Postal Museum has no record of the incident, so possibly it's a 19th century urban myth.

In 1824, John Dick was succeeded by Dr Alexander Wilson, who had been a surgeon on a whaling ship, then became medical officer to the Shotts Ironworks. In 1827, Dr Wilson found himself embroiled in an investigation into illegal carriage of mail. In an attempt to evade the high cost of posting letters, the Shotts Iron Company took to hiding its letters in parcels it was sending via the mail coaches. The parcels were delivered and uplifted by a private runner who came daily to Whitburn post office. Three times the Whitburn postmaster was investigated and each time was found to be innocent of any wrongdoing, as he could have had no knowledge of what the parcels contained.

With the arrival of motor transport, the walking or mounted postman became a thing of the past and multiple collections and deliveries each day enabled the post to be used for quick messages: a postcard could be sent and an answer received the same day. A telephone exchange opened at Whitburn post office in 1907, when there were 'no fewer than ten private connections'. Whitburn was upgraded to a main post office branch in 2013, offering postal, banking, savings, insurance and retail services and even mortgages. More recently the Whitburn branch has been run in tandem with a convenience store and continues to provide a valued service to the community, particularly since the closure of the banks.

City of Glasgow Bank collapse

As the number of businesses increased, there was a need for somewhere to deposit takings or negotiate a loan. The City of Glasgow Bank was the earliest bank to set up a branch in Whitburn: in 1846, local businessman Robert Gardner became its bank agent. He had a drapery business in Whitburn and later diversified into farming, leasing various farms on Polkemmet estate. For a few years he also mined some of the valuable oil-bearing Torbanite coal, a time best remembered for the spectacular fire in June 1872, when the Torbanehill bing caught fire and the ground flowed with burning oil. In addition to all these activities, Gardner was the first Provost of Whitburn (known then as the senior magistrate) and served from 1862 to 1882. As the leading man in town, he built a house to reflect his status (it's now the Cross Tavern), with a room at the back entered off Manse Road for transacting bank business.

Unfortunately, the City of Glasgow Bank collapsed in 1878, the result 'of utterly reckless and dishonest speculation on the part of the Glasgow Board of Directors'. The savings of its many investors were lost and, worse still, it was not a limited company, so all those who had bought shares in it were liable for its debts – some £6 million in all, an enormous sum in those days. As a result, many quite ordinary people who held shares were reduced to destitution by the crash. Robert Gardner was a prominent man, so 'the collapse of the bank created a great sensation in the town, especially amongst those who had any money in it.' A savings bank for small deposits had been part of the bank's business in Whitburn and even these small depositors lost their money. Robert Gardner, though an agent of the bank, had not bought shares in it; he survived the crash and was later associated with the Commercial Bank.

The Co-op

Like every West Lothian town of any size, Whitburn had co-operative stores: 'West Benhar [Co-operative Society] reigned supreme – and... had groceries, fruit and vegetables, butcher's, boots, shoes and clothing shops, all in West Main Street'. The society was founded in 1885 in the mining village of West Benhar, near Harthill, and first set up in Whitburn about 1898 in the former Inn buildings.

For five years, Whitburn also had its own Co-op Society. It began business in November 1934, in the Town Hall (the ground floor of the Masonic Lodge). During its short life, Whitburn Co-op managed to pay an average quarterly dividend of 2/9 (14p) per £1, but it was wound up in August 1939. With the West Benhar Co-op so well established, it was difficult for the new society to attract members, and it failed to grow large enough to be viable in the long-term. West Benhar continued to flourish under its president Christie Barras into the 1960s, when it was among the top four societies in Scotland for average weekly purchase per member. It merged with the West Lothian Co-op Society in the late 1960s and West Lothian Co-op became part of the Scottish Midland Co-operative Society (now Scotmid) in 1982. A Semichem store (part of Scotmid since 1995) continues to operate at West Main Street. The present Co-op supermarket is part of an English-based group of co-operatives.

A new town centre

By 1967, Whitburn's growth was such that the town council resolved to redevelop the town centre, with the aim of separating local and through traffic, providing an open civic space and a pleasanter environment for shoppers. The Cross was opened up by demolishing the buildings on the north-west and south-west corners. A new range of shops with flats above was built on the north-west side in 1966, while on the south-west side a new bank and hotel were planned (the latter never built) with an open space where pedestrians would sit. But the proposed pedestrianisation scheme was rejected, so the open space was next to a busy junction and the public declined to linger there. With their flat 1960s design and stained concrete, the new buildings form an undistinguished opening to West Main Street, out of date, out of line and out of keeping with the rest of the street.

Something of the character of the old Whitburn was lost in the redevelopment but Whitburn council was always confident that old was bad and new was good – particularly from 1968 to 1971 under Provost John Boyle, who is said to have had 'an insatiable hatred of old buildings' and believed that '20th century thinking had to be met with a 20th century environment'.

Hard times for local shops

Whitburn had 20 shops in 1871 and the figure rose gradually, reaching 67 in 1966. Of these, 58 were independent traders, plus four Co-op shops and only four multiples. Among well-remembered businesses in the town were Wood's Yetthouse bakery, Crawford's shoe shop, Boni's café, the chip shop at the West End and Dewar's haberdashery. The oldest shops still trading are the butcher's business in East Main Street, dating back to the 19th century and owned by Livingston's since 1948, and Fisher's bakery, in business at changing locations in West Main Street since 1929.

As the population rose, the number of shops increased, reaching 84 in 1981, probably the highest ever. Thereafter, two factors came into play: Livingston new town and more recently online shopping. Over the last 20 years, Livingston has become one of the largest indoor shopping centres in Scotland. Its effect has been to draw shoppers away from all the traditional town centres in West Lothian; but on the other hand, local people appreciate having such a good shopping centre at no great distance.

Online shopping has presented a challenge to high streets everywhere. Whitburn has lost its furniture and most of its clothing shops and can now cater only for everyday shopping, not for durables. Convenience stores continue to proliferate but there are as many service outlets as shops and several empty units – in 2012, shop occupancy was 81 per cent, the lowest rate in West Lothian, though far from the worst in Scotland. The siting of the two discount supermarkets outside Whitburn town centre has taken shoppers away from the Main Street but allows easier parking. The higher than average rates of deprivation in Whitburn, and the prolonged recession since 2008, have also affected the health of the Main Street. It's unlikely that the new residents of Heartlands will save Whitburn's Main Street: they are more likely to shop in Livingston or the cities.

Pubs and hotels

The Olde Market Inn is the oldest pub in Whitburn today but it was not the first to be established. Whitburn Inn preceded the building of the village of Whitburn and its original location is not certain. With increasing business from travellers on the new turnpike road, it was rebuilt (probably c.1760s) on the site between the present Cross Tavern and the former Clydesdale Bank building. It was the main inn in the village, sometimes referred to as the Head Inn, where public meetings and important social and civic occasions were held. It continued in business throughout the 19th century but, after the coaching era, business declined and it closed in about 1899. The building was converted to retail use and was demolished c.1969. The Boni and Franchitti families built new premises for their shops and café on the site.

There were dramshops at Polkemmet Toll and several other locations in the village but having no accommodation, they could not be called inns. Halfway House at the gates of Polkemmet estate operated as an inn from the 1820s till at least 1851, then reverted to residential use.

The Castle Inn was certainly in business by 1850 (possibly much earlier) under a woman owner, Mrs Susannah Muir. It may have been at the south-west corner of the Cross and closed down in 1881. In 1867 comes the first mention of the Commercial Inn which operated at 8 West Main Street until its closure in 1896, the year in which the Market Inn is first listed in the Valuation Rolls, indicating that it was built in 1895–6. The last tenant of the Commercial Inn, John Sharp, was also the first tenant of the Market Inn. If indeed the inn dates back to 1783 as is claimed on its east wall, then it was on a different site and under a different name.

In 1900, John Adam, the last tenant of the Whitburn Inn, bought the large house at the south-east corner of the Cross that had been the home of Robert Gardner and opened it as the Pretoria Inn in the summer of 1900, naming it in honour of the capture of Pretoria during the Boer War in South Africa just three weeks earlier. The name was retained until 1913 when it was changed to the Cross Tavern.

The Roadhouse originally opened as a filling station, tearoom and shop in 1934 and the Double Five pub opened in the mid 1950s in the former British Linen Bank premises at 55A West Main Street, hence the name. The Linden was opened in 1963 as a 'luxury pub' with function rooms upstairs. It closed down, but the building re-opened in 2002 as the Karma Indian Restaurant. The Clachan pub opened at 68 West Main Street in the mid-1950s. It was run by James Boyle, also notable as a county councillor and county council convener during the last year of his life. He died in 1974 and the tenancy was taken over by his wife Betty. Both were leading figures in the Scottish and local licensed trade.

Demolition of Whitedalehead Farmhouse began in December 1970 for the building of a new hotel, the Whit(e)dale, which opened in 1971. 'The handsome, modern, 12-bedroom hotel,' declared the *West Lothian Courier*, 'is the symbol of the new, progressive and expanding Whitburn.' The Whitdale was acquired in 1988 by John and Margaret Hilditch who greatly enlarged and upgraded it, renaming it the Hilcroft. Now part of the Best Western hotel chain, it has been an asset to the town, a popular venue for weddings, functions and special occasions. In 1981, the Hilditches opened the former Brucefield Nursery (beside the old Free Church manse and, before that, Eastburn House) as the Croftmalloch Inn.

Social clubs had their heyday in the 1970s and 1980s: the Miners' Welfare was the largest but there were also the British Legion, the Labour

Club, the Masonic, Whitburn Juniors and the Bowling Club. The last three are still in operation but the Miners' Welfare Club burned down in 2011 and was demolished. Though its glory days as a cinema, dance hall and social centre had passed, its closure was a great loss to the town.

Nightclubs had a brief popularity in the 1990s and early 2000s but Whitburn's clubs had a chequered history with several closed after incidents of disorder or drugs on the premises: the Anywhere Nite Club had its licence revoked in 2007, Club Class was shut down in 1998 and the Oasis club closed after a riot involving over 100 people on gala day night in 2003.

CHAPTER 23

Poverty, Poor Relief and Self-help

UNTIL 1845, CARE of the poor was the responsibility of the Church. The sums paid to them came mainly from weekly church offerings, fines for misbehaviour or fees for hire of the mortcloth. In effect, it was the money of the poor that was helping those who were poorer still. Occasionally, however, the landlords gave help in money or kind as, for example, in the severe winter of 1801, when they provided firewood, coal and grain to some of the poorest in Whitburn. Sometimes bequests were left to assist the poor of the parish, such as that of a Mrs Wilson who in the early 1840s bequeathed money 'for behoof of aged and indigent females in Whitburn, who may have seen better days'.

Poor relief amounted to about half the wage of an ordinary labourer – scarcely enough to live on – and was given only to the aged, sick or infirm. Those fit to work but unable to find any were not eligible, there being no understanding that trades such as weaving went through times of boom and bust beyond the power of ordinary people to control, and they might find themselves unemployed, however much they wished to find work.

After the Disruption of 1843 when the Church of Scotland split in two, the old system of church-run poor relief became unworkable. Responsibility for the poor passed from the Church to the state, to be administered locally by a parochial board (later called the parish council) in each parish. Occasionally the heritors continued to impose a voluntary tax on themselves in times of hardship – probably in their own self-interest, fearing a permanent increase in their assessments for poor relief. In 1846, their voluntary 'stent' allowed the board to make an extra allowance to each pauper because of the failure of the potato crop – fortunately the Scottish poor were not so dependent on potatoes as the Irish, who starved in their millions during the 1840s famine.

The parish councils continued to distinguish between the deserving and the undeserving poor. The drunk, the feckless, and unmarried mothers were the undeserving and were relieved at a lower rate than the respectable poor. Another distinction was made between 'indoor' and 'outdoor' relief. Outdoor relief was paid to the respectable poor so that they could continue to live in their own homes. Indoor relief required the poor person to move temporarily or permanently into the poorhouse.

Whitburn had no poorhouse within the parish but shared the use of Linlithgow Poorhouse in combination with seven other parishes. In order to discourage the poor from applying for relief, the poorhouse accommodation, diet and regime were made as harsh as possible. Men, women and children were separated; inmates were given rough and repetitive work, and not allowed to leave the premises without a special pass. As intended, it was perceived as shameful to have to enter the poorhouse, and most preferred to suffer rather than accept 'indoor relief'.

The day-to-day work of assessing who was poor enough to be helped and dividing the deserving from the undeserving was the work of an inspector of poor in each parish. They were often local men who knew the people and could shrewdly assess their cases. Whitburn Parish Council prided itself on keeping its poor relief costs low – helped by the fact that they paid the poor's inspector a very low salary.

In 1911, the government introduced a national insurance scheme to provide small benefit payments to those who were sick or unemployed. Strikers, however, were not entitled to benefits so during the long miners' strikes of the 1920s, the men and their families suffered great hardship. Whitburn town council undertook to provide meals at school for miners' children and the strikers themselves organised soup kitchens during the 1921, 1926 and the 1984–5 strikes. This was no small task: in 1921, the miners' wives produced some 750 meals daily at four soup kitchens in Whitburn parish, while groups toured local towns and villages to raise funds for them.

By the end of the 1920s, the government had recognised that its national insurance scheme was not working and replaced it with an unemployment benefit scheme. However, before assistance was granted, strict enquiries were made into the applicants' circumstances – the hated and humiliating Means Test. In 1939, there were 400 adults on the poor list in Whitburn, some 10 per cent of the population. All in all, the 1920s and 1930s were a wretched time for Whitburn's jobless.

After the war, the Labour government introduced the welfare state and the concept of 'cradle to the grave' welfare. Just as the worry of unemployment or illness was finally being lifted from the lives of ordinary people, a bequest was made to the poor of Whitburn in 1948 by a former resident. Captain Matthew White, son of a weaver, left the village as a young man, prospered as a master plasterer and died in Jersey. Although few people in Whitburn could remember him, he left £10,000 for the poor, to be administered by the town council. White Street in Whitburn was named in his honour, and his fund still makes grants to OAPs of 70 and over who have lived in Whitburn parish for at least ten years.

Self-help

Poverty carried a stigma, so people sought to maintain their respectability and guard against having to ask for church or state poor relief, by means of self-help and self-improvement. These might also provide a way for people to get on in life, and to improve their social and educational circumstances. Despite being sometimes viewed as a Victorian striving after middle-class respectability, the self-help movement relates to the radical strand in Whitburn's history; it was an effort by working people to retain their independence of church or state charity and to assist one another by banding together against adversity. The following were some of the ways they set about it.

Friendly societies

The earliest known friendly society in Whitburn was the Whitburn Whipmen's Society, formed by the local carters, cadgers and ploughmen (whose work involved the use of horses). It was formalised in May 1813 but was probably in existence earlier. The aim of friendly societies was to build up a fund of money by small weekly payments, from which members could claim an allowance during sickness or inability to work. In the event of their death, relatives would be given help to cover funeral expenses. Only those who could afford the entry money and the weekly payments could join, therefore they could not help the poorest, but they could save the respectable working man from falling into destitution. The Whipmen's Society survived for nearly 70 years, having opened up its membership to men of any occupation. It was wound up in 1882 as its membership had fallen too low to be viable.

In place of local societies, large national societies began to grow up, which, by virtue of their scale, were more financially secure. Whitburn had branches of four national friendly societies: the Gardeners, the Shepherds, the Good Templars (which demanded temperance of its members) and the Rechabites (which demanded total abstinence). The Templars and Rechabites admitted women; the other societies were male only. All flourished before the First World War, the Rechabites into the 1930s. The friendly societies adopted ritual and regalia similar to the freemasons and held social events and annual processions with colourful banners and bands.

The national societies did not become so strong in Whitburn as elsewhere in West Lothian, perhaps because of the success of the Whitburn Funeral Expense Society, the largest and longest-surviving of Whitburn's friendly societies. It was founded by nine working men in 1861 and offered benefits only in the event of death. Because of this the payments required were lower than other societies and by 1878 it had attracted the huge membership of 7,000, drawn from south-west West Lothian and North Lanarkshire. Why were so many willing to make financial sacrifice to ensure a decent funeral? If a family could not afford the burial, the parish council would provide it but a 'parish funeral' was considered as great a disgrace as having to 'go on the parish' or enter the poorhouse. And if there was nobody to claim the corpse, the parish council had the right to hand over the body to medical science for dissection, a practice which retained in popular memory the horror of the grave-robbing period. The ever-present fear of falling into poverty and shame was only removed by the coming of the welfare state in 1947; the Funeral Expense Society was wound up in 1958.

Freemasonry

In freemasonry there was a general expectation that masons would help their fellow masons get on in life and membership provided a certain status among the Protestant community. Lodge Polkemmet 927 was instituted on 1 May 1902 and its first temple was consecrated in December that year. Although a larger temple was created in an extension to the Institute in 1911, it was still not big enough, so in 1930 the lodge bought the town hall next door. After an ambitious fundraising campaign, a second storey was added to serve as the masonic temple, while the enlarged town hall below remained available for hire. The new temple was consecrated in October 1930 – a true square with an inner square formed by four pillars and a domed ceiling complete with echo.

Women being barred from lodge membership, local women in 1922 formed the Polkemmet chapter of the Order of the Eastern Star, which still survives – Polkemmet No. 195. In 1978, a Royal Arch Chapter (a progression of freemasonry) was set up in Whitburn – Polkemmet Chapter No. 84 – sharing premises with the existing lodge. The freemasons continue to be active and are generous in fundraising for local charities and good causes.

Self-improvement

In much of the social activity of the burgh, there was an underlying drive towards self-improvement. A Mutual Improvement Society was set up in the 1860s which discussed science, history and politics, and a Literary Association met weekly on Wednesday evenings in Lady Baillie's School to discuss the great literary works. The local ministers and other speakers offered lantern slide lectures on topics as diverse as Egyptian antiquities and political economy. The number of organisations and their breadth of interests were extraordinary: geology, horticulture, temperance, caged birds, rambling, Christian missionary work, ornithology – nothing was beyond the interest of some segment of Whitburn's residents.

Libraries

A library was certainly in existence in Whitburn by 1816 when James Wilson left it a bequest in his will. It was a collection of books rather than

> ### Keen readers
>
> A reprint of the works of a deceased English cleric published by Archibald Bruce in Whitburn in 1798 contains a list of subscribers, 101 of whom are from Whitburn parish. One of them, Mr Hamilton, ordered 33 copies, so was presumably going to sell them in his shop. That some 134 people out of a parish population of 1,537 bought or might buy such an abstruse book indicates a high level of literacy among the population.

a purpose-built building and was probably a subscription library, whereby users had to pay to join. Lady Baillie's coffee and reading rooms functioned like a reference library but there was no local authority provision of libraries in West Lothian until the 20th century. A small library was opened by the county library service in the Labour Hall in 1951 but a purpose-built one was not provided until 1965, when the county council built a new library on the site of Lea Street. Opening it, Councillor James Boyle firmly placed it within the tradition of self-improvement and self-education: 'it is to the public library that scores of thousands come for education and information. It is their college and university.' A major refurbishment in 1993 added a small museum telling the story of Whitburn past and present.

The Colliery Hub

The Colliery Hub is an interesting venture established in 2017 in the former Polkemmet colliery offices. Set up by Dave Gillan and his wife and Alex Smith, the charity and 'community interest company' is a not-for-profit venture started by local people for local people and run by local volunteers on a shoestring budget – but with ambitious ideas for the future. Beginning with a Monday night craft group, they now offer beekeeping courses, café, free clothing for young children, several hobbies clubs and soon, it's hoped, a community garden. It has attracted some 30 users, many of them unemployed, and makes its facilities and tuition free to those on benefits. A true self-help venture, it shows that the radical tradition of relying on community-led solutions rather than waiting for officialdom to deal with problems is far from dead in Whitburn.

CHAPTER 24

Keeping Whitburn in Order and in Health

Police

BEFORE THE MID-19TH century, there was no police service in Scotland outside the cities and public order was entrusted to a few respectable local men, sworn in and provided with batons (like police truncheons), and hence known as baton men. Detection of crime was left to local justices of the peace or the sheriff's officers, with the assistance of members of the public and, indeed, it was local men who captured the murderer of James Murdoch, a Longridge shop-keeper, in 1815. John Murdoch (no relation) was handed over to the Whitburn baton men, taken to Linlithgow jail, tried, found guilty and condemned to death.

The first policeman in Whitburn was probably a young man called Thomas Johnston who is listed in the 1841 Census as a rural policeman. His role probably included moving vagrants and beggars out of the county (to prevent their claiming local poor relief) and maintaining public order especially while railway navvies were in the area: they had a reputation for drunken disorder. A Linlithgowshire Police Force was formed in 1840 and the first of its constables was appointed to Whitburn in 1843 – James Barnes, a former Kirkliston baker.

The extent of poverty and the lack of material goods is indicated by the crimes of the time – stealing a pair of trousers from a dwelling house, a watch and a cap, a large cheese from a farmhouse, making off without paying for a drink. But more serious crime was not unknown: in 1866, Margaret Forsyth was arrested on suspicion of the murder of her new-born baby whose body had been found beneath a hedge in the village, apparently smothered.

The increase in population required a second police constable and a police station with cells was built adjoining the Baillie Institute in 1869. The first purpose-built police station and police houses were built on the north side of East Main Street in 1936 (east of the doctor's house, Craig-Uisk) and from there the police covered the whole area from Blackburn to Fauldhouse.

West Lothian Police became part of Lothian and Peebles (later Lothian and Borders) Police in 1950. The 1936 police station was replaced by the present station at the corner of West Main Street and Weavers' Lane in 1979, and today covers both Whitburn and Blackburn.

Health

The care of Whitburn's health was in the hands of surgeons for the first years of its existence. In 1850, the first fully trained general practitioner came to the village, Dr Alexander Clark, who built for himself Almondbank, the large stone house beyond the filling station. It fell to him to deal with an outbreak of smallpox in 1856. The cholera outbreak of 1853–4 seems not to have much affected Whitburn, though local people had died in the 1849 outbreak. In the absence of emergency services, Dr Clark was called upon to deal with the many accidents in the pits, the workplace or the home.

> ## Gunpowder at home
>
> In 1869, miner Walter Savage was in his house, emptying gunpowder from one paper bag into another containing a full pound of powder. Foolishly he threw the empty bag into the fire, where the remnant of the powder ignited and flashed out, causing the full bag in his hand to explode, severely burning him, his wife and his two young children. Since miners had to buy their own gunpowder and store it at home, this was in effect a mining accident.

As housing and sanitation improved, public health improved and provision of a clean water supply eradicated many diseases like typhus and typhoid. Infectious diseases such as scarlet fever, diphtheria and tuberculosis, however, continued a scourge especially among children. When the board of health directed local authorities to make provision for isolating these highly infectious diseases, Whitburn town council joined with Armadale and Bathgate and the county council to build a hospital at Tippethill, where sufferers could be isolated from their families and treated. The hospital opened in 1901 with 28 beds, staffed by a matron and nurses and overseen by one of the local GPs. It was enlarged in 1925 and again in 1937 to increase capacity to 75 patients. The children who were treated there must have found it an upsetting experience as they were allowed no visitors, not even their parents, who could only wave to them through the glass in the door.

By the 1950s, these diseases had been brought under control by vaccination and Tippethill became a geriatric hospital which also taught trainee nurses. In the 1970s, patient numbers had fallen so low that the health board proposed closure but after a campaign by local people, this was averted. The old buildings were demolished and replaced in 2000 by a new 60-bed unit caring for elderly patients with dementia or terminal illnesses. Two 2018 reports into Tippethill House highlighted some failures in nursing care and inadequate levels of staffing and psychiatric help, but these problems are now being addressed by NHS Lothian.

In 1936, Whitburn set up a nursing association, whereby local people subscribed a few pennies a week, entitling them and their families to the services of a district nurse when required. The first nurse was Elizabeth Russell who soon proved her usefulness by carrying out over 3,000 home visits in the first year. She also acted as midwife and child welfare nurse. In 1948, with the establishment of the National Health Service, medical, hospital and nursing treatments became free to all at the point of need. Demand has constantly increased until today the health centre in Weavers' Lane has eight doctors and 14 nursing staff and offers treatment, clinics and health advice. However, Whitburn still has an above average number of residents suffering from chronic health conditions, which correlates with its higher levels of deprivation and unemployment.

CHAPTER 25

Whitburn at War

First World War

THE FIRST WORLD War began on 4 August 1914 and affected not just the families who had a member serving in the forces. Every man, woman and child was affected in some way by the difficulties brought by war. Restrictions on everyday life were introduced immediately. In the very first week of the war, foreigners were required to register at the police station. To guard against Zeppelin bombing attacks, lighting restrictions were introduced and locals were fined if they failed to draw their blinds and showed a light at night. Pub opening hours were reduced, 'treating' was banned and alcohol content was watered down.

Scores of volunteers from Whitburn enlisted in the first 18 months of the war and many more were later conscripted. Twelve members of Whitburn Band enlisted to become the battalion band of the 3rd/5th Royal Scots and at least two of them, William Aitken and Smith Tennant, were killed.

Whitburn people enthusiastically and tirelessly raised funds throughout the war – for families whose breadwinner was away at war, for Belgian refugees, for the dozen or so Whitburn men who were POWs in Germany, Christmas boxes for soldiers – all kinds of wartime causes. Towards the end of the war, the government appealed for the nation to lend it money for the war effort in the form of war bonds. Whitburn achieved such a high total during War Weapons Week in 1918 that the War Office agreed to name a tank after the burgh.

The government was reluctant to introduce food rationing, fearing it would be unpopular but the severe shortage of food in 1917 caused by German submarine warfare forced them to introduce rationing. Local people were encouraged to grow vegetables in their gardens or take up the offer of an allotment and ordered to save and recycle anything of value – paper, glass, metal, wool, cotton, rubber, food waste, even animal bones. Petrol was also rationed and bus services were cut back.

The shortage of manpower caused by conscription was severe, so much so that Browning of Whitburn was fined for using his son to drive a motor car – he was just 13! Restrictions were introduced on many occupations, preventing people leaving them without official permission. With so many men away in the army, employers were forced to take on women in jobs they had never before been considered for: as bakers, shop assistants, clerks, delivery drivers, railway porters. Some Whitburn women worked in the foundries of Bathgate and Armadale and a dozen or more worked as VAD nurses at Polkemmet House when it was in use as a convalescent hospital for servicemen.

Men too old or too young to join the army, or who were in reserved occupations (like many miners) were recruited into the Whitburn Volunteer Force, a sort of First World War Home Guard, where they learned rifle shooting, bayonet fighting, and drill. By the time the Whitburn force was set up, all threat of invasion was over, so they served no very useful purpose.

Towards the end of the war, a Spanish flu epidemic affected much of the world, killing many more millions than died in the war. In Whitburn in October 1918, the school was forced to close because so many pupils and teacher were off with flu, coal output was affected because of miners being sick and the local doctor was overwhelmed with work. The disease particularly affected those in the prime of life, and probably claimed some 20 to 30 lives in Whitburn.

In November 1918 came the Armistice but one more Whitburn death was to occur. Dr Michie, the local GP, had been called up in the last weeks of the war and was sent as medical officer with the Royal Scots to fight the Bolsheviks in Northern Russia. As the nation celebrated peace he was going off to war and was killed on 31 December 1919, leaving a widow and an infant daughter.

The first Whitburn casualty – indeed, the first West Lothian death of the war – was Sir Gawaine Baillie of Polkemmet, killed in the second month of the war. He was the first of many and differed only in that his family could afford to bring his body home for burial in the mausoleum at Polkemmet (later reinterred in the South churchyard). In March 1915, the government introduced a ban on repatriation of bodies, so that all the dead, whether rich or poor, were treated equally. The number of First World War names on Whitburn war memorial is 63 but it's likely that several names are missing and that Whitburn lost perhaps as many as 10 per cent of its male population between the ages of 15 and 50. The total number of Whitburn men who served in the war certainly exceeded 200.

Second World War

By the late 1930s, it was evident that a second war with Germany was likely, and the government began to re-arm, and to prepare for the expected aerial bombing and gas attacks on the civilian population. An

Air Raid Precautions (ARP) committee was formed by Whitburn town council to recruit air raid wardens and make preparations. Gas masks were distributed and volunteers piled sandbags around the walls of the police station and the Baillie Institute as protection from air raids. Several dozen public air raid shelters were put up, the first two of them in Murraysgate Crescent and Manse Avenue.

The first sounding of the air raid warning sirens (on the police station in East Main Street and the Welfare Hall in West Main Street) came on 20 October 1939 but proved to be a false alarm. Whitburn never suffered bombing during the war but the blackout had nevertheless to be enforced and probably contributed to several civilian deaths. Robert Redmond (18) was killed while cycling in the dark and George Wood, Robert Crozier and William Heenan were killed by a car late one night in October 1943, while walking their racing greyhounds on the Glasgow road.

Some 80 Edinburgh school children (and 15 mothers) were evacuated to Whitburn in September 1939 and were billeted on private households. More children arrived later and most of them were moved to Polkemmet House which served as a school for evacuees until 1942.

As in the First World War, fundraising went on throughout the war, with concerts and dances held to benefit servicemen's and other wartime charities. Again on the model of the First World War, major savings campaigns were held to persuade people to lend their money to the government for the war effort – such as War Weapons Week in 1941, Warship Week in 1942 and Wings for Victory week in 1943. During these campaigns, surprising sums of money were raised in the town.

Wounded soldiers in Bangour Hospital were entertained, as when the South Kirk brought a party of soldiers to the Masonic Hall and supplied them with tea, a concert, dancing and games. The hundreds of Polish soldiers based at Polkemmet provided an exotic element at dances and other social events and special film shows (in Polish) were held for them at the Welfare. They also organised their own concerts and dances, to which Whitburn people were invited.

Rationing of food and fuel was introduced right at the start of the war and was extended to more and more foodstuffs as the years went by. Salvage – saving paper, metals, rubber, waste food, etc for recycling – became a way of life and sometimes involved young folk in its collection. But though an irritation, the early introduction of these measures was effective in avoiding the severe shortages of the First World War.

A company of the Home Guard was formed in Whitburn in 1940 – B Company of the 2nd West Lothian Home Guard – and made its base at the Baillie Institute. The men, too young or too old to join the regular forces or in reserved occupations, drilled, learned rifle shooting and grenade throwing, prepared to repel the expected invasion and guarded strategic or sensitive locations like collieries and railway junctions. They also had a large social element, holding dances, concerts and fundraising events.

As the threat of invasion or of bombing receded, most of the evacuees went back home to Edinburgh, and the ARP precautions began to seem redundant. In December 1944, the Home Guard was stood down, and to mark the occasion, the 2nd West Lothian Battalion, led by Whitrigg Colliery Pipe Band, marched along the main street where the Marquess of Linlithgow took the salute in front of the Baillie Institute.

In 1945, with the Allies sweeping across Europe, POW camps were liberated and the men began to come home. Archie Graham of the Black Watch, a POW since his capture at St Valéry in June 1940, arrived home in Whitburn on 23 April 1945, five years to the day since he had left.

> The first person he met on stepping off the bus... was his mother who was about to board the same bus on her way to East Whitburn to acquaint a friend about her son's expected arrival... Needless to say it was a joyful reunion.

When Victory in Europe (VE) day was finally announced in May 1945, Whitburn people decorated their houses with flags and streamers, dances were held in the Welfare, thanksgiving services in Brucefield Church and 600 Polish soldiers at Polkemmet paraded through the town, headed by the Miners' Welfare Silver Band. A vast children's pageant was arranged by James Sangster, preceded by parades through the streets of Blackburn and Whitburn accompanied by the Whitrigg Colliery Band. Victory in Japan (VJ) Day brought further celebrations:

> Children were busy all day collecting material for bonfires. These were kindled in the evening at different parts of the town and district, and nearly every bonfire had a dancing party of its own. Whitburn Miners' Welfare Band paraded the town, and discoursed lively music.

British casualties were on nowhere near the same scale as in the First World War but Whitburn lost at least 29 men. Walter Hodgekinson, a baker with James Wood & Sons, was a member of the Royal Army Service Corps and was killed when SS *Lancastria* was bombed as she evacuated civilians and soldiers from northern France. Somewhere between 3,000 and 5,800 died, 'the largest single-ship loss of life in British maritime history'. In December 1944, John McLean (19) was killed by enemy action while serving in the Royal Navy. An orphan, he lived with his grandfather, Mr P Wilson, in Armadale Road, and was a Co-op grocer before his call-up. In February 1945, fruiterer John Marshall and his wife, of Fairmont, West Main Street, received notification that their eldest son, Pilot Officer James Marshall, after surviving two operational tours in the Middle East, had been killed in a flying accident. Closer to home, an RAF plane crashed at Longridge in 1944 – a Wellington bomber on a training exercise from an RAF airfield near Doncaster – and a Canadian airman was killed.

After the war, the Women's Section of the British Legion prepared a list of the men from the burgh who had been killed. The 29 names were finally added to the war memorial in late 1950 and the memorial was re-dedicated on Armistice Day 1951. These were not the last Whitburn men to die in conflicts. In 1952, Private Robert Deans was killed while serving with the Black Watch in the Korean War. In the 1970s, the name of David Ferguson was added. The 20-year old private was serving in Northern Ireland in 1976 when a land mine exploded under the Land Rover in which he was travelling and killed him. He left a widow and six-month-old daughter. And in 2004, the name of Robert Thomson was added on a supplementary stone; the 22-year-old Sapper was killed while serving with the 35 Engineering Regiment in Basra during the Iraq war.

CHAPTER 26

Sports and Leisure

THE STRENGTH AND well-being of a community can be judged by its efforts to help itself. Sports and games were the first activities to be formally organised by public-spirited volunteers and, since then, many other kinds of clubs and societies have grown up and flourished in the town.

Fairs and Games

For about 150 years, Whitburn Games were held annually in July. Being organised by the Whitburn Whipmen's Society, they were sometimes known as the Whipmen's Play. Some claimed that the Games dated back to the 1760s or 1770s, originating in a wager between competing coachmen on the turnpike road.

Whitburn also had an annual Fair Day, which combined a hiring fair for farm servants with a sale of livestock and produce, as well as stalls and sideshows; it provided one of the few public holidays in the year. By the mid-19th century, the fair and games were held on the same day and, like fairs everywhere, attracted complaints of drunkenness, disorder and pickpocketing. The 1907 Games attracted some 1,500 spectators and, in addition to the main athletics, included other attractions such as a shooting gallery, switchback pulley, donkey races for the children, quoiting, shooting and football competitions and 'juvenile dancing'. Soon afterwards, the Games mutated into the annual Highland Gathering.

Whitburn Agricultural Society also held annual shows from c.1846 but both Society and shows were finally wound up in 1964 because of loss of interest by the public.

Sports

The earliest organised sport in Whitburn was probably curling. A Whitburn Curling Club was certainly in existence by 1838 when one of its members, Sir William Baillie, attended the first meeting of the Grand (later Royal) Caledonian Curling Club.

Bowling is another long-established game in Whitburn: early players claimed that it was first played in the village in 1779, when the bowls were simply 'whin bullets' shaped by the weavers. The game first became popular in Whitburn in the form of carpet bowling, of which Whitburn claimed to have the oldest club in Scotland, founded in Victorian times. The outdoor game got going in 1887, when the Baillies granted the playground of Lady's Baillie's former infant school for a bowling green. Whitburn has been the most successful club in the history of the Rosebery Bowl competition, with 27 wins to date. A public bowling green was opened on the site of the former mansion house at Polkemmet Country Park in 1982.

Various short-lived football teams came and went in the early years of the 20th century but Whitburn Juniors was formed in 1934 when land was leased from the Baillies and laid out as Central Park. The club came close to winning the Junior Cup in 1966, losing to Bonnyrigg in the replay of the final but finally won against Johnstone Burgh in 2000.

Swimming came to Whitburn when the pool opened in West Main Street in 1976 and the Amateur Swimming Club was founded in 1978. The club name was changed to the Trojans in 1995 and the club celebrated its 40th anniversary in 2018.

Martial arts have been sports in which Whitburn has excelled, in particular tae-kwon do, thanks to coach Les Hutchison who founded the local institute in 1973 and is a Grand Master ninth dan, the highest rank awarded in the sport.

In boxing, the best boxer to emerge from Whitburn was Johnny Flannigan, Scottish Welterweight Champion in 1947 and '48, the year he turned professional.

Volleyball flourished in the town in the 1980s and 1990s, supporting men's, women's and junior teams competing at national and international level.

Other sports clubs have come and gone in Whitburn: athletics, tennis, quoiting, cricket, cycling, angling, gymnastics, shinty, American football, homing, billiards, pool, draughts – and no doubt others as well which have left no trace behind them.

Gala Days

The first gala day was held in 1907, when a procession of some 600 children met at Whitdale School and, led by Whitburn Band, marched through the burgh. The teachers distributed milk and buns but the sports had to be postponed because of rain. The first ever arch was built in 1908 but arches did not become a regular feature until after the Second World War. As the years progressed, banners, bands and decorated floats were added and houses were decorated with flags and bunting.

The galas were interrupted by the First World War and, in the 1920s, by miners' strikes and hardship. In 1925, the gala settled on a date in early July and remained there till changed to the present late June date in 1968. The first gala day queen (Mary Dow) was crowned in 1934 and, by 1939, the number of children taking part was approaching 2,000.

Again, the gala was interrupted by war but resumed in 1947. The 1955 gala was a highlight, as guests of honour were the Queen and Prince Philip during their royal tour of West Lothian. Numbers of children taking part reached over 5,000 in 1964. In 1967, a Civic Week was introduced, the first such in West Lothian. The name was changed to Downdie Week in 1985 and events included torchlit processions, fireworks displays, gymkhanas, film shows, Songs of Praise services, a multitude of sports competitions, pram races, even piano smashing.

As costs inexorably rise year by year, the gala committee has to make ever greater efforts throughout the year to raise sufficient funds. The latest gala, with some 20 bands on parade, cost an estimated £30,000, of which less than a sixth is provided by West Lothian Council. Despite smaller numbers of children taking part and the loss of formal participation by the local schools, the gala continues to flourish, strengthening pride of place and community ties and its many local volunteers work hard each year to ensure it has a future.

Bands

Whitburn Band can trace its history back to 1871, when it was formed at a meeting in the Castle Inn and was given a set of instruments and uniforms by Robert Gardner, the Provost. In 1915, during the First World War, seven of the band members enlisted in the 3rd/5th battalion of the Royal Scots and with further enlistments 'almost to a man', the remnant of the band at home ceased to be viable. Some members did not survive the war, so the band was formally wound up in 1919. It was revived two or three years later and, with a few more interruptions, has continued ever since.

Its name has varied according to its sponsors – the Miners' Welfare, Murray International Metals, David A Hall, etc. Since the 1970s, the band has won the Scottish championship 20 times, as well as British titles and a second place in the 1990 European championships. It has broadcast on radio and television, regularly played at football internationals at Hampden, briefly dabbled in 'acid brass' in the late 1990s and took part in the Queen's Golden Jubilee Procession in 2002. In recent years, it has reached an extremely high standard musically, as shown by its invitation to play for an innovative collaboration with the Rambert Dance Company in 2015 on the theme of the miners' strike. In 2013, a brass band 'pathway' was set up in Whitburn with sponsorship from the Heartlands developers, whereby players young and old are trained and developed in three different bands. The band is currently ranked seventh in the world rankings – truly a band to be proud of.

Whitburn's pipe band was set up as East Whitburn Pipe Band in 1918 and made its first public appearance in 1920. From the late 1920s, it was sponsored by Whitrigg Colliery but when Whitrigg closed in 1972, Polkemmet colliery took over sponsorship of the band, changing its name from Whitrigg to Polkemmet Pipe Band. The band flourished, competing in local, Scottish and World Championships and attaining great success in the 1980s and 1990s. However, when Polkemmet colliery closed down in 1985, the band was again on the lookout for sponsorship and became in 1990 Polkemmet Grorud (under which name it came second in the World Championships in 1991), then in 1995, BT Polkemmet. When Pipe Major David Barnes left in 2006, so many of the members followed him to his new band that Polkemmet was wound up. It was briefly revived but has since folded.

Entertainments and parks

In the last decades of the 19th century, the working day shortened and a half-holiday on a Saturday was widely introduced. People now had leisure time and filled it with a huge variety of activities, secular as well as religious – lectures, soirées, dances, trips, choirs, concerts, amateur dramatics. In fact, a great deal more live entertainment and social activity was on offer in Whitburn in the past than today with all its television and online viewing.

Clubs have been set up over the years to cater for all ages and interests in society, from toddlers to pensioners. Church organisations have long played a prominent role, while the SWRI has been going since 1928. Uniformed organisations first appeared in Whitburn with the forming of a scout troop at the South Church in 1913. Since then Brownies and Guides, Boys' and Girls' Brigades have also been formed.

Once the Town Hall opened in 1866, larger concerts and functions could be held. Another important asset was added to the town in 1932 with the opening of the Miners' Welfare hall at 111–3 West Main Street. The funding came from the national Miners' Welfare Commission and as a source of income the committee installed cinema equipment. In fact, Whitburn had cinema showings from at least 1913 at the Whitburn Electric Theatre (in the Town Hall) and, in 1933, George Wright got permission to build the Picture House on the south of West Main Street. Both the Welfare and the Picture House continued to show films until about 1960.

Townhead Park opened in 1922, on ground gifted by Sir Adrian Baillie. Until 1948, the swings were chained up on Sundays to prevent desecration of the Sabbath! The council got funding from the

National Playing Fields Association to pay for the establishment of a King George v Playing Field (upgraded from the Bog Road playing field). Complete with heraldic panels on the gateposts, it opened at Baillie Street in May 1953. Since then, the local authority has provided a youth and community centre (1974), play areas in housing schemes and estates, assistance to sports and clubs and societies, a swimming pool and sports grounds. The schools continue to play a large part in nurturing sport in the young and introducing them to what for some will be lifelong activities. However, the main provision of leisure activities in Whitburn remains the work of many willing volunteers.

CHAPTER 27

Some Famous Natives and Local Notables

Famous Natives

FRANCHITTI, DARIO (1973–), racing driver. Son of George and Marina Franchitti, his family moved from Whitburn to Bathgate when he was eight. McLaren/Autosport Young Driver of the Year 1992; Indycar racing series champion in 2007, 2009, 2010 and 2011; winner of the Indianapolis 500 in 2007, 2010 and 2012; winner of the 24 Hours of Daytona race in 2008. After a serious accident in 2013, he retired on medical advice. He was married 2001–13 to American film star Ashley Judd and was awarded the MBE for services to motor racing in 2014.

Franchitti, Marino (1978–), racing driver, brother of Dario, cousin of racing driver Paul di Resta. Competed in sports cars and grand tourer racing, with highlights being second place in the American Le Mans Series – LMP2 in 2009 and winning the 12 Hours of Sebring in 2014.

Ingram, George (Dixie) (1937–2017), dancer. Born in Whitburn, father George was Area Chief Stores Inspector with the NCB. Took up Highland dancing as a child and won hundreds of prizes. Became a junior clerk with the NCB at Polkemmet Pit. Professional lead dancer with his Dixie Ingram Dancers, 1959–68, on the highly popular BBC television programme, The White Heather Club. Gave up dancing in 1970 and became a livestock auctioneer.

Jackson, Leon (1988–), shop-worker, singer, winner of television talent show The X-Factor in 2007. His first single was the third best-selling of 2007 but he struggled to maintain initial success. Probably too young to cope with the pressure, he's said to be the most forgotten X-Factor winner.

Lambie, John (1941–2018), footballer with Whitburn Juniors, Falkirk and St Johnstone, then coach at Hibs, manager at Hamilton Academicals and Partick Thistle (several times at each), then Falkirk FC. Stood unsuccessfully as an SNP councillor for Polkemmet ward in 1999. A larger than life personality, very popular, known for his love of homing pigeons, cigar-smoking, straight talking and profanity. One story about him has passed into football legend: when one of his players got concussed and confused, Lambie ordered, 'Tell him he's Pelé and get him back on!'

Lennon, Danny (1969–), footballer and football manager. Played for Raith Rovers, Partick Thistle and Cowdenbeath. Appointed manager at Cowdenbeath, went to St Mirren in 2010, where he led the team to the 2012–3 Scottish League Cup. After a spell as caretaker manager of the Scotland Under-21 team, went to Alloa Athletic in 2015. Since 2017, manager of Clyde.

Mooney, Andy (1955–) businessman. Born in Whitburn, father was a miner, mother was a quality supervisor at Levi's. Trainee accountant at Uniroyal, then Cameron Ironworks, then joined Nike UK as chief financial officer. Moved to the US and c.2000 became chairman of Disney Consumer Products Worldwide, overseeing the global promotion of the Disney brand. Left Disney in 2011 and is now CEO of Fender Musical Instruments.

Richmond, Christina (Ina) (1876–19xx), daughter of John Richmond, the gasworks manager at Whitburn for 27 years, assistant to her brother then manageress of the gasworks at Magherafelt, County Londonderry, from 1908 to 1914, the first woman gas works manager in the UK.

Wardrop, Alexander (1850–1924), poet. Born and lived in Whitburn till the age of 21. His best-known work was the book, *Mid Cauther Fair: Poems, songs and sketches* (1895).

Wardrop, James (1782–1869), surgeon and cardiologist. Son of laird of Torbanehill and related to William Wardrope, the surgeon apothecary. Apprenticed to his uncle Andrew Wardrop, an Edinburgh surgeon, studied anatomy and medicine there and was appointed House Surgeon to Edinburgh Infirmary aged 19. After study on the continent, went to London in 1808; appointed in 1818 a surgeon to the Prince Regent, later George IV. Set up and ran for ten years at his own expense a charitable hospitable giving free treatment to the poor and free tuition to medical students. Noted for various improvements in surgery and for a new method of operating on aneurysms – all this in the pre-anaesthetic era. Published on anatomy of the eye, heart diseases, etc. Sociable, quarrelsome, coarse in his language, an original thinker and a good storyteller but a poor teacher. Buried in Kirkton churchyard at Bathgate.

Local notables

Aitken, William (c.1900–44), Provost. Elected to the town council in 1929. Became Scotland's youngest Provost in 1935, aged 35. Served as Provost through the war until his death in 1944. Newsagent and tobacconist in West Main Street. Active in fundraising for troops' comforts fund, the war savings campaigns and in organising gala days.

Allan, Robert (c.1869–1949), overseer on Polkemmet estate for 40 years. Born in Whitburn, a joiner, then factor at Polkemmet, 1891–1931. JP and much involved in Whitburn life.

Barras, Christie (1900–73), miner, Co-operative Society insurance agent. Councillor and Bailie, president of West Benhar Co-operative Society and stalwart of Whitburn Miners' Welfare. Founder of the old folk's treat and supporter of Whitburn Burgh Band.

Bell, Alex (19xx–2004), last Provost of Whitburn, town and district councillor, last vice-convener of Lothian Regional Council. Vice-chair of the campaign to save Tippethill Hospital from closure in the mid 1990s and its subsequent rebuilding.

Boyle, James (19xx–1974), miner, Labour county councillor for East Whitburn, last convener of West Lothian County Council, 1973–4. Businessman, partner with depute convener William Connolly in the County Printers and County Tavern in Blackburn, and owner of the Clachan Bar in Whitburn.

Boyle, John (c.1915–95) Miner, then shop steward at British Leyland. Town councillor and Provost 1968–71; noted for his work on overspill agreement with Glasgow and the industrial growth of Whitburn and redevelopment of its town centre. Brother of James Boyle, above.

Dean, Margaret K (1876–1972), a teacher in Whitburn from 1903. VAD nurse at Polkemmet Hospital 1915–8; fundraised for Whitburn war relief and comforts fund, 1939–45. Active on the gala day committee, in charitable work, fundraising and community causes. After standing unsuccessfully in 1933 and 1934, she was co-opted onto the town council in November 1934 on the death of another councillor, thus becoming the first of only two female town councillors but lost her seat the following year. (The second woman was Nan Lees, from 1951–5.) She died in 1972 at the age of 96. Dean Street was named after her.

Douglas, Henry (c.1817–70), the original Downdie. His father was a tailor, who married a near relation, so all four sons and one daughter born to them were 'of weak intellect'. The 1851 Census describes three sons as 'unable to follow any trade', and their early nickname, usually written as Doundy or Dundy, may have come from the word dunderhead – a foolish person.

> Doundy [Henry Douglas] was *the* character of Whitburn...
> He was... very harmless, and has never been known to be
> violent except when he was tormented by the boys of the
> place, when he would defend himself with might and main.
> He will be greatly missed in Bathgate... [where] for a great
> many years past he headed the procession, gaily decked with
> sash and rosettes and carrying a white rod... This celebra-
> tion of Newlands' birthday was somewhat peculiar, because
> he rarely if ever joined in any of the sports or processions
> in Whitburn itself.

It seems likely that the nickname Doundy began to be given by Bathgate in mockery of all Whitburn residents, and that Whitburn folk jokingly adopted the term for themselves.

Drysdale, David (c.1894–1969), Provost. An official with the Scottish and Motormen's Union, associated with Labour and trade unionism all his life. Served for over 30 years on the town council, the last nine as Provost, 1944–53. Convener of the West Lothian county education committee 1945–c.1955.

Fairley, Archie (19xx–2000), miner, then a builder, then a full-time official of the GMB union 1969–92. Councillor for Whitburn, active in the local Labour party, election agent for Tam Dalyell at five successive elections and convener of the West Lothian District Council planning committee; instrumental in setting up community councils and in establishing Polkemmet county park.

Flannigan, Terry (c.1922–73), coal industry contractor, then welder. Appointed manager of newly opened Labour Club in 1966. Supporter of many sports and community groups. Father of eight children, his son Danny was a Labour councillor on West Lothian District Council, 1980–8.

Flemington, James. The first James Flemington (17xx–18xx) served in the Peninsular Wars; the second (1788–1860) served in the Royal Artillery, then set up a drapery business in the town; the third (c.1813–95) was a draper, one of the promoters of Whitburn as a burgh and a founder of Whitburn Gas Co; the fourth (1844–1915) was town clerk then Provost of Whitburn and a draper; the fifth (1883–1917), born but not resident in Whitburn, was killed in the First World War.

Gallagher, Margaret (c.1901–80). Supporter of the Trefoil School, demonstrator with the Women's Rural Institute, helper with the WRVS, Meals on Wheel, Darby and Joan Club and wartime comforts fund, blood donor and organiser.

Gamble, Robert (c.1935–). Came to Whitburn as part of Glasgow overspill to work at British Leyland. Councillor for Whitburn 1969–92 and 1995–2007, involved in much community and charity work in the town, county and district. A supporter of Whitburn Band and instrumental in the West Lothian twinning partnership with Hochsauerland. Has done more than anyone to encourage an interest in the heritage of the burgh and to record its past in his various books.

Gilchrist, Dr Thomas (c.1884–1943), GP. Footballer with Rangers, Third Lanark and Motherwell, then studied medicine. Assistant to Dr Anderson in Armadale, came to Whitburn in 1919. Bowler, golfer, president of Whitburn Ex-Servicemen's Association, lecturer in first aid, medical officer for Whitburn Home Guard, raised funds for the local ARP Ambulance. Built and lived at Craig-Uisk, East Main Street. Killed in 1943 in a car crash.

Griffith, William (1910–78), businessman and Provost. Started as a bus driver with Browning's, then set up as a coal merchant and contractor, bought several bings and sold the spent shale for road bottoming, earning the nickname King of the Bings. Town councillor and Provost, 1953–5. Chair of West Lothian licensing court and JP. A sometimes controversial figure, straight-talking, energetic, generous, didn't suffer fools gladly. Donated new Provost's robes and chain.

Hilditch, John (1948–2003) and Margaret. A maintenance fitter at Ravenscraig and British Leyland. In 1978, they purchased the Royal Bar in Harthill, then the Croftmalloch Inn and the Hilcroft Hotel, giving employment to over 100 people. John was also a keen football supporter and golfer. A founder member and past president of Whitburn Rotary

Club, he received a Paul Harris Fellowship from Rotary International for charity work and service to the community.

Kearsley, Herbert (c.1877–1966), band leader. Born in London, came to West Calder in 1900 as a Co-op painter. Conductor of West Calder Public Band, then of Whitburn Band, which he led to great success; the first Scottish Band to win the Brass Band Championships in London in 1954.

Liddell, Ivor (1939–98), PE teacher at Whitburn Academy from 1967 and then assistant rector. He and his wife Eleanor, also a teacher, were widely known for their work at summer school camps at Meigle and Dounans in Aberfoyle.

Nicolson, James (c.1816–87), crewman on the steamer *Forfarshire*, wrecked on the Farne Islands in 1838. He was one of those rescued by Grace Darling. Lived for 28 years at East Whitburn, buried in Whitburn cemetery.

Shanks, William (c.1863–1929), blacksmith. Town councillor for 40 years and Provost, 1917–29. Instrumental in first two council housing schemes and in erection of war memorial. A wide knowledge of horticulture and breeding collies; 'a rare pawky wit… ever ready with a good story… a capital singer'.

Stevenson, George (1923?–1999), miner. A faithful fundraiser for Tippethill Hospital, stalwart of Whitburn Juniors FC, well-known as MC at the Miners' Welfare and led Whitburn's gala day parades in fancy dress for many years.

Swan, Jim (1940–), union convener at British Leyland. As convener of the joint shop stewards committee, fought to prevent the closure of the factory and its thousands of jobs. A stalwart of the Labour and trade union movements, campaigned for health and safety improvements and instrumental in establishing the annual International Workers' Memorial Day across Scotland. A local councillor for Whitburn and Blackburn for 13 years until retirement in 2012; secretary of West Lothian Trades Council.

Radical past, radical future?

It would require many volumes to capture the variety and complexity of Whitburn's history – this book can only give a faint indication of how much has happened over the last 300 years of Whitburn's history and why the town developed as it did. So many of its people lived, died and left no trace behind but it's hoped that this book has suggested something of what their lives were like.

The mid-19th century change from self-employed weavers to waged miners meant that Whitburn's strong radical streak was re-directed from political reform to a concern with jobs and social and economic conditions. Local people dared to call for radical changes to the injustices of their time and challenge the powerful, whether churches, lairds, councils or employers. It may be that their experiences, achievements and failures will open young people's eyes to the realisation that injustices should be challenged and that ordinary people can do it.

Some of the religious beliefs and political divisions of the past have tainted Whitburn's story with narrowness, sectarianism and bitterness; on the whole, however, there has been remarkably little conflict among its population. The town has successfully integrated successive waves of incomers and it's hoped it will continue to do so. It has a record of care, kindness and community-mindedness – from the lairdly benevolence of successive Lady Baillies, to the miners' families helping out one another during the strikes, to the hundreds of volunteers who give up time and effort each week for voluntary, charitable and community causes.

Whitburn still has many problems; not least the hidden poverty of the unemployed and the in-work poor. It's concerning that 11 of the 13 data zones that make up Whitburn are within the lowest third in Scotland and four are among the worst 20 per cent in Scotland, based on their levels of income, unemployment and ill health. In addition, Whitburn has a greater proportion of older people than the Scottish average, a much lower number of people with access to the internet than the West Lothian average and double the West Lothian average of benefit claimants. It's evident that a great deal still needs to be done by the council, public bodies and by community self-help to provide Whitburn's people with a fairer share of jobs, income and well-being – that, and not just new shops and houses in Main Street, will be *real* regeneration.

Work is underway. A charette (a major public consultation) was held in Whitburn in the spring of 2015 and from this a master plan with a community-led vision of the future of Whitburn has been created and a Whitburn Regeneration Group set up. The Burgh Chambers are being converted into a partnership centre, bringing together various council and hopefully other public services. Whitburn community council is active as a bridge between the council and the community, making people's views and concerns known so that these can help shape the council's decisions. Non-party political, it aims to involve locals in solving local problems and finds that people respond most readily to short and specific projects such as the town clean-up or the recent two-year twinning with Oswaldtwistle. Whitburn Community Development Trust was formed with the help of the community council to take on larger projects and seek funding for them. Whitburn Traders' Group works specifically for town centre regeneration and much good work is done by the community centre management group, including setting up a children's club two days a week that provides activities and a free lunch during the school holidays. All these groups work together and also liaise with the council and the police and they are working towards the regeneration of the town centre, the green network of paths which will link the town with Polkemmet country park and surrounding villages, dealing with anti-social behaviour and improving the town's environment. The community council is also part of the Heartlands liaison group. The Heartlands development will change the area in a way that will only be to the benefit of the whole town if means can be found to integrate the two communities and it will require much goodwill on both sides.

Whitburn has a great deal in its favour – just 20 miles or so from both Glasgow and Edinburgh, with 80 per cent of Scotland's entire population within a one-hour drive from the town and Polkemmet country park on its doorstep. A clear sense of identity, active community and voluntary groups, its strong people and its community spirit will be what pulls it through – as they have during the upheavals and hardships of the past.

Whitburn's history reveals that its people have always brought forward radical solutions to the problems of their day. They have not waited for the powers-that-be to address their difficulties but have been proactive in seeking their own solutions and have shown a notable lack of deference to authority. Today, the town still needs radical answers to its problems; if the past is anything to go by, Whitburn's people will find them.

Further reading

Whitburn kirk session records
Whitburn heritors' records
West Lothian Courier, 1872 to date
Whitburn burgh police commissioners' minutes 1862–1901
Whitburn town council minutes 1901-75
Old Statistical Account, parish of Whitburn
New Statistical Account, parish of Whitburn
Third Statistical Account, parish of Whitburn
Censuses of Scotland
Valuation rolls, 1855–1979
Ordnance Survey maps
Ordnance Survey namebooks (1855–9)

Cochrane, William P *West Lothian postal history, 1661–1925* (Scottish Postal History Society, 2016)

Crawford, Mary A (ed) *The beginnings and early history of the Trefoil School by Those who still remember* (Trefoil Guild, 1954)

Danskin, John *A History of Brucefield* (Brucefield Parish Church, 2017)

Gamble, Bert, JP *Burgh with a history* (The author, 1995)

Gamble, Bert, JP *Photographic history of Whitburn* (The author, 2001)

Gillespie, Robert *Round about Falkirk* (Dunn & Wright, Glasgow, 1879)

Knox, Harry *Vanished railways of West Lothian* (Lightmoor Press, 2017)

McCallum, Mark *The miners' strike of 1984/85: as interpreted through local and national newspapers available in West Lothian, Scotland* (Unpublished thesis, submitted for MLitt in Journalism Studies, Strathclyde University, September 2004.)

McCracken, Gordon A *Whitburne: ane histore o' its auld paroch kirk* (The author, 2000)

McMartin, William B *Brucefield Church, Whitburn, 1857–1957: a history of the congregation* (Brucefield Church, 1957)

Smith, Mark *A thorn in the flesh: exploring the closure of Polkemmet colliery against a national crisis, 1984–85.* (Thesis, MA (Hons), Dept of History, Univ. Glasgow, 2012)

West Lothian Council *Placemaking in Whitburn, Final report, 8 December 2015*

West Lothian County Council *A physical, economic and social survey of West Lothian* (WLCC, 1958)

West Lothian County Council *County survey report* (WLCC, 1970)

West Lothian Trades Union Congress *Unity is strength: West Lothian memories of the Miners' Strike, 1984–85* (WLC Museums, 2004)

Whitburn Local History Group *Farming in Whitburn past and present* (The Group, 1994)

Workers' Educational Association/West Lothian District Council Museums Service *Levi's Uncut: memories of some Levi's workers, Whitburn plant, 1969–1999* (WEA, 2007)

INDEX

A

Accidents, 80–1
Adams, John, 140
Agriculture, See Farming
Aitken, William, 160, 172
Allan, Margaret, 99
Allan, Robert, 103, 172
Almond River, 27, 32, 72, 97, 114
Almondbank, 119, 158
Anderson, Alex, 38
Andrew, Peter, 69
Auld, William, 53

B

Bailie, or Barony officer, 37, 41
Baron Court, 16, 37
Baillie family of Polkemmet,
    16–7, 48, 63
Baillie, Adrian (6th Bart), 106,
    107, 168 & image
Baillie, Gawaine (5th Bart),
    104–5, 161 & image
Baillie, Gawaine (7th Bart), 107
Baillie, George (3rd Bart), 104
Baillie, Lady (wife of 1st Bart),
    48, 64–6, 115
Baillie, Lady (wife of 2nd Bart),
    96, 102–4, 141
Baillie, Lady (wife of 4th Bart),
    105, 106
Baillie, Penuel, 48
Baillie, Robert (4th Bart), 104
Baillie, Thomas, 16, 17, 21
Baillie, William
    (Lord Polkemmet), 22, 51, 52
    63, 64 & image

Baillie, William (1st Bart), 48,
    60, 64–5, 69–70, 71, 84, 115,
    140, 165
Baillie, William (2nd Bart), 91, 96,
    102 & image
Baillie, William (wright), 16
Baillie Institute, 103–4, 162
    & images
Bain, Robert, 61
Bald, Robert, 68–9
Banks, 147
Barnes, David, 168
Barnes, James, 157
Barracks, The, 43, 117–8
    & image
Barras, Christie, 125, 148, 172
Barron, Rev William, 28–9
Barry, James, 25
Bathgate militia riot, 51–2
Bell (handbell), 15, 98, & image
Bell, Alex, 93, 98, 99, 172
    & image
Belmos, 132
Beveridge, Robert, 69, 70
Bevin Boys, 75, 100
Biblewoman, 103
Bird, Rev John, 79
Bishop, Elizabeth Burns, 57–8, 64
    & image
Bishop, John, 58, 83, 93, 140
Bishop, Robert H., 93–4
Bishop, Thomas, 69, 70, 80, 94
Bishop, William, 17
Blaeberryhill Farm, 27, 96
Blaeberryhill Road, 114, 128

BMC/British Leyland, 77, 127,
131, 132, 134, 135, 136, 172,
174, 175
Bogle, Margaret, 17
Bowling, 110, 165–6
Boyle, James, 128, 150, 156, 172
& pic??
Boyle, John, 99, 148, 172
Brewery, 55
Brice, Helen, 140
Brice, William, 25
Brough, Rev Robin, 119
Brown, James, 25, 99
Brown, Rev John, 45–6, 93
& image
Brown, Robert, 25, 48, 139
Brownhill, 19
Browning's, 113, 131, 160, 174
Bruce, Rev Archibald, 40, 42,
43–5, 48, 117, 118, 156
Bryce, William, 60
Buchanan, Rev J.L., 116
Burgh boundaries, 109, 126
Burnhouse School, 145
Burns, Robert, 20, 53, 57–8, 140
Burnwynd, 39
Bus services, 113–4

C
Cadden, Patrick, 80
Calder, John, 39, 59, 84
Calder, Robert, 83
Campbell, William, 139
Campbell Bros, 114, 131
Cappers, 62, 71
Car ownership, 114, 128, 129–30
Carlyle, Alexander, 19–20
Carriers & carters, 27, 32, 55,
113–4, 131, 154
Catholicism, 41–2, 90, 119–20
Chalmers, Thomas, 117
Chartism, 83–5

Christmas tree, 142
Churches, 11–16, 28–9, 37–40,
115–121 Brucefield/Free,
117–9 & image; Burgher
& Anti-Burgher, 43–46, 93,
117–8; Catholic, 119–20;
Gospel Hall, 121 & image;
Parish/South, 11–6, 27,
28–9, 37–40, 115–7 & image;
Pentecostal, 120; See also
Seceeders & Secession churches
Churchyard (South), 30, 46,
58, 141
Cinemas, 151, 168
Clachan, 150, 172
Clark, Dr Thomas, 95, 158
Cleugh Road, 26–7, 112
Climate, 20, 36
Clearances, Lowland, 25, 46
Clubs & societies, 165–6, 168
Coaching era, 20, 26–7, 40, 54–7,
111–2, 146 & image
Coal mining, 67–82, 87, 88–9,
111; mining accidents, 80–1,
158; coal miners, 68, 70,
76–8, 81, 87, 93, 122–3
& image; child & female
labour, 69–70 & image
Coffee House & Reading Rooms,
See Baillie Institute
Colliery Hub, 156
Common, 18
Community Centre, 104, 169, 177
Cook, Robert, 120
Co-operative, 147–8, 172
Cotton manufactory, 31–2;
Cotton jeanie, 31–2, 33
& image
Council housing 123–8; individual
streets, 124; Overspill, 125–8;
Right to Buy, 128–9
Countryside belt, 137

Covenanters, 13, 42, 86
Cowhill Farm, 136, 137
Crane Fruehauf, 132, 136
Crime, 37, 56, 157
Croftmalloch, 24, 132,
Croftmalloch Inn, 150, 174
Croftmalloch Primary School, 145
Cromwell's invasion, 12
Cross Tavern, 147, 150
Crozier, Cameron, 127
Crozier, Robert, 162
Cult, 13, 93
Cult(rigg) mine, 62, 68, 70–1
Cunynghame, David, 18, 21, 28
Cunynghame, Lady Mary, 21, 28
Cunynghame, James, 15, 16,
    18–9, 21
Cunynghame, William Augustus,
    21, 22, 26–9, 31, 63, 67 &
    image
Curling, 66, 105, 165

D
Dalyell, Tam, 79, 173
Dalziel, James, 93
Damhead, 17
Dardanelles, See Polkemmet
    Colliery (new)
Darroch, Rev Richard, 119
Davidson, George, 140
Dean, Margaret, 172 & image
Deans, Charlotte, 40–1
Deans, Robert, 164
Deprivation, 9, 138, 149, 153,
    159, 176
Dick, James, 25, 99
Dick, John, 31–3, 83, 146 & image
Dickson, Jim, 137
Dickson, William, 46–7
Distillery, 23
Dixon, William, & Co. 73, 123
Dixon Terrace, 43, 80, 123, 143

Doctors, 84, 95, 99, 106, 118,
    146, 158–9, 161, 174
Double Five, 102/3
Dow, Mary, 167
Douglas, Henry (Downdie), 173
Downdies, 167, 173
Drove Loan, 14, 26
Drysdale, David, 99, 125, 173
Dumback, 82
Duncan, Thomas, 82, 118
Dundas, Robert, 64
Dykehead, 19

E
Eardley, Father, 119
East Benhar, 82
East Main Street, 27, 103, 112,
    149, 157, 162 & images
East Whitburn, 21, 27, 36, 63, 64,
    112, 168, 172, 175 & image
Easton, James, 25
Easton, Nan, 106 & image
Edmiston, William, 38
Edmistone, John, 54
Emigration, 93–4, 104
Employment, 31–5, 79, 88–9,
    131–6
Evacuees, 107–8, 162–3

F
Fairley, Archibald, 173
Farming, 17–18, 23, 36–7, 88,
    103, 165, 178
Fauldhouse, 11, 71, 75, 79, 85,
    103, 119, 120, 141, 145, 157
Ferguson, David, 164
Feuing of land, 19, 21, 23–6, 27,
    66, 83
Fin(d)lay, John, 44–5, 53 & image
Findlay, Neil, 79
Fire service, 31, 100–1 & image
Flannigan, Johnny, 166

Flannigan, Danny, 173
Flannigan, Terry, 173
Flemington, James, 33, 84,
    99, 174
Flowerers, 32, 33–4, 60, 62
Food, 37
Football, 165, 166, 170–1, 174
    & images
Forrest, Alexander, 80
Forrest, Rev Gavin, 117
Forsyth, Margaret, 157
Frame, William, 24
Franchitti family, 92, 149, 170
Freemasonry, See Masonic
French Revolution, 44–5, 49, 52–3
Friendly Societies, 104, 142,
    154–5
Friends of the People, 49–51, 52
    & image

G
Galas, games and fairs, 165–7
    & image
Gallagher, Margaret, 174
Gamble, Robert, 110, 137, 174,
    178 & image
Gardner, Robert, 95–7, 99, 147,
    150, 167
Garibaldi, Giuseppe, 85 & image
Gas company, 97, 171, 174
Gateside, 49, 56, 63, 90, 127
Geddes, Alexander, 70–1
Geddes, Thomas, 95
General Strike, See Miners' strikes
George V Park, 169
Gilbert, James, 59–60, 61, 140
Gilchrist, Thomas, 174
Gillan, David, 156
Gilmour, Allan, 24
Gordon, Lord George, 42
Gordon, Thomas, 63–4, 67
Gourlie, Thomas, 55

Graham, Archibald, 163
Graham, James, 83
Grave-robbers, 29–30
Greenrigg, 64, 123
Greenrigg Mine, 68, 70, 81, 88
Greenshiel(d)s, Samuel, 29, 83,
    139–40
Griffith, William, 99, 132, 174
    & image

H
Halfway House, 27, 39, 57–8, 66,
    150 & image
Hamilton, John, 25
Harthill, 72, 82, 103, 118, 141
Handloom weaving, See Weaving
Harper & Sons, 131, 135
Hazelton, James & Anne, 127
Health, 135, 143, 158–9, 161
Heartlands, 129, 136–8, 168, 177
    & image
Heenan, William, 162
Home Guard, 162–3
Houghton, Rev Christine, 117
Heritors, 12–5, 139, 152
Hilditch, John & Margaret, 150,
    174–5
Hodgekinson, Walter, 163
Houlden, James, 25
Housing, 26, 98, 109, 122–130
    & images; for miners, 122–3;
    Council, 123–9; private,
    129–30; sheltered, 128
Hume, Rev William, 116–7
Hunter's Close, West Main Street,
    image
Hutchison, Les, 114

I
Immigration, 25, 89–91,
    92–93, 120
Industrial estates, 101, 132, 134

Industrial Revolution, 31–2, 33, 59–62
Industry, 31–3, 62, 67–76, 79–80, 81–2, 88–9, 131–8
Ingram, Dixie, 170
Inns, 20, 21, 23, 27, 149–51; Whitburn Inn, 27, 46, 55, 56, 63, 111, 149 & image; Castle Inn, 150, 167; Commercial Inn, 150; Halfway House, 27, 58, 150
Ireland, Rev John, 96, 99, 116,
Ireland, 89–92, 58, 59, 113
Ironstone mining 71–2, 88–9, 112
Italian immigration, See Immigration

J
Jackson, Leon, 170 & image
Jacobite Rebellions, 41
Johnston, Thomas, 157

K
Karma, 150
Kearsley, Herbert, 175
Kelly, Thomas, 96
Kerr, Rev Angus, 117
Kinghorn family, 70
Kinloch, Henry, 37
Kinloch, William, 24
Kirk Sessions, 12, 14, 28, 33, 37–40, 139

L
Labour Party, 75, 86–7, 98, 153
Lambie, John, 170–1 & image
Lambie, Robert, 99
Lawson, Jean, 54–5
Lea Street, 97, 124, 156
Leeds Castle, 106–7
Leggat, John, 62
Leggat, Mr, 142

Leggatt, Mrs, 33
Leisure 66, 165–9
Lennon, Danny, 171
Levi Straus, 132–4, 136, 178 & image
Libraries, 86, 103, 141, 156
Liddell, Ivor, 175
Linden, 150
Literacy, 34, 143, 156
Little, Andrew, 142–3
Livingston Parish, 11–2, 13, 15
Livingston New Town, 127, 128, 131, 132, 136, 149
Loch, David, 31
Lockie, Isabella, 39
Lollards, 13
Longridge, 45, 46, 103, 112, 157, 164

M
McCabe, Godfrey, 127
McCallum, Father, 119
McCracken, Rev Gordon, 92, 117
McGregor, Father, 119
McGuinness, Father, 119
McIntyre, Jimmy, 108
McKenna, Joseph, 127
MacKenzie, Archibald, 32
MacKinnon, Rev Robert, 116
McKnight, Rev John, 118
McLean, John, 163
McMartin, Rev J.B., 118–9
Mains, Agnes, Jean & Nelly, 25
Maps, 21, 88, 111 & images
Market Inn, 24, 150 & image
Market Place, 23–4, 63, 90
Marshall, James & John, 164
Marshel, Elizabeth, 39,
Marshel, Thomas, 28–9, 40
Martial arts, 166
Martin family, 30, 39
Martin, David, 21

Masonic Lodge, 117, 144, 151,
   154, 155
Melvin, William, image
Michie, Dr John, 106, 161
   & image
Mickel, Robert, 99, 132
Miley, Father, 119
Militia, 51–2, 53, 66
Millbank, 125
Milne, William, 83
Miners' Strikes, 74–5, 76–78,
   153, 166 & image
Miners' Welfare: Club, 101, 150–1,
   168, 172, 175 & image; Fund
   78, 81, 163, 168
Mitchell, Alexander, 98
Mitchell, Rev Graham, 71, 84, 95,
   115–6
Mooney, Andy, 171
Muir, Susannah, 150
Muir, Thomas, 49–50
Murdoch, James & John, 157
Murray, Peter, 34, 97
Murraysgate: Houses, 123–4,
   127; Mine, 82; Toll, 54,
   67, 150; Women's Social
   Club, 128
Myreton, Robert, 22

N
Newcastle Waggon, 40
Newton, John, 98
Nicol, George, 38
Nicolson, James, 175

O
Oil States Industries, 138
Orange Order, 91–2
Oswaldtwistle, 177
Overspill, 125–8, 172, 174
   & image

P
Paine, Thomas, 44, 50
Park Lane, 62, 97, 124
Parks, 168–9
Patrick, young, 17
Patronage, church, 13–15, 16,
   28–9, 43, 46, 63, 115–6
Pipe band, 163, 168
Pirn winders, 34, 59, 60, 62
Police, 30, 77, 90, 157–8
Police Acts, 95
Police college, 109–10, 125
Polish immigration, 92–3; troops,
   92, 108–9, 162, 187
Polkemmet Colliery, C19th, 68–72,
   111, C20th, 73–81, 93,
   123, 124, 135, 136–7, 168
   & image; miners' strike, 76–80
   & image; nationalisation/
   NCB, 75–6, 81; & images
Polkemmet Country Park, 110,
   166, 177
Polkemmet Estate, 13, 17, 58, 71,
   102–3, 104–5, 107, 110, 172;
   race track, 107; squatters, 109
Polkemmet House, 66, 104–5,
   107–8, 110 & images; WW1
   hospital, 105–6, 161, 172
   & images
Polkemmet Primary School, 144–5
Polkemmet Rows, 71
Pollution, 72, 82, 97–8
Poverty & poor relief, 18, 36, 38,
   152–5, 176
Popery, See Catholicism
Population, 10, 15, 36, 79, 88–9,
   93, 95
Postal services, 56, 146–7
   & image
Pottishaw, 82
Pretoria Inn, 150

Priests, 119–20
Pringle, Adam, 84
Pringle, David, 61
Printers – See Fin(d)lay, John
Provosts, 99, 125. See also
    individual provosts
Pubs & Hotels, 54, 148,
    149–51, 174
Purdie, Robert, 51–2, 53

Q
Queen, HM, 85, 103, 108, 167

R
Radicals & radicalism, 9, 13, 34,
    43–53, 83–7, 94, 154, 156,
    175–6,
Railways 68, 111–2, 113 & image
Ramsay, John, 95
Rattray, Father, 119
Redmond, Robert, 162
Reform, 44–5, 49–52, 83–6, 176
Rhind, Rev James, 29
Richardson, Davie, 33
Richmond, Christina, 171
Roadhouse, 93, 114, 150
Roads, 20, 26–7, 113, 114;
    turnpike/toll roads, 54–56,
    112; A8 & M8, 27, 114, 132
Robertson, Bethia, 24, 25, 27
Robertson, John, 21, 24, 25, 27
Robertson, Walter, 80
Roger, Rev Alexander, 119
Roy, Stephen, 120
Royal Mail coaches, 27, 55–7,
    65, 146
Russell, Alexander, 24, 26
Russell, Elizabeth, 159
Russell, James, 56

S
Sabbath Observance, 40–1, 168
Sangster, Christina, 103

Sangster, James, 163
Sangster, Robert, 113
Savage, Walter, 158
Schools, 37, 61, 107, 139–45;
    Catholic, 145; Dr Gillespie's
    117; Junior Secondary, 99,
    144; Lady Baillie's, 121,
    142 & image; Parish/Public
    School, 96, 142–4 &
    image; Sabbath School, 28;
    Secondary education, 99, 143,
    144; Venture schools, 14–1;
    Wilson's schools, 141–2, 143
    & image
Scott, James, 113
Seceders, 34, 46, 52; Secession
    churches, 43–6, 117–8
Self-help & self-improvement,
    152–6
Sexual misconduct, 17, 38–9
Shanks, John, 84
Shanks, William, 99, 175
Sharp, John, 150
Shaw family of Polkemmet, 13
Shaw, James, 49
Shaw, Rev Robert, 117–8
Shops, 88, 92, 103, 147–9
Shotts, 15, 26, 29, 54, 67, 68,
    71, 146
Shuttle Row, 62, 90, 97, 124
Slavery, 22, 46–9, 68, 93–4, 139
Smallpox, 65–6, 158
Smart, James, 39
Smith, Alexander, 156
Smith, Andrew, 120
SNP, 87, 170
Social Clubs, 150–1
Soldiers, 12, 32–3, 53, 108,
    160–1, 163–4
Somerville, D.K., 144
Somerville, Rev James, 15

Soup kitchens, 74, 78, 153
& image
Spanish flu, 161
Sports, 105, 165–6, 169
Squatters' camp, 109, 125
SSHA/Weslo, 125, 127, 129
St Joseph's Primary School,
144, 145
Stafford, William, 80
Stagecoaches, See Coaching era
Starch Works, 33
Stark, John, 49
Station, See Railways
Statistical Accounts: First/Old, 25,
29, 33, 34, 67; Second/New,
67, 115
Steel, Ebenezer, 62
Stepends, 27
Stevenson, George, 175
Storrie, James, 19
Suffragettes, 86
Swan, Jim, 175
Swimming, 101, 144, 166
SWRI, 168, 174

T
Tambourers, 34, 62
Taylor, James, 25
Tennant, Ian, 108
Tennant, Smith, 160
Thatcher, Margaret, 9, 76, 77,
128, 134–5
Thomas, Joe, 137
Thomson, Robert, 164
Thornton, John, 39
Thuruthipillil, Father Sebastian,
Tippethill, 91, 158–9, 172, 175
Tollbars & tollhouses, 54–5,
112–3, 150
Torbanehill, 62, 72, 82, 147, 171
Town Centre Development, 114,
138, 148–9, 177 & image

Town crier, 15, 98
Town Hall, 98, 148, 155, 168
Townhead, 63; Gardens, 100, 109,
124, 125 & image; Park, 168
Trade Unions, 60, 74–5, 76–7, 87,
93, 133, 134, 173, 175
Tranent, 52
Trefoil School, 107–8 & image
Trotter, James, 36–7, 52, 68
Turnpikes, See Roads

U
Unemployment, 9, 61–2, 77,
79, 132, 134–5, 136, 153,
159, 176,
Uniformed organisations, 117,
119, 168
Union Canal, 68
United Collieries, 81, 123

V
Volkswagen (GB), 134
Volleyball, 166
Volunteers, 52–3, 161

W
Waddell, George, 50, 53
Waddell, James, 53
Walker, Alastair, 109
Walker, James & Thomas, 56
Wallace, Alexander, 39
Wardrop, Alexander, 171
Wardrop, James, 171
Wardrope, Rev Alexander, 15, 28
Wardrope, William, 13–4, 15, 19,
28, 43, 187
War memorial, 161, 164, 187
Wars: Napoleonic/Peninsular,
32–3; WW1, 73, 105–6,
160–1, 167, 174; WW2, 75,
92, 100, 107–8, 161–4
Water supply, 95–6, 97, 98

Waterloo, 32
Waterston, John, 140
Waterstone, William, 84
Watson, Rev James, 29–30,
  64, 115
Weavers, 30, 31–2, 33–5, 46, 48,
  49, 56, 59–62, 72, 83, 84, 86,
  88–9, 122, 176 & images
Weir, Margaret, 54
Weir, Robert, 39
West Lothian Housing
  Society, 123
West Main Street, 25–6, 62, 90,
  92, 97, 103, 123, 148, 149,
  150, 166, 168 & images
Wester Whitburn, 14, 21, 24, 39
Whitburn: development of, 88–9;
  new village, 21, 23–6, 31–2,
  67, 122
Whitburn Academy, 144
Whitburn Band, 86, 160, 166,
  167–8, 175
Whitburn, Barony of, 16, 37
Whitburn, Burgh of, 87, 95–100;
  Burgh Chambers, 103–4, 110
Whitburn Burgh Commissioners,
  See Whitburn Town Council
Whitburn Cemetery, 97, 175
Whitburn Community Council,
  137, 173, 176–7
Whitburn Community
  Development Trust, 138, 177
Whitburn Inn, See Inns
Whitburn Mill, 19, 63
Whitburn Mutual Improvement
  Society, 85, 155

Whitburn parish, 11–15
Whitburn Parochial Board/Parish
  Council, 152–3, 155
Whitburn School Board, 96,
  99, 143
Whitburn Town Council, 91,
  95–100, 103, 104, 113, 116,
  122, 123–9, 131, 148, 153,
  158, 162
Whitburn Traders' Group, 177
Whitdale/Hilcroft Hotel, 150, 174
Whitdale Primary School, 144
Whitdalehead, 67, 124, 141,
  143–5 & image
White, John, 70–1
White, Matthew, 125, 153
Whitefield, Rev George, 28
Whitrigg Colliery, 81, 168
Wilson, Agnes, 38
Wilson, Dr Alexander, 84, 146
Wilson, Ian, 92
Wilson, James, 141, 146, 156
Wilson, John, 38, 84
Wilson, Mrs, 152
Wilson, P, 163
Women, 106, 128, 154, 155, 164;
  Women's work, 34, 37, 69–70,
  89, 106, 132, 133–4, 142,
  161; political involvement, 78,
  85, 86, 97, 99, 172
Wood, George, 162
Wood, James, 71, 99, 163
Wright, Bethia, 24, 25, 27

Y
Yetthouses, 19, 63

Luath Press Limited

committed to publishing well written books worth reading

LUATH PRESS takes its name from Robert Burns, whose little collie Luath (*Gael.*, swift or nimble) tripped up Jean Armour at a wedding and gave him the chance to speak to the woman who was to be his wife and the abiding love of his life. Burns called one of the 'Twa Dogs' Luath after Cuchullin's hunting dog in Ossian's *Fingal*. Luath Press was established in 1981 in the heart of Burns country, and is now based a few steps up the road from Burns' first lodgings on Edinburgh's Royal Mile. Luath offers you distinctive writing with a hint of unexpected pleasures.

Most bookshops in the UK, the US, Canada, Australia, New Zealand and parts of Europe, either carry our books in stock or can order them for you. To order direct from us, please send a £sterling cheque, postal order, international money order or your credit card details (number, address of cardholder and expiry date) to us at the address below. Please add post and packing as follows: UK – £1.00 per delivery address; overseas surface mail – £2.50 per delivery address; overseas airmail – £3.50 for the first book to each delivery address, plus £1.00 for each additional book by airmail to the same address. If your order is a gift, we will happily enclose your card or message at no extra charge.

Luath Press Limited
543/2 Castlehill
The Royal Mile
Edinburgh EH1 2ND
Scotland
Telephone: +44 (0)131 225 4326 (24 hours)
email: sales@luath. co.uk
Website: www. luath.co.uk